After Justice

Catholic Challenges to Progressive Culture, Politics, Economics and Education

Thomas A. Michaud, Ph.D.

En Route Books and Media, LLC
Saint Louis, MO

⊕*ENROUTE*

Make the time

En Route Books and Media, LLC
5705 Rhodes Avenue
St. Louis, MO 63109

Contact us at **contact@enroutebooksandmedia.com**

Cover Credit: Sebastian Mahfood

Copyright 2022 Thomas A. Michaud

ISBN-13: 978-1-956715-92-7
Library of Congress Control Number: 2022947904

Table of Contents

Foreword

Peter Redpath

Toward the start of his "Introduction" to this book *After Justice: Catholic Challenges to Contemporary Culture, Politics, Education and Economics*, Thomas Michaud immediately and rightly identifies contemporary 'Progressivism' as a *political ideology*, not a *political philosophy*, having its "roots"—that is, proximate first principles that spawned it—in the "Modern Rationalism and Positivism of the seventeenth and eighteenth centuries." No wonder should exist, then, as Michaud states, that, once Progressivism secured somewhat of a foundation so that in the early twentieth century, especially in the United States, "it shed any vestige of its origins as a philosophy to morph into a thoroughgoing political ideology. As such, it actually spawned an official political party—The American Progressive Party."

Due to its many intellectual and political inconsistencies as an uneasy "olio of ideas" mistaking itself for a political philosophy championing *social justice*, in the spirit of Alasdair MacIntye in his celebrated book, *After Virtue*, Michaud rightly observes that, acting according to its real nature, during the twentieth- and twenty-first centuries, Progressivism has devolved into a fragmented, increasingly more becoming authoritarian "collectivism." Specifically, within the past few decades, he notes these tendencies expanding within: (1) Postmodernism—which he understands to be simply what our colleague John N. Deely correctly labeled 'Modernism on steroids' and Michaud succinctly summarizes as, "anti-Modernism with its rejections of Rationalism, Scientific Positivism and any traditional-based metaphysics"; 2) the authoritarian Politically Correct and Cancel Culture standards of moral righteousness; and, 3) the Woke mentality that employs social and mainstream media to transform the "people" into a "conformist, hive-minded ruling mob."

After finishing the general summary of his "Introduction," Michaud specifies the nature of his book as a work in what has come to be known as 'Traditional Catholic Philosophy'—common and uncommon commonsense realism in the classical tradition of Socrates, Plato, Aristotle, and Saint Thomas Aquinas; and, in contemporary times by *another sort of learning*, though uncommon commonsense philosophers like Gabriel Marcel, Fr. James V. Schall, Michael J. Novak, Mortimer J. Adler, and Pope Saint John Paul II (Karol Wojtyla). Considered as such, he identifies its chief aim to be to expose and drive into its coffin, Progressivism as a political ideology that, due to its lack of philosophical carriage: poses "a serious threat to individual autonomy, family identity, cultural and political heritage, the integrity of education, and economic stability and growth."

Michaud's collection of essays and lectures offers a comprehensive critique of the politicized ideological facets of Progressivism. From its 'Green' environmentalism, through its revolutionary transformation of culture, to its redefinition of the human person, Michaud effectively shows that Traditional Catholic Philosophy does have the principles and morally normative standards to challenge and dismantle Progressivism. Readers of this book, especially those who feel beleaguered by Progressivism's incessant assaults on their core beliefs and their Faith, will be edified and energized by the hope that this work imparts.

Foreword

Curtis L. Hancock

Echoes of Saint Augustine for Our Times

In his book *The City of God*, Saint Augustine advised how Christians could cope with disturbances in the ancient Roman Empire during its decline. Augustine's book comes to mind since some historians have compared America's own apparent decline to ancient Rome. Thomas Michaud's *After Justice* advises Christians today in a way that is analogous to Augustine's advice. Michaud would no doubt blush at the comparison with Augustine. Nonetheless, there is a fitting parallel: his book is filled with wisdom, providing intellectual, practical, and spiritual direction. This book will fortify readers in an age of crisis and anxiety.

Like Augustine, Michaud exercises a humility about the human condition, recognizing (1) that we are limited in our ability to change the world for the better, and (2) that we must have a deep trust in Providence. In the writings of Gabriel Marcel, one finds these two convictions significantly developed. Since Michaud has long been influenced by Marcel, it is not surprising to see him affirm these beliefs. Marcel suggests that the arc of history has taught us to be blithely *hopeful* but cautiously *optimistic*. Hope is not the same as optimism. Michaud understands this distinction because hope is a *theocentric* matter, while optimism is *anthropocentric*.

Our hope is in God and God cannot fail. "We know that in all things God works for the good of those who love Him, who have been called for his purpose." (Romans 8:28) On the other hand, optimism is a sought-for human outcome. Optimism is the belief that human beings can act individually or communally to produce good results. But in a fallen world, human endeavor risks being compromised. Because optimism relies on human effort, it is never secure. Hope, however, is grounded in Revelation's promise that God's aims for the world will surely be realized. God will win, and he has promised that the faithful will share in the victory. Before that eschatological outcome, human beings, provided they work hard and cooperate with God's grace, might also gain some victories of their own along the way. Hope is certain. Optimism is ironic. It is worth noting that Michaud is always aware of these distinctions when he writes about government, economics, and culture.

A close reading of the essays in this collection show that Michaud has assimilated three of *The City of God*'s central teachings about social life. First, Augustine teaches that justice in society is temporary. Human persons must be tireless in their labors to perpetuate justice. Justice can be achieved for a while, but it is penultimate, awaiting the next iteration of injustice to make social life problematic. Hence, the pursuit of justice is a struggle that endures across the ages. Christians must transmit the habit of patience so that the generations cooperate in their effort to advance justice. Secondly, Augustine warned against the delusion of utopia, an ideal politically perfect world. Such a world will never exist, Augustine insisted. Such a world can only exist in God's heavenly kingdom. Utopia, in other words, is God's business. For humans it is an impossible dream. Human beings cannot bring about utopia because our actions, despite our good intentions, will always be compromised at some point by our ancestral human sin. As an American patriot, and as one schooled in American history and political thought,

Michaud understands these constraints implicitly. Michaud appreciates why the Framers of American government insisted on limited government and separation of powers. Michaud also appreciates the sentiments of John Adams and James Madison who believe that the success of the American experiment depends on Americans remaining a virtuous people. Thirdly, Augustine warns that Christians should not tie their happiness to the promises of politicians. Christianity is about transforming the heart of the individual person into a new creature in Christ. In essence, Christianity is not a political project. Jesus understood this; hence he disappointed zealots who hoped he would be a revolutionary politician. For Augustine, Jesus' Parable of the Wheat and Tares is definitive. The lesson of the Parable is that evil in this world will always be "coincidental with good." In other words, no political system, nor its agents, can get rid of evil or justice permanently. In the next life, in God's Kingdom, God will correct once and for all the imbalances of injustice. However, on this side of Heaven, while human history rolls along, humankind will have to wrestle with evil. There is irony in Christian social life. We are called to cope with evil, realizing that we can never conquer it on this side of the vale. And yet, by cooperating with God's grace, we can nonetheless improve this profane world.

Our struggle in history is filled with drama and meaning, but Augustinian irony measures the struggle. Peace, prosperity, and justice may exist for a while. But be sure the other shoe will drop soon enough. Then the Christian will have to respond anew. Michaud understands that we must prepare for this, asking what, as a Christian individual, one is expected to do as a participant in the drama of history. This sense of mission will keep one well-adjusted and focused. It will keep one from imagining that the point of life is to be comfortable and pampered by utopian dreams of perpetual justice and peace. It is not that easy.

The reader will find engaging how Thomas Michaud weaves these themes of Augustinian wisdom into his Collection.

Introduction

As a political philosophy Progressivism has its origins in Modern Rationalism and Positivism of the seventeenth and eighteenth centuries.[1] Since then, it has evolved as a shifting and uneasy blend of mainly left-wing ideas. With the nineteenth century's Age of Ideology, as Henry David Aiken names it,[2] Progressivism secured some of a foundation so that in the early twentieth century, particularly in the United States, it shed any vestige of its origins as a philosophy to morph into a thoroughgoing political ideology. As such, it actually spawned an official political party, The American Progressive Party.[3]

As an ideology, Progressivism was and is a leftist populism that seeks social justice above all else.[4] The transformation of the meaning and principles of justice into its ideological social justice is the reason for the title of this volume, *After Justice*. Progressive populist social justice is mostly unrecognizable as justice from the perspective of philosophical evaluation. As a mere ideology without philosophical self-examination, Progressivism's olio of ideas is uneasy due to many inconsistencies. A major one is that its populist "for the people" social justice orientation is devolving into a collectivism that is more and more becoming authoritarian.

In recent decades in the United States, various derivative forms of Progressivism have emerged that manifest its lack of philosophical cohesion and authoritarian proclivity, such as: 1) Postmodernism, which was actually anti-Modernism with its rejections of Rationalism, Scientific Positivism and any traditional-based metaphysics and ethics; 2) the authoritarian Politically Correct and Cancel Culture standards of moral righteous-

1

ness; and, 3) the Woke mentality that employs social and main-stream media to transform the "people" into a conformist, hive-minded ruling mob.

Most of the works in this volume challenge Progressive ideology in its various forms. Those challenges mainly issue from what has come to be known as Traditional Catholic philosophy. The challenges aim to expose Progressivism as it is, a mere ideology that lacks philosophical carriage and whose desired outcomes pose a serious threat to individual autonomy, family identity, cultural and political heritage, the integrity of education, and economic stability and growth. The principles of Traditional Catholic philosophy are shown to be a sound and hopeful foundation for resisting Progressivism and correcting its reformist and revolutionary agenda.

In Spring 2004, I travelled for the first time with my colleague Peter Redpath to the Catholic University of Lublin (KUL: Katolicki Uniwersytet Lubelski).[5] Since then, in almost every other year I visited KUL and other Catholic universities in Poland and Spain. Still, it was that first experience that inspired and graced me with a renewed devotion to follow the mission and teachings of one of my personal heroes, Saint John Paul the Great. KUL is the academic home of Rev. Professor Karol Wojtyla, and since the late 1970s, I have favored his philosophical works. Later when he became Pope John Paul II, I continued to be edified by his encyclicals, letters, books and teachings. In fact, in October 1978, I was writing my Ph.D. qualifying paper and researching my dissertation at the Edmund Husserl Archives at the Catholic University of Leuven (Louvain), Belgium. My qualifying paper was on the philosopher Max Scheler and I had come across an essay about Scheler by Karol Wojtyla.[6] I was literally studying Wojtyla's Scheler article when I learned through a radio broadcast that he had been elected Pope. I truly believe that the Holy Spirit illumined me at that spiritually propitious moment.

During my visits to KUL, I became immersed in the academic world of Rev. Professor Karol Wojtyla. I was able to sit at his desk, teach and lecture in the seminar rooms where he taught, and come to know colleagues who were his students and friends. KUL and the surrounding neighborhood of Lublin were alive with philosophical discourse. Even the street news kiosks sold philosophy books and journals. My travel American philosopher friends, Redpath and Curtis Hancock, as well as other friends, students and family who accompanied me on various trips to Poland were captivated by the intellectual and faithful atmosphere of KUL. Our host, Professor Piotr Jaroszynski, initiated the annual International Congress of Philosophy on the Future of Western Civilization, which each year had a specific theme dedicated to addressing cultural issues chiefly from the perspective of Traditional Catholic thought. Most of my papers in this volume were written for presentation at, and subsequent publication in, the Congresses' volumes. In 2004, for instance, it was the third Congress and the theme was Philosophy and Education. The International Congresses are now in their 21st year. Because of the International Congresses, the opportunities to lecture and deliver courses in KUL's Graduate English Program in Philosophy, the most gracious hospitality of our Polish colleagues, and the robust welcoming of Traditional Catholic thought, my American and international colleagues found a home at KUL.

There are at least three other Catholic philosophers who had a profound influence on my philosophical development and whose thought is applied in some of the essays in this volume. They are, Gabriel Marcel (1883-1973), Michael Novak

(1933-2017) and Rev. James Schall, S.J. (1928-2019). I first became involved with Marcel's philosophy in the early 1980s through my interests in the topic of intersubjectivity in existential phenomenology. I found his "journalistic" style of writing, his creativity and his concrete philosophy to be a fertile alternative to so much of the overly abstract, systematic phenomenology of that time. In addition, Marcel's Traditional Catholicism was not covert in his works, but overtly evident in his critiques of contemporary culture, morality and politics. Through his faith-filled philosophy he defended a pro-life stance, astutely assessed science and technology, and strongly warned against the rise of political collectivism in the forms of socialism and communism. Unlike so many philosophers of his day, moreover, he offered sound wisdom in facing the vicissitudes of contemporary life. Over the years, I became fully engaged with Marcel's works and legacy. I was a founding member of the Gabriel Marcel Society, its Secretary/Treasurer and then its President. I remain most grateful to the Gabriel Marcel Society for supporting my efforts to enliven and extend Marcel's legacy, which deserves to be furthered as a hopeful philosophical pathway for treading through the Progressive wildlands.

I had the privilege of spending much personal time with Michael Novak and Fr. James Schall. They were both most congenial gentlemen, and always willing to discuss my interpretations and applications of their writings. Both had, moreover, a gifted sense of humor, which was frequently woven into the stories they told, and, especially with Fr. Schall, displayed in their delightful quips about current events. Although they do not necessarily identify Progressivism by name, Progressivism and its derivative forms are clearly the critical focus of their writings on social justice, political economy, ordered freedom, egalitarian tolerance, the nature of human relationships, and the importance of religion and morality for the survival of a democratic republic.

This volume is organized into six thematic sections. Each section has an Introduction that addresses the section's theme and provides some background on the selections in it. The selections are grouped in the chronological order of when they were written. The earliest overall selection is from 2004 and the latest from 2021. Except for the first and last sections, the selections are philosophical papers. In the first section, the selections are editorials written for a newspaper and lectures given at various Catholic organizations. The last section is a short story that is included simply because it is hopefully entertaining, although it does have a serious message. Most of the selections have been published in an international magazine or journal, and most of those selections were published in the Polish language.

There are many people I must acknowledge and thank. First, my wife Kim who has been my loving partner, supporter, editor, philosophical interlocutress and Catholic role model for the past 50 years. With Kim, I understand the meaning of piety in human relationships: piety is the disposition one has toward another who gives one so much that no expression of gratitude can ever adequately measure up to what one receives. I would like to thank my children, Maxwell, Adrienne, Yvette and Gabriel. Each of them in their own way has contributed to my philosophical work and whatever wisdom I might have acquired. With them, I have a wealth that goes beyond whatever I could express in words. With Peter Redpath and Curtis Hancock, my friends, intellectual confreres and traveling companions for more than 25 years, philosophy became an international adventure, though perhaps more of an escapade than adventure at times.

There are many colleagues I must recognize and thank for their collegiality, support and publication permissions: my friend Piotr Jaroszynski of KUL has had a life-altering personal and professional effect on me; Fr. Pawel Tarasiewicz, formerly of KUL, editor of various international journals and a long-time friend, stands out as one of the very best Catholic priests I have known; Professor Imelda Choldna-Blach of KUL is a philosopher whose potential as a teacher and writer will carry her far beyond the quite respectable academic status she has already earned; and, finally, Prof. Henrique Martinez, Abat Oliba University, Barcelona, Spain, graciously permitted me to publish my article that appeared in a volume he edited. My Program Coordinator, Harold Ellifritt has been invaluable in assembling this volume with his advice and publishing experience, and my former Program Assistant, Mary Lou Conley, whose "wizardly" word-processing skills produced the original versions of most of the selections in this volume.

As a final note in this Introduction, I must say that I hope this volume can help some of those Traditionals who are struggling because they feel displaced in or alienated from our society. Perhaps understanding the multifaceted objectives of the Progressive ideology will enable them to recognize, challenge and resist the Progressives' aims to cancel their beliefs in what truly is the common good for society.

References and Notes

1. For an overview of the origins and history of Progressivism see the article, "Diversity within U.S. Culture and Politics" in Section V of this volume.
2. Henry David Aiken, *The Age of Ideology* (New York: New American Library: The Mentor Philosophers, 1956).
3. This party was short-lived, but the Progressive Congressional Caucus is alive in the U.S. Congress. It currently has at least 100 members, most of which are from the House of Representatives.
4. This definition of Progressivism as well as what is offered in the first paragraph of this Introduction are based on: "Progressivism," available online at http://www.progressiveliving.org/progressivism
5. KUL is now officially named: John Paul II Catholic University of Lublin. However, the acronym, KUL, is still commonly used.
6. Karol Wojtyla wrote his habilitation thesis on Scheler at Jagellonian University in 1952 entitled: An Attempt to Develop a Christian Ethics Based on Max Scheler's System. A more recent work has English translations of essays Wojtyla wrote on Scheler: *Catholic Thought from Lublin: Person and Community - Selected Essays* (Dordrech, Holland: Peter Lang Publishing, 1993)

Section I

Lectures and Editorials

Section Introduction

This Section is a collection of editorials and lectures. The editorials were solicited by and published in Polish in a Traditional Catholic Polish national newspaper which appears daily throughout Poland and, in digital form, in many other nations. The editorials were written before and after Barack Obama's election to a second term as US President. Obama's two-term administration ensconced Progressivism as the leadership ideology in the USA and, perhaps, in various other nations as well. All of the editorials consider the serious challenges to Traditional Catholics that Obama's Progressivism posed, especially the direct assaults on the Culture of Life. Some of the editorials also present disturbing data from the Catholic voting patterns in the Obama elections. These data show that Catholics in general were unaware of the threats to their faith leveled by Obama's Progressivism.

In 2013-2014, I gave a series of "Thinking Catholic" Lectures to various Catholic organizations and parishes. I believed that if I could educate adult Catholics about some fundamentals of their faith pertaining to the nature of the soul, ethics and economic justice that are particularly relevant to opposing Progressivism, they could perhaps better understand the threats they are facing. I found that plain-spoken applications and interpretations of the *Catechism of the Catholic Church* were highly successful and appreciated teaching methods. The final lecture on "Sports" was a hit. I taught a Philosophy of Sports undergraduate course for many years using Michael Novak's *Joy of*

Sports as a text. The lecture audience, which was sizable, had no idea that the Church actually had teachings about sports. It was certainly one of the most popular lectures I have ever delivered.

Editorial

Catholics and Public Life
June 2012

What are the responsibilities of faithful Catholics in public life? Although this question poses profound issues today with governments and economic unions enacting policies that promote the "Culture of Death," it is not by any means a new question. As Fr. James Schall, S.J., reminds us in his article "Political Withdrawal?" (*The Catholic Thing*, 21 February 2012), St. Augustine actually struggled with this very question during his time of the collapsing and corrupted Roman Empire.

In Book 3 of *The Confessions* Augustine relates his reaction to reading the *Life of Anthony*, the Egyptian monk (250 – 356 A.D.) who withdrew from involvement in public life. Augustine concluded that he too must withdraw. G.K. Chesterton in his *Saint Francis of Assisi* also recalled the same St. Anthony. Chesterton affirmed that in the warped culture of the late Roman Empire, withdrawal was the only option.

Is withdrawal from public life the option today? Should faithful Catholics not become politicians or government agents? Should they not strive for moral change and true justice? Should they now retreat in the face of governments and economic unions which promote abortion, euthanasia, sterilization, fetal experimentation and same-sex marriage?

In *Deus Caritas Est* (28), Pope Benedict XVI teaches that, "It is not the Church's responsibility to make its teaching prevail in political life. Rather, the Church wishes to form consciences in political life and to stimulate greater insight into the authentic requirements of justice as well as greater readiness to act accordingly, even when this might involve conflict with situations of personal interest."

The Holy Father continues by saying that, "The Church cannot and must not take upon herself the political battle to bring about the most just society possible. She cannot and must not replace the State. Yet at the same time she cannot and must not remain on the sidelines in the fight for justice. She has to play her part through rational argument and she has to awaken the spiritual energy without which justice, which always demands sacrifice, cannot prevail and prosper."

These words of Pope Benedict are an exhortation for Catholics to continue to fight for authentic justice and moral change. This is a fight that should be prosecuted with reason, rational argumentation and canny political organization. This fight must be based on the formation of consciences of faithful Catholics, and in accord with the principle of subsidiarity, it should begin within the most basic communities, namely the parishes.

Catholics need to realize that rational argumentation issuing from a well-formed conscience can seriously challenge the policies of the Culture of Death. With the leadership of their pastors and priests, parishes should: 1) design and distribute voters' guides about the beliefs and records of political candidates; 2) invite faithful Catholic clergy, leaders and professors to present lectures which teach the rational arguments against the Death policies; 3) organize workshops and discussion groups so that parishioners can educate each other in the rational ways of opposing the Death Culture; 4) and, parishioners should encourage their pastors and priests to deliver sermons and homilies which expose rationally the immorality of the Death policies.

With the grace of the Holy Spirit, a faithful Catholic's well-formed conscience engaging in public life can indeed establish powerful resistance to the spread of the Death Culture. This is now the calling and responsibility of faithful Catholics.

Editorial

Will it be Obama's America
October 2012

All presidential elections in any nation have some historical significance. What the USA faces on November 6, 2012, however, has significance of such magnitude that it eclipses most of the presidential elections in USA history. The very nature of the USA as a constitutional republic, as a free-market economy, as a nation informed by Judeo-Christian moral principles, and as a world leader, is at stake.

Honest political pollsters and pundits claim that the election is too close to call. The partisan mainstream media and biased polls overtly side with Obama, covering up his failures and concealing what he really believes in order to propagandize gullible Americans.

What these naïve, mind-clouded Americans fail to understand is that the upcoming election is not about "politics as usual," Democrats typically battling Republicans. The election is actually about the survival of the USA as it is and has been since its founding.

In a remarkable film, *2016: Obama's America*, Dinesh D'Souza and John Sullivan expose Obama's operative ideology. The film is a cautionary tale, warning us about what America and the world would be like if Obama wins a second four-year term. This ideology, in which Obama was educated and to which he still clings, is post-colonial globalism. It maintains that the power of developed nations must be radically diminished because they have amassed that power by exploiting "colonized" underdeveloped nations. To compensate for such injustice, the wealth of the USA and some European nations must be reduced through globally enforced redistribution measures. The military power, which protects their exploitive colonialism, must also be decreased by dismantling military bases, cutting military budgets and missile disarmament.

This ideology is driven by a socialist zeal; it is a Marxist liberation ideology, anti-capitalist, anti-individual freedom, and, in many ways, anti-Judeo-Christian morality. It is the ideology of Obama's biological father, and the ideology of various activists and university professors who Obama idolized, such as Edward Said, Derrick Bell and Frank Marshall Davis.

Although critics dismiss *2016* as election year slander, it is indisputable that many of Obama's presidential actions manifest this ideological motivation. Obama has corrupted or simply ignored the USA Constitutional legislative process as with "Obamacare" and overriding the Defense of Marriage Act. He has fully supported the Muslin Brotherhood in Egypt and other extremist Muslim groups in the Middle East. He has banned oil drilling and pipelines in the USA for "environmental" reasons, but given taxpayers' dollars to fund drilling in countries like Brazil. He has refused to enact effective policies to limit illegal immigration into the USA. He has incited class envy and antagonism in the USA without admitting that his redistributionist policies have actually caused escalating unemployment and declining standards of living.

So conned by the media and Obama's charming facade, too many Americans can't or won't perceive what is really at stake with his ideology. Among those whose minds have been distorted are, unfortunately, almost half of the USA's Catholic voters.

In spite of courageous efforts by some bishops, clergy and faithful lay Catholics in opposing the mandated death-culture of "Obamacare" and his support of gay marriage, the Center for Applied Research in the Apostolate reports that the Catholic vote is virtually split: 47% for Obama and 45% for Romney.

The non-Hispanic Catholic vote is probably the ultimate swing group for the election. If it were to shift by six or more percentage points in favor of Romney, it is probable that Obama would lose. But will this happen?

It is possible but unlikely that there will be such a substantial shift. Liberal progressive Catholics, the clergy and the lay, believe in Obama's socialist redistribution of wealth and power. They believe that "Caesar" and his big government can create a utopian heaven-on-earth.

Does this mean, then, that Obama will win, and his vision of a diminished America and world will prevail? Not necessarily, because at this time it really is too close to call.

Editorial

A Nation Divided
November 2012

Not since the Civil War has the USA been such a starkly divided nation. The Presidential Election confirmed that there are two Americas, the Red and the Blue.

The Blue, mainly centered in large urban areas throughout the nation, seeks a Progressive Utopia, a centralized, secular, unionized socialist state: BIG Government, Obamacare's Socialized Medicine, Impractical Green Energy Projects, abortion, same-sex marriage and always HIGHER taxes. It is the "empathetic" Nanny State, which seduces Blues with alluring "freebies" paid for by wealth redistribution and entitlements for the favorite voting blocks.

The Red seeks limited government, adherence to the Constitution, "one nation under God," entrepreneurs, a solid work ethic, the right to life, the defense of traditional marriage and family, and ordered freedom and liberty.

With the Blues currently in power, however, the Reds, in their suburbs and rural areas, must accept that they will be paying for the Blues in the financially distressed urban centers. Reds will be working and paying the always HIGHER taxes so that the Blue leaders can continue and even increase their freebies for the entitled.

In Book VIII of his *Republic*, Plato examines the transition from democracy to tyranny. The principal means of this transition is the leader, who changes from being a Protector to becoming a Tyrant. To interpretively paraphrase Plato, a protector is at first a champion. He calls for change and dispenses hope, as if he were tossing pieces of candy to a crowd. He is full of smiles, well-liked by those he meets, and making promises that people want to hear, such as liberating debtors from "unfair" financial burdens and distributing wealth to his followers. He eventually learns that resistors can be so impoverished by always HIGHER taxes that they must devote themselves almost entirely to making a living and, thereby, will be less likely to campaign against him. By such financial oppression and by eliminating from power any of those who rule with him but criticize his policies, the Protector finally becomes the Tyrant.

Plato's insights are ominous for the USA today. But the BLUES are in charge, and what the Ancient Athenian could not know is the extent of the influence that solidifies the Blue power. That SUPER INFLUENTIAL power is the so-called "private" media, namely most news outlets, TV shows, Hollywood films, and magazines. With a Pravda-style allegiance, the Blue media protect and serve Obama and the Blue agenda like a Praetorian Guard. It is more powerful than even Orwellian Newspeak; it is all-encompassing Culturespeak. Words, images, and tactics are fabricated and inserted into all media to subjugate the hearts, minds and behaviors of the people – only Blue People are wanted, Red People do not belong. For instance, Reds who are right-to-lifers, defenders of traditional marriage, and opponents of government-freebie contraception are, according to Blue media Culturespeak, prosecuting a "War on Women". They are enemies who must be defeated for the sake of protecting "Women's Rights".

Before the Election, Catholic voters were identified as a very important group which could potentially curb the Blue rise to power. Faithful believers and some Catholic Church leaders hoped that because of the Obama Administration's assault on religious liberty, blatant promotion of abortion, same-sex marriage and free contraception, Catholic voters would wake up, take their Faith seriously, and reject Obama's radical anti-life agenda. Some Bishops challenged Catholics as to how they could support a regime whose Obamacare mandates that Catholic hospitals and colleges provide insurance coverage for contraception for all employees and students.

Those efforts, some very courageous indeed, were unfortunately in vain. Perhaps this is because the Church's efforts were not supported by all of the clergy and certainly not by all of the Catholics. Maybe too many Church leaders were just too timid, cowardly, or just did not understand what was at stake. In the Election, Catholic voters chose Obama over Romney, 52% to 45%. The 7% was even a greater margin of difference than the 1%-2% with the general population vote.

In this Election, the Catholic vote as a defender of Catholic moral principles proved itself to be ineffectual at best and scandalous at worst. The Church should recognize seriously that this Election has forced a mission upon it. It is a mission which must carried out in the most effective ways possible, otherwise the Church's fundamental moral teachings in America will devolve into irrelevance. The Blue agenda will overwhelm it and it will stand for nothing more than a Marxist version of "social Justice."

Is there hope for the USA? Can the divide between the Blue and the Red ever be bridged, if not healed? At this time, the future is bleak. Still, we must remember that the virtue of hope is a supernatural one and its energy is the Grace of the Holy Spirit. For many decades, the future of many nations and the world itself looked very bleak with the tyrannous Soviet Empire, but the USSR did collapse. Strong Faith and Prayer enabled people to endure during those oppressive times. The USA must find genuine hope once again, the hope that with Divine

Grace, His *LOGOS* of Truth and Righteousness will ultimately triumph.

Editorial

Where is "Mud" in Negative Campaigning
May 2014

In most democratic republic nations today the opposition between the political left vs. right has become intense. In the USA the mainstream media that typically supports the left, the liberal Democrats, and opposes the right, the conservative Republicans, fuel this intensity. In collaboration with leftist politicians, the media aim to convince voters that all negative campaigning is not civil, not fair and not even ethical. The media have established themselves as the judges of what is or is not negative campaigning, and sadly their judgments usually obey what the political left commands.

So what is real and not merely media-made mudslinging? In general, mudslinging toward politicians is character assassination, intentional misrepresentation of their voting records, positions and statements, and focusing on politically or ideologically irrelevant incidents from their personal past. Another way politicians and their media lackeys throw mud is to castigate an opposing ideology to influence voters to believe that anyone advancing political positions within that ideology is morally corrupt. It is not mudslinging, however, to cite accurately politicians' voting records or their political influences through close personal associations.

Although the left would certainly disagree, the vast majority of mudslinging today in the USA does indeed come from the left. The mainstream media wield enormous power, the power to reinforce their predominate ideology and promote their political agenda. Consequently, the following examples concentrate on mudslinging from the left, since their mudslinging is so frequent and has such a powerful national impact.

As the self-appointed judges of what is uncivil negative campaigning, the media have decided that to cite one of their favored politician's voting record on an issue they oppose is mudslinging. As an Illinois State Senator, Obama, for example, voted "present" in 1997 on a bill banning partial birth abortion, a political strategy to disguise his actual opposition to the ban so that he could then say that he had not voted against it.

Subsequently from 2001-2003 he voted three times against the Illinois Born Alive Infant Protection Act. When this horrific voting record was cited in the 2008 and 20012 Presidential campaigns, the mainstream media accused Obama's opposition of negative campaigning. The media denounced the opposition's claim that Obama had voted to allow infanticide by insisting that the opposition was only intending to smear Obama's character, and his voting record on the issue should not even be raised or questioned.

Related to this partial birth abortion issue is the left's rendition of the right's opposition to Obamacare's proposed funding of birth control for women, which includes the abortifacient "morning after pill." Taking their marching orders from the Democrats, the media proclaimed that any politician, who opposed Obamacare on such grounds, was participating in a morally egregious "War on Women." These politicians, males and females alike, were and still are accused of being morally flawed, as being anti-women and oppressors of woman's rights. The media abet the Democrats in assassinating the characters of their ideological opponents, which is mudslinging of a most heinous sort.

The media's mudslinging advocacy of Obamacare, however, doesn't stop with their "War on Women" accusations. They also denigrate morally those politicians who oppose Obamacare on most any grounds as being against the poor and even racist. The media have shown themselves to be relentless in their negative, mud-filled campaigning for Obamacare.

Beyond the so-called "women's reproductive rights" issues, the media have also succeeded in actually altering the common language of other issues so that they can support their ideology and the politicians who believe in it. Mainly because of the power of media influence, it has become accepted in the USA to call someone who opposes same-sex marriage "homophobic." But consider that word: a phobia, according to psychology, is an irrational fear. It is an extreme fear that normal, rational people do not have; it is a psychologically disordered fear. For the media to accuse a politician who has a rational moral opposition to same-sex marriage of being homophobic is to claim that the politician is to some degree or in some way psychologically disordered, or perhaps even crazy. What more blatant mudslinging could there be?

The leftist media dismissed as negative smear campaigning any attempts to expose Obama's politically influential close associations. For instance, though he attended religious services for 20 years at Pastor Jeremiah Wright's church, and Rev. Wright baptized Obama's children, the media aggressively insisted that Obama really did not know about Rev. Wright's anti-American themes in his sermons. Rev. Wright is of course the radical preacher who proclaimed that the USA deserved what it got with the 9/11/01 terrorist attacks, and that it is not "God Bless America" but "God Damn America."

With Mitt Romney, on the other hand, the media focused for days during the 2012 campaign on an irrelevant incident from his past. Romney once put his family dog in a carrier attached to the top of his van to let the dog enjoy the rush of air while driving. Although the dog was unharmed, the media accused Romney of animal cruelty and alleged the incident was a sign of his anti-animal rights and overall anti-environmentalism ideology. Incredible, fabricated mudslinging, for which the media was never held accountable!

With the staggering power of the leftist media, the standards of ethical propriety in political campaigns have not been just violated but dramatically redefined. The traditional democratic process itself has become unrecognizable under the cover of its thick coat of media-made mud. Only a thorough "power-washing" coming from the electorate, the people themselves, could possibly cleanse our sullied democratic republic.

Thinking Catholic

Economic Justice and its Types

June 2013

A. Justice in general is a virtue. It ought to be cultivated as a trait of a person's character so that the person acts habitually in a just manner. Though there are many ways in which justice can be defined, it is, most basically, "right relations between people." A person acting with the virtue of justice seeks "to conform to" (synonyms = to establish, to engender, to follow) right relations with others. It is very important to remember that as a virtue, justice is principally a character trait, principally a disposition within oneself. (See below: **CCC #1807**)[1]

---

[1] "CCC" refers to the *Catechism of the Catholic Church*

B. It is also important to note that the principal quality of justice within an economic context is FAIRNESS. Fairness, however, has at least two meanings EQUALITY (sameness) and EQUITY (deservedness). Moreover, equity is morally prior to equality in the sense that equity morally justifies equality. To be more specific the argument runs: People ought to be treated equally. Why? Because they all possess a fundamental human dignity, and thereby they deserve (equity) equal treatment.

1. In doing ethics, it is important to recognize the distinction between equality and equity and make prudent judgments about which type of fairness applies to the situation at hand.

2. In recent years the fairness meaning of "equity" has been changing due to various groups, organizations and movements. "Equity" is being redefined as ensuring an equality of outcomes. Equality of opportunity means that each person or group has access to the same resources to fulfill their social and economic ambitions. Equity, now, however, is understood as ensuring that a person or group has access to whatever resources that are needed in their situation so that they can have achieve outcomes that are equal to the outcomes that "privileged" persons or groups achieve.

C. The Preferential Option for the Poor (**CCC #2448**)

D.The Four Types of Justices (Economic Applications)

1.**Contributive Justice**: The availability (synonyms = willingness, disposition, character, habit of justice, the habit of beneficence) to contribute proactively to the economic well-being of another (others) and/or the economic common good of society.

NOTE: Contributive justice is a necessary condition for acting for, with and on all of the other justices. Without the disposition to seek justice, to act justly, the other types of justices will not matter to a person. Or, if they do matter, without the disposition of contributive justice, they will be more of a matter of politics and ideology than virtue. Sometimes this view of contributive justice is identified with **legal justice** (see reference to **CCC #2411** below), but this notion of contributive justice actually expresses a more fundamental understanding of justice as a virtue of character rather than merely a type of "legal" requirement.

2. **Commutative Justice**: The justice of "fair" economic transactions, which in general would involve no force or fraud, voluntary agreement, fair prices and wages, and honesty. (**CCC #2411**)

3. **Distributive Justice**: The "fair" distribution of wealth in a society, which would include access to wealth and opportunity for wealth. This is mostly applied as a **corrective justice**. (**CCC #2411**) Corrective justice involves actions (e.g., political, legislative, peaceful and/or riotous protests) taken to correct a perceived economic injustice in the present and/or from the past.

4. **Compensatory (Reparative) Justice**: "Fair" compensation to individuals and/or groups who have been "stolen from" in the past by a person, society at large and/or the government. This is entirely a **corrective justice**. (**CCC #2412**)

References and Comments from CCC:

CCC #1807: "Justice is the moral virtue that consists in the constant and firm will to give their due to God and neighbor…Justice toward men disposes one to respect the rights of each and to establish in human relationships the harmony that promotes equity with regard to persons and the common good. The just man, often mentioned in the Sacred Scripture, is distinguished by habitual right thinking and the uprightness of his conduct toward his neighbor." [Comment: Justice demands integrity of character.]

CCC #2448: "…those who are oppressed by poverty are the object of a *preferential love* on the part of the Church which, since her origin and in spite of the failings of many of her members, has not ceased to work for their relief, defense, and liberation through numerous works of charity which remain indispensable always and everywhere." [Comment: Notice that the emphasis here, as it is in other contexts, is on works of charity; there is no mention of government systems or programs that would be part of a "welfare state."]

CCC #2411: "Contracts are subject to *commutative justice* which regulates exchanges between persons in accordance with a strict respect for their rights. Commutative justice obliges strictly; it requires guarding property rights, paying debts, and fulfilling obligations freely contracted."

CCC #2411: "One distinguishes *commutative* justice from *legal* justice, which concerns what a citizen owes in fairness to the community, and from *distributive* justice which regulates what the community owes its citizens in proportion to their contributions and needs."

CCC #2412: "In virtue of commutative justice, *reparation for injustice* committed requires the restitution of stolen goods to their owner."

Thinking Catholic

Social and Economic Justice
March 2014

A. Background on Social Economic Justice: A Clash of Political Ideologies

1. Progressivism vs. Magisterial Catholicism: Progressivism has grown substantially since the 1960s in parishes, dioceses, seminaries, religious orders and especially Catholic universities. It has at various times and under various circumstances called itself or been called by others Catholic/ Christian Marxism, Catholic/Christian Humanism, Catholic Liberationism. Today it is commonplace, and many Catholics simply accept its views on morality and economics as true and authentic teachings of the Faith.

2. Magisterial Catholicism today (with qualifications, a.k.a., Traditional Catholicism, Orthodox Catholicism, Conservative Catholicism) has been gradually diminishing in numbers and is a minority voice, if a voice at all, at most Catholic universities. In fact, many dioceses, religious orders, seminaries and universities today will intentionally and publicly identify themselves with progressivism or magisterialism, if not in "word" then in "deed."

3. The tension within the Church has made it confusing and challenging to understand what Catholic Social/Economic Justice holds and what it obliges us to believe in order to act morally.

B. The Church and Politics

1. Catholic teaching is that the Church must remain outside of politics, but not remain outside of social matters of morals. Political developments are not the province of the Church, but matters of morality, such as moral justice, are part of the Church's God-given mission. Benedict XVI taught in <u>Deus Caritas Est</u> (28) that: "It is not the Church's responsibility to make its teaching prevail in political life. Rather, the Church wishes to form consciences in political life and to stimulate greater insight into the authentic requirements of justice as well as greater readiness to act accordingly..."

2. Pope Benedict continued by saying that, "The Church cannot and must not take upon herself the political battle to bring about the most just society possible. She cannot and must not replace the State. Yet at the same time she cannot and must not remain on the sidelines in the fight for justice. She has to play her part through rational argument, and she has to awaken the spiritual energy without which justice, which always demands sacrifice, cannot prevail and prosper."

3. Key here is the notion of forming consciences for political life through rational argumentation. What is not mentioned is for the Church to organize and participate in such activities as: labor strikes, voter registration and training, and lobbying government for special

assistance programs. Benedict's words call for a reasoned approach, one that requires education in the
Catholic tradition which will enable the formation and
exercise of informed consciences.

4. So, what should an informed Catholic conscience
    know about issues of social and economic justice?
    What rational arguments should be taken into account
    in forming consciences?

C. What do CCC & CA[2] teach us about social/economic justice?

1. The Church believes in the *preferential love of the poor*.
    CCC #2448: *In its various forms — material deprivation, un-
    just oppression, physical and psychological illness and death —
    human misery is the obvious sign of the inherited condition of
    frailty and need for salvation... This misery elicited the compas-
    sion of Christ the Savior, who willingly took it upon himself and
    identified himself with the least of his brethren. Hence those who
    are oppressed by poverty are the object of a preferential love on the
    part of the Church...*

2. The Church opposes Marxism, socialism and com-
    munism which "deify" the State. The Church favors a
    market economy which is ordered by reasonable laws
    and regulations but rejects an individualistic capitalism
    which selfishly exploits human labor and puts profit
    above all else.
    CCC #2425: *The Church has rejected the totalitarian and
    atheistic ideologies associated in modern times with "com-
    munism" or "socialism." She has likewise refused to accept, in*

---

[2] "CA" refers to the Papal Encyclical of John Paul II, *Centesimus
Annus* (1991)

the practice of "capitalism," individualism and the absolute pri-
macy of the law of the marketplace over human labor. Regulating
the economy solely by centralized planning perverts the basis of
social bonds; regulating it solely by the law of the marketplace
fails social justice, for "there are many human needs which cannot
be satisfied by the market." Reasonable regulation of the market-
place and economic initiatives, in keeping with a just hierarchy of
values and a view to the common good, is to be commended.

3. The Church emphasizes the traditional principles of
    solidarity and subsidiarity. Solidarity is a bond of
    friendship, and the disposition of social charity: it in-
    volves the sharing of material and spiritual goods, the
    spiritual even more than the material. (CCC #1937,
    #1939 & #1948) With subsidiarity, a community of
    higher order should not interfere with a community of
    a lower order, or deprive the latter of its function.
    (CCC #1883) Subsidiarity is opposed to all forms of
    collectivism, sets limits to state intervention, and aims
    at harmonizing the relationships between individuals
    and societies. (CCC #1885)

4. These reasonable laws and regulations must be estab-
    lished within a democratic order wherein the role of
    the State is to guarantee a certain economic security,
    such as with individual freedom and private property.
    Still, the moral conditions of human rights, including
    justice and equality, are areas for private citizens and
    groups in civil society.

    CA #48: *These general observations also apply to the role of the*
    State in the economic sector. "Economic activity, especially the
    activity of a market economy, cannot be conducted in an institu-
    tional, juridical or political vacuum. On the contrary, it presup-
    poses sure guarantees of individual freedom and private property,

as well as a stable currency and efficient public services. Hence the principal task of the State is to guarantee this security, so that those who work and produce can enjoy the fruits of their labors and thus feel encouraged to work efficiently and honestly....Another task of the state is that of overseeing and directing the exercise of human rights in the economic sector. However, primary responsibility in this area belongs not to the state but to individuals and to various groups and associations which make up society." **(This embedded quote is contained in CCC #2431)**

5. The State should also limit its intervention into the economy because expanded intervention can create the Welfare State, a.k.a., the Social Assistance State. CA #48 invokes the principle of subsidiarity to help explain this.

6. In recent years the range of such intervention [intervention of the State into the economy] has vastly expanded, to the point of creating a new type of state, the so-called "Welfare State." This has happened in some countries in order to respond better to many needs and demands, by remedying forms of poverty and deprivation unworthy of the human person. However, excesses and abuses, especially in recent years, have provoked very harsh criticisms of the Welfare State, dubbed the "Social Assistance State." Malfunctions and defects in the Social Assistance State are the result of an inadequate understanding of the tasks proper to the State. Here again the principle of lower order, depriving the latter of its functions, but rather should support it in case of need and help to coordinate its activity with the activities of the rest of society, always with a view to the common good.

7. By intervening directly and depriving society of its responsibility, the Social Assistance State leads to a loss of human energies and an inordinate increase of public agencies, which are dominated more by bureaucratic ways of thinking than by concern for serving their clients, and which are accompanied by an enormous increase in spending. In fact it would appear that needs are best understood and satisfied by people who are closest to them and who act as neighbors to those in need.

8. Further comment on CA #48: The bureaucratic mentality of an inordinate number of State Social Assistance agencies drains human energies and diminish personal responsibility. The agencies are also expensive, which, of course, translates into ever higher taxes and diminishes the "fruits of one's labor."

9. What at this point can we conclude generally? For the Church, social economic justice is not the principal task of the State. It is principally the moral obligation of persons acting within a well-ordered juridical framework of democratic market economies. We can conclude, moreover, that economic systems and political welfare programs by themselves cannot bring about justice and equality and actualize the "preferential love of the poor."

D. Excursus: Reflections on EG[3] and Pope Francis

1. In regard to substance, EG appears to convey the teachings of CCC and CA. As an Apostolic Exhortation, EG does aim to form moral consciences through rational argumentation. There is nothing in EG that is exceptional or is not consistent with the magisterial CCC. Consider the following excerpts:

202. *The need to resolve the structural causes of poverty cannot be delayed, not only for the pragmatic reason of its urgency for the good order of society, but because society needs to be cured of a sickness which is weakening and frustrating it, and which can only lead to new crises. Welfare projects, which meet certain urgent needs, should be considered merely temporary responses. As long as the problems of the poor are not radically resolved by rejecting the absolute autonomy of markets and financial speculation and by attacking the structural causes of inequality, no solution will be found for the world's problems or, for that matter, to any problems. Inequality is the root of social ills.*

Comment: Pope Francis expresses serious cautions about regulating the economy "solely by the law of the marketplace." **(See above CCC #2431)** He also emphasizes that welfare projects are merely "temporary responses," which implies that a "permanent" Welfare State would be morally problematic.

189. ...*The private ownership of goods is justified by the need to protect and increase them, so that they restore to the poor what belongs to them. These conviction and habits of solidarity, when they are put into practice,*

---

[3] "EG" refers to the Apostolic Exhortation, *Evangelii Gaudium* (2014), of Pope Francis.

open the way to other structural transformations and make them possible... **(CCC #2431)**

Comment: Pope Francis does uphold the right to private property especially because the private, as opposed to the collective, ownership of goods is the best and perhaps most efficient way to protect and increase the goods so that in solidarity, they can be shared with the poor.

203. ... *Business is a vocation, and a noble vocation, provided that those engaged in it see themselves challenged by a greater meaning in life; this will enable them truly to serve the common good by striving to increase the goods of this world and to make them more accessible to all.*

Comment: Pope Francis does not castigate business as intrinsically immoral.

204. ... *Growth in justice requires more than economic growth, while presupposing such growth: it requires decisions, programmes, mechanisms and processes specifically geared to a better distribution of income, the creation of sources of employment and an integral promotion of the poor which goes beyond a simple welfare mentality. I am far from proposing an irresponsible populism, but the economy can no longer turn to remedies that are a new poison, such as attempting to increase profits by reducing the work force and thereby adding to the ranks of the excluded.*

Comment: Pope Francis once again denounces a welfare mentality, while exhorting us to recognize with good conscience "a new poison" that is advanced as an economic remedy.

240. *It is the responsibility of the State to safeguard and promote the common good of society. Based on the principles of subsidiarity and solidarity, and fully committed to political dialogue and consensus building, it*

plays a fundamental role, one which cannot be delegated, in working for the integral development of all. This role, at present, calls for profound social humility.

Comment: Pope Francis affirms the traditional principles of subsidiarity and solidarity.

241. *In her dialogue with the State and with society, the Church does not have solutions for every particular issue. Together with the various sectors of society, she supports those programmes which best respond to the dignity of each person and the common good. In doing this, she proposes in a clear way the fundamental values of human life and convictions which can then find expression in political activity.*

Comment: Pope Francis confirms that the principal responsibility of the Church is not to replace the State with solutions for every particular issue, but to awaken moral consciences to fundamental values which can then find expression in political activity. (**See above Pope Benedict from** *Deus Caritas Est*)

208. *If anyone feels offended by my words, I would respond that I speak them with affection and with the best of intentions, quite apart from any personal interest or political ideology. My words are not those of a foe or an opponent. I am interested only in helping those who are in thrall to an individualistic, indifferent and self-centered mentality to be freed from those unworthy chains and to attain a way of living and thinking which is more humane, noble and fruitful, and which will bring dignity to their presence on this earth.*

Comment: Pope Francis does not align himself with the ideologies of communism or socialism in his opposition to individualistic capitalism. It appears clearly that he endorses a reasonable regulation of the marketplace and economic initiatives in keeping with a just hierarchy of values and a view to the common good. (**See above CCC #2425**)

Thinking Catholic: Applying Catholic Ethics
March 2014

NOTES: "**CCC**" refers to the *Catechism of the Catholic Church* and "**ST**" refers to *Summa Theologica* of St. Thomas Aquinas

A. The main source of moral confusion today: moral relativism

B. St. Thomas Aquinas (1225-1274) differentiates between three kinds of laws (ST, Q. 91, A. 1 & A. 2).

1. **Eternal Law** (Divine Law) is the WORD of GOD and God is His Word. Eternal Law is revealed by Scripture and it is the source, in God, of all law.
2. **Natural Law** is a rational creature's participation in Eternal Law. Only rational creatures (human beings in this world) are governed by the Natural Moral Law, and, thereby, only human beings are capable of acting morally or immorally. All non-rational creatures are amoral (morally neutral) in whatever they do. See below: **CCC #1951, #1955, #1956 & #1958**
3. **Law of Nature:** All that is, is governed by the Law of Nature. This Law is the order, the design, which God infused into nature when He created the universe.

C. What is **EVIL?** Evil in general is **PRIVATION**; it is **NOTHING**, but the lack of what is good. Now, since all that is, is the creation of God, and God is all good, all of His creation is good. Nothing in the universe was or is created as evil. Evil emerges whenever any thing or action does not fulfill the God-created natural design (the **law of nature**) of that thing or action. That thing or action is naturally deprived, though that privation is **immoral** only if it pertains to a rational creature's chosen conduct because it violates **natural law**; it is **amoral** if it does not pertain to a rational creature's chosen conduct, but still deprived because it did not conform to the **law of nature**.

D. The natural law is knowable by the natural "light of reason," an intellective process involving speculative and practical reason. (The following is based on *ST, Q.94, A. 2, 3, & 4.*)

1. **Practical reason** poses the question, "What is the natural good of X?" "X" refers to any natural thing or action.

2. **Speculative reason** contemplates the essence, the "whatness," of X which yields an essential definition of X. Such a definition expresses the God-given, God-created "reason-for-being," the natural design and purposes, of X. The truth of such essential definitions is accepted as "self-evident." A self-evident truth is actually true in that it accurately asserts some relevant feature of reality. It is recognized as true once a reasonable person understands it, and with such recognition, any attempted denial of it would be patently absurd.

3. **Practical reason** accepts and applies the essential definition as an **objective standard** for determining the good of X. This objective standard is a natural law in regard to a "human" X. If the human X does not conform to its essential definition, then it is evil, immoral, and deprived.

4. For instance, consider the question: Why is lying wrong? Lying is a type of human communication, but what is the essence of communication? The natural design purpose of acts of communication is to convey information about reality. But when one lies, the information communicated is not about reality; it is disinformation. A lie communicates unreal information, a fake reality, so a lie is deprived and thereby immoral since does not conform to the natural design purpose of communication.

E. St. Thomas makes further relevant distinctions (*ST, Q. 94, A. 4*). **Virtue** is the **natural good,** the **natural perfection,** of anything. It is virtuous and good for anything to fulfill its natural design, its natural purposes, as defined by the **law of nature**. This is what St. Thomas labels as an **aspect of virtue**. But this virtue must also be understood in regard to the **proper species**, so we must understand what is good in terms of the species we are considering. In the case of the human species, we have to consider what is naturally good in terms of our species trait, namely our ability to reason. In this way we can discover what the **natural law** is for us.

Consider, *ST, Q. 94, A.3, Respondeo Se*: I answer that we may speak of virtuous acts in two ways: first, under the aspect of virtuous; secondly, as such and such acts considered in their proper species. If then we speak of acts of virtue, considered as virtuous, thus all virtuous acts belong to the law of nature (*legem naturae*). For it has been stated that to the law of nature (legem naturae) belongs everything to which a man is inclined according to his nature. Now each thing is inclined naturally to an operation that is suitable to its form: thus fire is inclined to give heat. Wherefore, since the rational soul is the proper form of man, there is in every man a natural inclination to act according to reason: and this is to act according to virtue. Consequently, considered thus, all acts of virtue are prescribed by the natural law (*lege naturali*): since each one's reason naturally dictates to him to act virtuously. But if we speak of virtuous acts, considered in themselves, i.e., in their proper species, thus not all virtuous acts are prescribed by the law of nature (*lege naturae*): for many things are done virtuously, to which nature does not incline at first but which through the inquiry of reason, have been found by men to be conducive to well-living.

F. Example: **Human Sexuality**

- **ASPECTS of VIRTUE** (Law of Nature)
- **PROPER SPECIES** (Natural Law)
- **PROCREATIVE**, pleasure, tension release. For the human species, sex infused with reason. All are good under the law of nature.
- **UNITIVE** virtue, is the proper good which entails commitment (fidelity), mutuality and love

G. Comments on and Interpretation of **Human Sexuality**
Sexual relations in marriage have a twofold end in regard to the aspects of virtue and its proper species: The unitive (fidelity) and procreative (fecundity) significance are both inherent to the marital conjugal act. The pleasurable virtue aspect of marital conjugality does actually heighten its unitive virtue. Each and every marital conjugal act must remain open to the transmission of life and nurture the marital unity. (See, **CCC #2366**) "By safeguarding both these essential aspects, the unitive and the procreative, the conjugal act preserves in its fullness the

sense of true mutual love and its orientation towards man's exalted vocation to parenthood." (**CCC #2369**) Accordingly,
each and every act, whether as an end or as a means, that intentionally aims to render procreation impossible is intrinsically deprived (evil). (See, **CCC #2370**). Still, responsible
parenthood does include the regulation of births (such as natural family planning) for just reasons such as the health (mental
and physical), economic well-being, and prudent spacing of the
births of their children. With such regulation, that is always
open to the possibility of procreation, parents must make certain that their desire to regulate births is not motivated by selfishness but is in conformity with the generosity appropriate to
responsible parenthood. (See **CCC #2368**).

References from CCC

1. **CCC #1951:** ... The moral law presupposes the rational order, established among creatures for their
   good and to serve their final end, by the power, wisdom and goodness of the Creator. All law finds its first
   and ultimate truth in the eternal law...
2. **CCC #1955:** ...This law is called "natural," not in reference to the nature of irrational beings, but because
   reason which decrees it properly belongs to human nature...
3. **CCC #1956:** The natural law, present in the heart of
   each man and established by reason, is universal in its
   precepts and its authority extends to all men...
4. **CCC #1958:** The natural law is *immutable* and permanent throughout the variations of history; it subsists
   under the flux of ideas and customs and supports their
   progress...

5. **CCC #2366**: This particular doctrine…is based on the inseparable connection established by God, which man on his own initiative may not beak, between the unitive significance and the procreative significance which are both inherent to the marriage act.

6. **CCC #2370**: … every action which, in anticipation of the conjugal act, or in its accomplishment, or in the development of its natural consequences, proposes, whether as an end or as a means, to render procreation impossible is intrinsically evil.

7. **CCC #2368**: A particular aspect of this responsibility concerns the *regulation of births*. For just reasons, spouses may wish to space the births of their children. It is their duty to make sure that their desire is not motivated by selfishness but is in conformity with the generosity appropriate to responsible parenthood.

Thinking Catholic: What is the Soul?
April 2014

NOTE: "CCC" refers to the *Catechism of the Catholic Church*

A. What the soul is **not**: some "popular" misconceptions - - not the inner seat of emotions/feelings, not a bundle of perceptions, not the mind or brain, not 21 grams of something, not biochemical electrical impulses, not a ghost in a bodily machine, not the source of musicality, and not the spirit. St. Paul speaks of the spirit, soul and body (*1 Thess. 5:23*), but the spirit is the "heart" which spawns a person's orientation to a supernatural end; it is sometimes described as the "depths of one's being where the person decides for or against God." (**CCC #368**)

B. Describing the soul: **The soul…**

1. **is** the *anima* (the first principle of human life); it is the human essence/*whatness* which causes matter (the *conceptus*) to be **a human kind of living being.**
2. **is** incorporeal (non-physical, immaterial) and immortal (indestructible). (**CCC #366**)
3. **is** a rational soul for a rational creature [In this 'sublunar' world only humans are rational creatures with an immortal, spiritual soul: "All dogs go to heaven" if we in heaven create them to be with us (In heaven, we are co-creators with God.).]
4. **has** the essential properties of intellect and free will. (See below **CCC #1711**)*
5. **is** directly and immediately created by God for each person and God has made man in His own image. He created man as male and female. The soul is that by which man is most especially in God's image. (**CCC #355 & #363**)

C. The embodied soul: life, death and eschatology

1. The spiritual soul is within the physical body but there is not a kind of dual nature to us, such that soul and body are in any way opposed as substantially different entities or different natures. The rational soul needs to be humanly embodied; it is designed and created by

God to be embodied. The human person is a composite being: the unity of body and soul. (See below **CCC #365)****

2. The death of a person is the separation of the soul from the body. But the soul does not depart because the body is dying (gradually losing its physical functions); as long as there are signs of life, the soul is present and the person is alive.

3. The disembodied soul at the time of our death is in an **unnatural** state; it is lacking its **natural** state until it is reunited with the body at the final Resurrection and that would be a *glorified body*. (**CCC #366**).

SOME RELEVANT QUOTES FROM CCC

*CCC #1711: "Endowed with a spiritual soul, with intellect and with free will, the human person is from his very conception ordered to God…"

**CCC #365: "The unity of soul and body is so profound that one has to consider the soul to be the 'form' of the body: i.e., it is because of its spiritual soul that the body made of matter becomes a living, human body; spirit and matter in man are not two natures united, but rather their union forms a single nature."

Thinking Catholic: A Catholic View of Sports
April 2014

NOTES: "CCC" refers to the *Catechism of the Catholic Church;* influential work, Michael Novak, *The Joy of Sports* (New York: Madison Books Inc., 1993).

I. Do We Take Sports Too Seriously? Actually, We Don't Take Sports Seriously Enough.

A. How many hours a week does your family spend on sports (including "fan" hours)? Probably at least 25-40 hrs.

B. Why aren't sports studied in any formal academic way in our education systems?

C. The "deeper," more serious meaning of sports:

1. Can we even define what a sport is? Are all competitions which require physical exertion sports?
2. A possible definition: SPORT = A rule governed athletic competition requiring high levels of physical exertion, training and practice. Some might argue that various sorts of competitive dancing require all of the elements of this possible definition of a sport. The difference here would be what the prime purpose is: With such dancing the prime purpose is the overall aesthetics of the dance, not the athletic degree or control of the physical exertion itself. Still, there are gray areas or crossover activities such as ice dancing, rhythmic gymnastics, or perhaps even synchronized swimming.
3. Also, all sports are games but not all games are sports, sport and game are not univocal in meaning. Board games are not sports, but even a game with oneself, such as practicing tennis against a wall by oneself can be a game. If a score is kept which counts the number of times a hit is good based on striking the wall above or below a net top line painted on the wall, then there is a game against yourself. Shooting free throws to beat

one's own percentage of makes would be another example of solo game-playing.

D. Michael Novak believes sports are major civilizing agents.
Sports are greenhouses for nurturing and growing our understanding of ordered freedom. We learn about establishing
rules that govern our liberty, which helps us realize that in
society, as in sports, there are norms for what we should and
should not do in order to be civilized.

E. The deeper meaning of "play": something we should understand to take sports more seriously

1. Should we "Play in order to work OR work in order to
    play?" Some folks believe that, for example, a vacation
    to play is a time to recharge so that one can work bet-
    ter. But that is not truly play. That is play as a work
    strategy. It can be helpful for work, but it is using play
    as a means to an end and is not as satisfying as playing
    for its own sake. Our work should be a way to free
    ourselves so that we can play. Retirement, for instance,
    is and should be ideally the best playground and play-
    time we have since we were kids.

2. Our work ethic should be complemented by a just-as-
    strong play ethic: Play is part of the essence of free-
    dom; play is our space for free choices and creativity;
    play should not be engaged in as a means to an end,
    but as an end in itself; play is its own reward.

3. A culture which has lost its appreciation of play is a lost
    culture. It is lost because it has no appreciation
    for what freedom really is at its most basic level.

4. Play is human inventiveness, intelligence, creativity; the
    love of challenge and contest (the *agon*).

II. Why Is God a Sports Fan?

A. A sacramental view of sports: Sports spirituality is profound; the body must be included in a robust spirituality which enables a holistic union with God. The spirituality of sports play helps us accept absolute concepts of winning and losing, discipline, hard work; it nourishes the soul and can make time irrelevant allowing us to transcend temporal secular struggles. *Sport, properly directed, develops character, makes a man courageous, a generous loser, a gracious victor; it refines the senses, gives intellectual penetration, and steels the will to endurance. It is not merely a physical development then. Sport, rightly understood, is an occupation of the whole man, and while perfecting the body as an instrument of the mind, it also makes the mind itself a more refined instrument for the search and communication of truth and helps man to achieve that end to which all others must be subservient, the service and praise of his Creator.* (Pope Pius XII, "Sport at the Service of Spirit," July 1945).

B. **CCC #1882:** *Certain societies, such as family and the state, correspond more directly to the nature of man; they are necessary to him. To promote the participation of the greatest number in the life of a society, the creation of voluntary associations and institutions must be encouraged "on both national and international levels, which relate to economic and social goals, to cultural and recreational activities, to sport, to various professions, and to political affairs." (John XXIII, Mater et Magistra, 60) This 'socialization' also expresses the natural tendency for human beings to associate with one another for the sake of attaining objectives that exceed individual capacities. It develops the qualities of the person, especially the sense of initiative and responsibility, and helps guarantee his rights.* **Comment:** Organized sports are natural for human beings; they can contribute to actualizing our free-dom and solidarity in the social sphere.

CCC #2289: *If morality requires respect for the life of the body, it does not make it an absolute value. It rejects a neo-pagan notion that tends to promote the* cult of the body *to sacrifice everything for its sake, to idolize physical perfection and success at sports...* **Comment:** The cult of the body in sports is indeed prevalent today and is a corruption of the deeper meaning of sports: e.g., Terrell Owens, Ochocinco, Lolo Jones, Dennis Rodman, others?

C. Ancient Greek and Roman cultures recognized the kin-ship between sport and religion: e.g., the Olympics.

D. What is a root meaning of "fan?" The word "fan" is ety-mologically derived from the Latin, "fanum" which means a "sacred place," like a temple. Fans going to a sports stadium are like religious temple-goers. A "fanatic" was originally a super-zealous, all-in religious devotee.

E. Like religion, sports have rituals and ceremonies that are structured: there are formalized rules of action, moments of silence and jubilation.

1. Athletes and officials wear uniforms that are like cleri-cal "vestments".
2. ASCESIS: Greek word for the regimen of discipline athletes imposed on themselves, which became in Latin, "ascetic" which referred to a cleric's life of self-discipline and self-denial.
3. Sports and religion both channel our senses of fate and destiny: what is (was) meant to be! Athletes frequently

invoke God and spirituality. Fans and athletes sometimes make "deals" with God to bargain for a victory.

4. Like religions, sports deal with human dreads, aging,
    dying, injury/health, pressurized performance, cow-
    ardice, etc. There is also "sin" and "redemption" in
    sports: e.g., in football the safety is beaten for a long
    play (the sin), but later in the game he makes a "pick 6"
    (redemption).

5. There are sports SAINTS and HAGIOGRAPHIES!

6. Like in religion, in sports there are chants, songs, and
    a sense of worshipful oneness.

F. The metaphysical in SPORTS: There is "sacred time" in
sports; we can leave ordinary time and get glimpse of eternity. Time can seem to slow down extremely or even stand
still. "8 seconds left, but 8 seconds can be an eternity!" Base-
ball batters report that when in a "zone" a 99-mph fastball
seems to be moving so slowly and appears so large like a can-
taloupe that they get a bead on it and smack a hit or home
run. When time seems to stand still, we have a glimpse of
being outside of time: a most exhilarating human experience.
"Being in a zone" can be a profound "metaphysical" experience.

Section II

Marcelian Perspectives

Section Introduction

All of the selections in this Section are about Gabriel Marcel or apply his thought in a substantial way in the context of the philosophical essay. In "Critiquing 'Politically Correct' Justice" Marcel's critical assessment of "rights contests" in egalitarian democracies is an aspect of his thought that has not been explored sufficiently, but certainly deserves greater attention. It is also interesting to note that this essay applies the thought of Pope John Paul II and Fr. James Schall as well.

The second selection adapts Marcel's thought to a current philosophy of political economy, economic personalism. Marcel rejected both individualism and collectivism as extremes in that they deform the human person. His economic personalism preserves the spiritual integrity and personal identity of the free person, which reinforces an economics of abundance rather an economics of scarcity. This essay's application of Marcel's thought to political economy is, perhaps, unique in Marcelian scholarship.

The final essay in this Section was written for a *Festschrift* in honor of Peter Redpath. A major theme in Redpath's works is the contemporary crisis in Western civilization. This is also a principal theme in Marcel's thought, and Marcel is a philosopher who Redpath admires greatly. Marcel and Redpath, moreover, both believe that at the core of the crisis is the deformation of traditional Christian metaphysics of the free individual human person in favor of a collectivist abstract humanism.

This abstract humanism supports a utopian global socialism and affirms the collectivist spirituality of an integral ecology, which is advanced in Progressive Catholic environmentalism.

Critiquing "Politically Correct" Justice[1]
April 2008

The terms "politically correct" and "political correctness" (or "PC" for either) have been in use for almost twenty years, although they have rather indefinite, fluid meanings. Depending upon context and the user's intent, they can mean, among other things, what is culturally fashionable, what favors the ideology of a current political administration, or whatever a majority of people accept. Still, all of these meanings, if not most of the possible meanings of PC, imply a fundamental meaning of PC which underlies its uses.

What is 'correct' in PC can be contrasted to 'truth.' As Robert Trundle explains, "when truth is politicized, there is a political correctness whereby what is 'correct' may be false in respect to empirical reality. Since false beliefs are ignored in regard to what is 'correct,' the correctness may vary in one culture at different times or at the same time."[2]

Trundle's explanation of PC exposes its pernicious epistemological implications: With most renditions of PC, what is PC replaces what is true of reality, what corresponds to the facts of reality. In this way, PC represents a politically charged anti-realism since PC ideology determines what reality is, and what really is does not bear on what is affirmed as true of reality.

When what is PC loses contact with reality, the search for truth is deformed into quests for power to dictate what is true. To paraphrase The Holy Father, John Paul II from *Centesimus*

Annus (#34): If objective truth is not acknowledged, then the force of power takes over and people tend to make full use of the means at their disposal in order to dictate truth by imposing their own interests or their own opinions.

Pope John Paul II recognized, moreover, that in regard to justice, if there is no objective truth, in obedience to which persons actualize their individual and human identities, then there is no sure principle for establishing right relations between people. In short, if no objective truth, then no justice.

The virulent anti-realist strain of PC infects society and culture with a psuedo-justice, a power-driven justice that debilitates right relations between people by imposing its ideological dictates on reality. This malignant effect of anti-realist PC is detectable in its widespread ideologies of fairness, rights, friendship, and peace through global economic development. By critiquing these ideologies, it becomes clear that they ignore or simply reject relevant aspects of reality, and thereby, fail to affirm what justice really should be.

A prominent PC version of justice identifies it with fairness, and fairness is advanced as being virtually synonymous with equality. As Piotr Jaroszynski states, however, "Justice is not based on equality but equity."[3] Equality, such as with PC models of socialistic egalitarianism, promotes sameness, while equity stresses the fairness of deservedness. Equity is more basic than equality because equality is a condition, which depending on circumstances, we deserve. To re-express Jaroszynski's points, PC socialist ideology rejects any form of inequality and proposes that the government's power should force everyone to the same level, usually the level of the lowest common denominator. But such equalization leads nowhere and ends only by impoverishing everyone and destroying culture. PC egalitarianism, unfortunately, rejects the fact of reality that people are different and must remain different.[4]

Equity, on the contrary, prudently considers the different circumstances in which people live, how they work, and what they contribute to society and culture as a whole. People do indeed deserve equal treatment from government, such as equality before the law, but this equal treatment does not entail that people be equalized in all or even most of their different socio-economic circumstances. Truly there are those, like the disabled and sorely disadvantaged, who deserve government support to reach a relative level of equality with others. Still, the total equality that the "justice" of PC egalitarianism imposes contradicts the individual dignity of human persons, a dignity which affirms and celebrates the differences between individuals. As Pope John Paul II teaches in *Centesimus Annus* (#13), "The fundamental error of socialism is anthropological in nature. The individual is an element, simply a molecule in a social organism," so that the good and dignity of the individual is completely subordinated to the functions of the socio-economic mechanism.

Another way in which PC egalitarian justice asserts itself in society and culture is with its redefinition of rights. More than 50 years ago the philosopher Gabriel Marcel recognized that democratic societies can all too easily become embroiled in destructive rights contests when egalitarian ideology holds powerful sway.[5] Marcel warned that egalitarianism encourages the claiming, the demanding, of rights, and brings a mercenary attitude into social relationships. As Marcel cautioned, "Each individual claims from the start to enjoy the same consideration and same advantages as his neighbor; and in fact, his self-respect tends to resolve itself into an attitude which is not only

defensive but ever claiming rights from others.[6]" In such an
egalitarian democracy, rights competition is played out as a
zero-sum game wherein the government's protection of an individual's rights is accomplished only at the expense of denying
another's rights.

This mercenary competition spawns an *ethos* of distrust and
conflict, which subverts what justice really is and ought to be.
Justice, the right relations between people which embrace propriety and a respect for others, becomes a distrustful, defensive
attitude because people are afraid that if they graciously extend
themselves to serve others, they will be "unjustly" exploited.
Thus, people begin to consider it beneath their dignity "to do
anything whatever for nothing."[7] Justice, then, is oddly connected with the anxiety not to be duped, not to allow another
person to take advantage of one's simplicity or one's good nature.[8]

Marcel's insights are practically prophetic in regard to their
accuracy about present day egalitarian democracies. PC entitlement-thinking is precisely a phenomenon about which Marcel
warned. When rights are understood and asserted as social entitlements, which the government must fulfill, the responsibilities of justice are ignored or rejected. For example, a common
PC entitlement is based on diversity. The claim is that one's
diversity entitles one to government-enforced social privileges
and government-fulfilled social benefits. This claim, however,
causes the social fragmentation of diverse groups, and separatism and even "tribalism" begin to dominate. Such a fractured
society loses touch with the reality of justice: the truth of right
relations, which embodies propriety and respect for others, is
undermined by the struggle between tribes to get from the government that to which they believe they are entitled. The tribes

are not really seeking justice since they have no sense of responsibility to respect the well-being of other groups: they seek only the advantageous power which comes with government-enforced and government-fulfilled entitlements.

Another PC effort to determine reality is with friendship and other human relations. In the former Soviet Union, the PC ideology required that all persons view each other as "comrades." In some current social movements and groups, members follow their PC version of solidarity and call each other "brothers" or "sisters." Such practices aim at redefining politically the meaning of friendship so that friendship serves the interests of the state's movements or group's ideological agenda. With the insights of James Schall, however, these practices are recognizable as PC ploys, which actually pervert the human reality of friendship. Schall cites Samuel Johnson to remind us that "He, who has friends, has no friend."[9]

Using Aristotle as his guide, Schall explains that within the reality of human experience, it is impossible for us to be friends with everybody in any deep sense. We need friendship to flourish and be happy, but friendship is a free choice, and it cannot and should not be dictated by any controlling PC ideology. Exclusivity among friends and having just one or a few friends are basic realities of human relations because friendship, in its most noble form, has a dignity that is grounded in the real existence of truth and goodness. Their existence is known and chosen by the friends as their own highest purpose. As Schall states, noble friendship "can exist only if something higher than friendship exists, something the friends are seeking as the purpose of each of their lives."[10]

When a PC ideology dictates that everyone should be comrades, or brothers and sisters, people's sights are lowered because most people do remain fundamentally unknown to each other at the deepest levels. The exclusivity of noble friendships is replaced by a shallow "friendliness" of PC tolerance and political conformity. This, however, is desirable for a PC ideology since its social and cultural power is threatened by noble friendships. Noble friendships are devoted to truth and goodness, which are beyond, higher than, an ideology. A PC ideology cannot control or fathom such "higher things." Consequently, it has to redefine and corrupt the most exalted human relationship in order to secure its power and prevent its PC "truths" from being questioned or even resisted by those who are committed to something other than the PC agenda.

In this context, the aims of various international organizations and unions to redefine the human relations of marriage and the family become transparent. When marriage and family are committed to the noble truth and moral goodness of the natural law, they are beyond the control of the organization's or union's PC ideology. Their foundation in an objective, higher moral order transcends mere political dictates. Therefore, in order to maintain their authority, the power-driven international organization or union must reorder the morality of marriage and family according to its self-serving standards, regardless of what the reality of marriage and family is and should be.

Friendship is also related profoundly to justice. A maxim, which perhaps once had important significance, has become more and more of a PC slogan, namely, "If you want peace, work for justice." Referencing Aristotle, however, Fr. Schall observes that civil societies depend for their peace more on friendship than on justice.[11] Justice, Fr. Schall claims, is a harsh virtue because it is blind to the persons involved in the exchange. Justice does not consider the individual peculiarities of persons, but looks at the relationship between persons; it looks at each person's part in the situation to ascertain what is "due." To be just to one another we do not need to know one another as persons: indeed, knowing one another may actually corrupt justice's objectivity. Justice, then, deals with strangers and decides what is just regarding their circumstances. This is why, as Schall explains, something more than justice is needed for human completion: the highest things are not conceived in justice alone."[12]

To employ a German language distinction, justice alone yields a *Gesellschaft*, when what is more conducive to human flourishing is the *Gemeinschaft*. Schall's thoughts can illumine this distinction as he indicates that the relationship of justice, what would be the harshness of the *Gesellschaft*, is softened and deepened by friendship, what would be the interpersonal *Gemeinschaft* relations. Economic commerce, for example, usually requires detailed contracts and civil enforcement when breaches occur. At its best, however, commerce is not based merely on exchanges of just and fair price, but on a friendship that would unite seller and buyer, or worker and owner, in a bond of more than simple justice. Therefore, when utilitarian friendship, is added to a commercial transaction based on justice, it mitigates the abstractness and harshness of the exchange. Commerce, industry, and work are based in justice, but seek more, namely the mitigation and understanding of friendship, albeit friendships of utility and even pleasure, since such friendships are not blind to persons.[13]

Schall notes that Aristotle believed that societies are safest and most bound together because of the people's friendships, which include utilitarian and pleasurable ones. "A world full of friendships of utility and pleasure is not a disordered world, but a world that recognizes the kinds of relationships we can and ought to have with many people whom we cannot know well enough to be friends in the deepest sense."[14] Such a society or world, moreover, is open to affirming and encouraging noble friendships, which nourish the pursuit of truth and goodness that transcends what is dictated by PC ideology. These friendships acknowledge that the highest things are given to, not made by man, thereby the reality of what is to be praised and affirmed is not merely an object constructed by purely human powers.[15]

The aforementioned slogan, "If you want peace, work for justice," should perhaps be replaced by the norm, "If you want peace, make friends." The PC spin on the original slogan does not consider friendship and the ways it softens justice by recognizing the individuality of persons. Without an interpersonal dimension, justice tends to become blindly and even ideologically egalitarian to maintain its "objectivity." As discussed earlier in this paper, ideological equality in socio-economic matters ignores or rejects equity. Unlike ideological equality, equity is not depersonalizing because it respects what individual persons are due, what they deserve, in their particular socio-economic circumstances. The best possibility for such equity, however, is only with a society which encourages the freedom of friendships and does not impose redefined meanings of friendship, or reordered standards for marriage and family.

A final issue for consideration is also related to peace, justice, and friendship. This is the PC view of achieving international peace through global economic development, or as the slogan says, "Peace through economic development." The presumption, which indeed has merit, is that vast inequalities of wealth between nations is a cause of strife, conflict, and the exploitation of poor nations by rich ones or by huge multinational corporations.

PC egalitarian ideology has maintained, sadly, that the way to correct wealth inequalities and protect lesser developed countries (LDCs) from exploitation is for the governments of wealthy nations to transfer, by means of grants and loans, massive amounts of wealth to the governments of LDCs. The PC strategy is that only such government-to-government transfers can ensure an egalitarian objectivity of just wealth distribution. The historical reality, however, is that after almost five decades of such transfers, many LDCs have not developed significantly, and strife, conflict, and exploitation still prevail. The PC commitment to the "objective" egalitarian justice of governments ignores the reality of power-driven political corruption. It further ignores the reality of needy persons in the LDCs, who actually deserve the aid.

Thomas Woods effectively exposes the numerous real problems with this way of PC economic development.[16] With many references to relevant studies and data, Woods identifies some of the problems: 1) To ensure the success of their foreign aid, wealthy nations tend to prop up brutal and corrupt regimes and shelter the regimes from the ruinous economic consequences of their interventionist policies. 2) Massive infusion of wealth into LDCs tends to weaken, if not destroy, their export sectors, since the countries lose motivation to generate wealth through exports. 3) Life in the LDCs becomes highly politicized since hostile groups struggle to seize power over the countries' increasingly lucrative coffers. 4) Even food aid becomes a political instrument, because food is made available to groups that will support the LDCs' controlling government.[17] 5) And, going beyond Woods, government officials welcome multinationals to take advantage of the cheap labor or resources in their countries, so that the officials can receive kick-backs to increase their personal wealth and the wealth of their regime.

Woods also cites the work of Hernando de Soto, who did an extensive study of economic development in his native Peru. De Soto discovered that with the transference of wealth to Peru's government, the government initiated a complex system of legal and not-so-legal regulations to protect the wealth for itself so that individual citizens could not easily access it for their entrepreneurial projects. Quoting de Soto, Woods notes that it took "the equivalent of 289 work days, 81 meters of forms, and eight overt bribes to legally establish a small clothing factory."[18]

The fundamental issue with all of these problems is that the PC strategy of achieving "Peace through economic development" ignores or rejects reality since it is premised on abstract egalitarian justice and not on the concrete reality of persons: what individual persons who have entrepreneurial ambitions can and will contribute to economic development. This is why some alternative strategies which focus on equity, what persons are due, have been and are more successful. The micro-loans or micro-grants given to deserving persons or small communities for developing small businesses or civic improvements are examples of successful equity-based aid. Another example is when communities are permitted to negotiate with multinationals which aim to locate a factory, for instance, in their community. The community is able to obtain from the multinational such civic goods as road development, or medical and educational facilities, as conditions for locating the factory.

These micro-development realities are examples of a type of equity-based subsidiarity. They are proven ways of overcoming some of the problems when wealth is given to a LDC's government, which is alienated from the personal concrete realities of the country's people. They aid persons on a local level, and facilitate their personal, their family's and their community's socio-economic flourishing. This flourishing strengthens friendships of all sorts since it does encourage a genuine interpersonal respect and cooperation, and this is the surest way to peace.

As long as PC definitions of justice according to ideological dictates about fairness, rights, friendship, economic development, and peace, continue to expand their power, people in real concrete situations will be depersonalized. Only a recovery of a robust realism, which defers to reality's order and design as the foundations for the truth, can empower persons to recognize, and reject PC's pseudo-justice.

References and Notes

1. "Critiquing 'Politically Correct' Justice" ("Krytyka sprawiedliwosci 'poprawnej politycznie'"), trans. by Rafael Lizut in Justice: Theories and Reality (*Sprawiedliwosc – idée a rzeczywistosc*), ed. Piotr Jaroszynski et al. (Lublin, Poland: Katedra Filozfi Kultury, 2009) pp. 37-44. Originally presented at the VIIth International Congress on the Future of Western Civikization: Theme, Justice. Published with permission.

2. Robert Trundle, *A Theology of Science* (Boca Raton, FL: Brown Walker Press, 2007) p. 79.

3. Piotr Jaroszynski and Mathew Anderson, *Ethics: The Drama of the Moral Life* (Staten Island: Alba House, 2003) p. 99

4. Ibid. See also my review of *Ethics: The Drama of the Moral Life* in *The Review of Metaphysics*, December 2005, pp. 432-434.
5. For a more fully developed presentation of Marcel's political theory, see my article "Gabriel Marcel's Politics: Theory and Practice" in the *American Catholic Philosophical Quarterly*, Vol. 80, Summer 2006, pp. 435-455.
6. Gabriel Marcel, *Homo Viator*, trans. Emma Craufurd (Gloucester, MA: Peter Smith, 1978) pp. 56-57
7. Ibid., p. 57.
8. See ibid.
9. James Schall, S.J., *At the Limits of Political Philosophy* (Washington, D.C.: Catholic University of America Press, 1996)
10. Ibid., p. 219.
11. Ibid., p. 225. Fr. Schall cites Aristotle's *Nicomachean Ethics* at 1155a25-28.
12. See ibid., pp. 225-26.
13. See ibid., p. 226.
14. Ibid., p. 227.
15. See ibid., pp. 235-36.
16. Thomas Woods, *The Church and the Market* (Lanham, MD: Lexington Books, 2005). See especially Chapter Four, "The Economics and Morality of Foreign Aid," pp.129-149
17. See ibid., pp. 130-134.
18. Ibid., p.130.

Marcelian Economic Personalism[1]
May 2010

Although the study of political economy emerged historically from Ancient and Medieval sources, it was captured by the Modern era, and, as such, it divorced itself from its ancestral heritage. Its genealogical origins in a metaphysically rooted anthropology and moral axiology were disowned in favor of adopting politicized ideologies and quantifiable certainties. For today's students of business and economics, in fact, philosophical reasoning and, even more so, metaphysical reasoning are vacuous unknowns. Moral axiology, moreover, is reduced to emotionally charged claims about what the state ought to legislate to ensure "social justice" and economic rights.

Without solid metaphysical foundations, academic studies in business and economics have become anarchic[2] social sciences wherein competing paradigms are accepted or rejected simply on the basis of political proclivities, prevailing mathematical constructs or conventions, and practical expediency. No "first principles" are acknowledged, much less philosophically assessed; no serious attention is paid to critiquing what the studies presuppose about human nature and moral values; and no effort is made to recover the missing "human person" in these depersonalized social sciences of political economy.

Economic personalism, or EP, is a relatively recent approach to political economy, which offers an alternative to the philosophical anarchy that has infected the studies of business and economics. This essay will concisely define EP by adapting it to the personalism of Gabriel Marcel (1889-1973) and proceed according to the following three rubrics: 1) The prevailing opposition in political economy between individualism and collectivism will be critiqued in regard to how their presumed anthropologies are correlated with their moral views on the common good. 2) The "first principles" of a Marcelian way of EP with a moral axiology of solidarity will be developed. And finally, 3) a Marcelian EP will suggest a sketch of an economics of abundance contrary to today's regnant, but depersonalizing, economics of scarcity.

Although Marcel never produced a treatise or even an essay specifically devoted to politics or political economy, his writings are laden with reflections on political principles, and economic theories and practices. For him, politics and economics were bound together, and his reflections on political economy were grounded in his metaphysics of the person.[3]

In an autobiographical essay Marcel offered a clear identification of his political stance: he confessed that in broad terms he considered himself "a liberal who has become more and more painfully aware of the limits of liberalism but who at the same time has remained convinced of the absolutely maleficent character of Totalitarian regimes of any sort."[4] Although Marcel affirmed and defended the reality of the individual person, he rejected the distortions of individualism, namely the painful limits of liberalism, which lead to a fragmented and hyper-competitive society of depersonalized atomic individuals.[5] He condemned, moreover, all collectivisms because they engender a totalitarian mass society, an extreme egalitarianism wherein individuals believe that the depersonalized and equalized aggregate is more real and more morally valuable than any of its constituents taken individually.[6] It was these deformations of individualism and collectivism that Marcel labeled as the "present universal crisis" of politics, a crisis that can be overcome only by getting people "out of the false dilemma between an imaginary individualism and a collectivism that denies the human personality."[7]

Neither individualism nor collectivism properly appreciates the human person. They also do not recognize the philosophical tendencies inherent in the co-relationships between their

anthropologies, their political economies, and their moral axi-
ologies of the common good. Those philosophical tendencies
can be exposed critically, which will facilitate definition of a
Marcelian way of economic personalism that does respect the
nature of the human person.

Modern individualisms and collectivisms generally presuppose one of two typical anthropologies: materialism or a Cartesian-like dualism, which can tend toward transcendentalism.
Each of these anthropologies yields a certain view of political
economy and the common good which denatures the person.
Materialism, which denies or simply ignores a person's spiritual
soul, is correlated with both individualism and collectivism.
Materialistic individualisms, like many libertarian views and the
objectivism of Ayn Rand, assert the absolute priority of the
individual. And though they negate or are just confused about
the nature of a person's free will, they propound that individual
liberty is of supreme moral value. They, accordingly, define the
common good as that which serves individual liberty, since for
them, liberty is a good that all individuals should have in common. Of course, then, they endorse thoroughgoing laissez faire
free-market capitalism. As Marcel would agree, however, such
extreme individualism atomizes society and reduces persons to
discrete window-less monads, competing with one another to
realize their absolute autonomy and achieve superiority. Persons become soul-less economic "erg units" acquiring as much
material capital as their "liberty" allows.

Materialistic collectivisms do not even bother with liberty
or free will. They maintain an anthropological determinism,
usually under the aspect of an evolutionary naturalism. Marxist
political economies, for instance, reduce persons to instantia-
tions of a collective "species being" and the common good is

what serves the evolutionary progress of the species. Moreover, since the advance of the species as such is of paramount value, egalitarianism reigns because no individual can truly advance unless all members of the species advance. Such materialistic collectivism is widespread in the social sciences today as they generally have adopted a scientific naturalism as their foundation and propound a distributionist political economy to fortify their belief in egalitarian evolutionary progress. The continued influence of B. F. Skinner's deterministic anthropology and his collectivist political economy, as posed in his utopian work Walden Two,[8] evidences the prevailing ideology of most of the social sciences. For Skinner, and much of social and behavioral science, statist redistribution of wealth is a necessary condition for the evolutionary progress of the species.

Cartesian-like dualisms incline towards locating the essence of the person in an immaterial soul or mind, or a universalized transcendental ego. In all cases, the mind or transcendental ego is a collective entity into which all persons are absorbed, and which establishes the ultimately real nature of persons. Such views, accordingly, subordinate individual personal identity to the collective soul, mind or universalized consciousness of a transcendental ego. They further maintain that since such a collective essence is shared by all persons equally, their ideal state and ideal political economy is an egalitarian collective in which wealth, capital, and even moral values are held in common by all. This view is manifest in varying degrees and varying renditions in the practical political economics of, for instance, the Kantian "realm of ends," the Hegelian State imbued with the Absolute Spirit, various other 19c German idealists such as Fichte, Schelling, and Bruno Bauer, and even American Transcendentalists, as with Emerson's "over soul" and Thoreau's "Walden" political economy.

The ideal of the common good in all of these types of dualisms is ironically similar to the materialisms discussed above
because egalitarianism prevails, and variations of distribution-
ism are valued morally. The difference with the materialisms,
however, is that the common good is grounded in a transcendental collectivism. All persons are one within the overarching
transcendental mind, soul or ego. Their personal identities are
ultimately dissolved into a faceless transcendental mass, and
thusly, depersonalization results.

A Marcelian EP does avoid the depersonalization of individualisms and collectivisms because its metaphysical ground
respects and preserves the person. Marcel held as a "first principle" that "Incarnation [is] the central 'given' of metaphysics."[9] For him, the person is an incarnate spirit, a composite
being: a body/soul unity, which has the spiritual faculties of
intellect and free will, and whose personal identity is a metaphysical constant never erased by an all-consuming collective
or reduced to an atomic individual. Marcel would accept that
the individual is a free knower, a volitional actor or agent.

Since human esse is co-esse, however, the individual has the
innate teleology to become a person: indeed, the entelechy of
the individual is personhood. Personhood is the perfection of
the individual. A chief virtue of personhood is solidarity, which
involves fulfillment of responsibilities to the "we," or the common good. Individuals reach the fullness of their being, their
co-esse, when they choose and act in solidarity with and for
others. This, however, is an ongoing process because as persons we are in continuous becoming; persons are always working to improve solidarity and actualize more and more of their
individual identities as persons. Solidarity does not deperson-
alize. Individual identity is not dissolved into some equalized
collective, and the individual is not absolutized as an atomic

monad which manipulates, subordinates or collides with others. Solidarity is the axiological condition of the metaphysics of the acting person.

A Marcelian EP founded on the metaphysics of the acting person resists the depersonalizing excesses of naturalistic individualisms and egalitarian collectivisms. It does not elide the essential spiritual aspect of the identity of the person, it does not subvert personal free will and volitional agency, and it does not yield an egalitarianism which calls for statist redistribution of wealth. Marcel was unambiguous in his denunciation of egalitarian collectivisms. He, for instance, rejected the consecrated formula of the French Revolution because, for him, equality and fraternity, which was usually his term for "solidarity," are oriented in opposite directions. Equality is basically egocentric. It fuels envious ego-driven claims which breed a resentment of those groups who supposedly "have" by those who believe they "have not." Fraternity, in contrast, is heterocentric since it affirms that "you are my brother and because you are my brother, I am capable not only of recognizing your superiority but of rejoicing over it."[10]

Marcel especially admonished philosophers who advanced egalitarianism. He charged that:

> Never could a philosopher who deserves the name take seriously the thought of equality in its application to human beings . . . To say that human beings are equal is just as unreasonable as to desire their becoming so (which by the way makes no sense whatsoever). Therefore, let us speak rather of a brotherly world, where everyone can enjoy finding qualities in his brothers, he does not possess himself.[11]

Marcel translated his opposition to egalitarian collectivism into concrete criticisms of socialistic political economies. Socialisms undermine persons' freedom to conceive and seek an "idea of a better life."[12] Their personal initiative to pursue a higher quality of life is stunted for two principal reasons: 1) ". . . whenever egalitarianism prevails, rooted as it is in envy and resentment, the sense of quality tends to vanish."[13] And, 2) socialism manages "to subordinate personal initiative in every field to state control."[14]

Marcel also exposed socialism's confused social justice ideology that is based on an egalitarian common good and advocates statist redistribution of wealth, so that all people have a right to have as much wealth as anyone else.[15] He bluntly stated that, "Nothing could ever convince me that a cleaning woman should earn as much as a professor."[16]

Egalitarian collectivisms, whether rooted in anthropological materialisms or transcendental dualisms, are depersonalizing. Personal identity, freedom, dignity, and the common good of solidarity are eroded as thoroughly as with individualisms. These forms of political economies persist nonetheless and are entrenched within the social science studies of economics and business. One main reason for their persistence is due to the presumption that "scarcity" is axiomatic. A Marcelian EP, however, can challenge the presuppositions upon which scarcity is based and lead to at least a sketch of some of the first principles of an economics of abundance.

In the USA, a widely used textbook in economics proclaims:

Economics is a social science. It examines the problems that societies face because individuals desire to consume more goods and services than are available, which creates a problem of relative scarcity. Wants are generally unlimited and apparently insatiable, whereas resources are limited."[17]

The text then describes ways in which the problem of scarcity has been and can be addressed. It argues that "social mechanisms" are required for allocating limited resources. Prominent among those mechanisms are market forces managed or controlled by state central planning, which, of course, is tantamount to some brand of socialism.

Modern political economy typically holds such claims about scarcity and its underlying view of wants. A Marcelian EP, however, questions whether for persons, wants are truly unlimited and insatiable. As rational creatures and volitional actors, are persons not able to choose to exercise the temperance of self-governance over wants? The modern social science view that we are determined, insatiable consumers, whether individually or collectively, is an anthropological presumption which obviously contradicts a personalist understanding of who and what we truly are. Since this presumption, moreover, justifies some sort of socialism as a mechanism to manage human wants in the face of scarce resources, to reject the presumption weakens, if not denies, the social scientific justification of socialism.

A Marcelian EP suggests an economics of abundance and begins with the principle that as persons with free will, intellect and a fundamental dignity, human beings are, in an economic sense, assets not liabilities. Persons are creative and productive, and thusly, for example, centrally planned mass population control programs to reduce the numbers of insatiable resource-consumers, ultimately depress, if not destroy, an economy. Modern Malthusian tenets of economic social science need not be accepted as "givens" and population need not be viewed strictly as an economic factor which must be controlled by central planning to manage scarcity.

A second principle of a Marcelian EP of abundance asserts that scarcity is fundamentally a moral issue and not a physical one. Scarcity is, then, mainly a result of the mismanagement of resources by governments or market agents (including corporations and financial institutions), of the vice of greed, and of the failure of economic social science to maintain a morally normative axiology rooted in its anthropologies. Marcelian EP's axiology of solidarity prescribes beneficence, charity, as a moral condition of personhood. Solidarity obligates persons to share resources and wealth as they are best able. This is an obligation which redounds upon persons themselves, their choices and actions for the sake of realizing their personhood. If charity is deemphasized in favor of centrally planned national or global redistribution schemes, high-tax statist economies too often result. These economies sadly engender the mentality that "Why should I be charitable? I pay my heavy taxes. It's the government's responsibility to deal with social problems, both domestically and abroad." Charity, then, and persons' efforts to realize solidarity are actually occluded by such redistribution schemes.

Finally, a third basic principle of an economics of abundance is that virtuous stewardship of technology-enhanced production and use of resources can and does yield abundance. The philosopher Alfred North Whitehead once cautioned that we should not let technological development outdistance our wisdom to manage it.[18] He meant, among other ideas, that the rapid pace of technological development can lead us to overlook the negative affects technologies can have on persons, communities, nations and the environment. Some technologies can actually accelerate resource depletion or enable wealth-generating control of resources by some populations while marginalizing others. Virtuous stewardship of technology, however, would be carried out within the charity of solidarity so that, for instance, persons and organizations which have control of agricultural, energy, and information technologies would share their developments with populations that do not have such capabilities.

This sketch of an economics of abundance through a Marcelian EP is indeed merely a sketch. Practical application of the principles obviously calls for much more detail. What remains important, however, is that scarcity, in economic social science is not axiomatic if a Marcelian EP is adopted as foundational. In addition, the depersonalizing effects of modern economics with its anthropologies of individualism and collectivism can be circumvented, if in education and practice, political economy is reordered to appreciate and respect the real nature of persons and the moral axiology of the solidarity of personhood.

References and Notes

1. This paper is reprinted with permission and originally published in: "Economic Personalism: A Marcelian Approach," in *Una Sociedad Despersonalizada? Propuestas Educativas (A Depersonalized Society? Educational Proposals)*, ed. Enrique Martinez (Barcelona, Spain: *Biblioteca Filosoficade Balmesiana*, Series I – Vol. VIII, *Editorial Balmes, Duran i Bas*, 2012) pp. 279 – 287

2. This use of "anarchic" recovers an etymological meaning of the term, "without principle."

3. For a detailed study of Marcel's political philosophy, see Thomas Michaud, "Gabriel Marcel's Politics: Theory and Practice," *American Catholic Philosophical Quarterly*, 80:3 (2006), 435-455.

4. Gabriel Marcel, "An Autobiographical Essay," trans. Forrest Williams, in *The Philosophy of Gabriel Marcel*, ed. Paul Schilpp and Lewis Hahn (LaSalle: Open Court, 1984), 62-3.

5. See John E. Smith, "The Individual, the Collective and the Community," in *The Philosophy of Gabriel Marcel* (op. cit.), 337-51, at 337.

6. See Gabriel Marcel, *Man Against Mass Society*, trans. G.S. Fraser (Chicago: Regnery, 1962), 166

7. Gabriel Marcel, *Searchings*, ed. Wolfgang Ruf (New York: Newman Press, 1967), 88.

8. B. F. Skinner, *Walden Two* (New York: The Macmillan Co., 1948).

9. Gabriel Marcel, *Man Against Mass Society*, 37.

10. Gabriel Marcel, *Awakenings*, trans. Peter S. Rogers (Milwaukee: Marquette University Press, 2002), 203. For more on Marcel's explanation of the connection between egalitarianism and resentment, see: Gabriel Marcel, *Tragic Wisdom and Beyond*, trans. Stephen Jolin and Peter McCormick (Evanston: Northwestern University Press, 1973), 30.

11. Gabriel Marcel, *Philosophical Fragments*, ed. and trans. Lionel A. Blair (Notre Dame: University of Notre Dame Press, 1967), 8-9.

12. Gabriel Marcel, *The Decline of Wisdom* (New York: Philosophical Library, 1955), 44.

13. Ibid.

14. Gabriel Marcel, *Homo Viator*, trans. Emma Crauford (Gloucester, Mass.: Harper and Row, 1978), 55.

15. Gabriel Marcel, *Philosophical Fragments*, 10.

16. Gabriel Marcel, *Awakenings*, 203.

17. Harry Landreth and David Colander, *History of Economic Thought*, Third Edition (Boston: Houghton Mifflin Co. 1994), 1.

18. Cited in Thomas Michaud, *The Virtues of Business Ethics*, Third Edition (Acton, Mass.: Copley Custom Textbooks, 2009), 157

The Missing Person in Catholic Spirituality[1]
Fall 2015

ABSTRACT

Peter Redpath and Gabriel Marcel warn that the West is engulfed in a crisis. From their various philosophical perspectives, they identify the source of the crisis as a distortion of traditional Christian metaphysics of the human person as a free individual capable of pursuing truth and entering into relations of community with others. The distortion is caused by an abstract humanism that rightly denounces individualism, but as an alternative promotes a socialistic collectivism. This essay argues that this distortion is further causing the emergence of a collectivist spirituality which loses the individual, free human person. This spirituality is shown to be particularly manifest in various Catholic approaches to socioeconomics and environmentalism.

Throughout his writings, lectures, public debates and personal discussions, my teacher, co-adventurer and, most importantly, friend, Peter Redpath, has issued a philosophically charged alarm: Something is radically wrong with Western culture! What that "something" is, is the loss of the metaphysics of the human person.

Redpath exposes this loss as the source of a degenerative crisis which has debilitated philosophy, science, education and political economy. Its historical genealogy extends back into Ancient times with the Sophists, but became most pervasive with the Modern Enlightenment. Redpath urges that an accurate understanding of the acting person, the sentient, embodied individual actively engaged in free, personal relationships must once again become a founding metaphysical principle of philosophy.[2] He exhorts all who have perceived in any depth this roiling crisis to strive to re-establish the primacy of the individual, embodied human person engaged in free personal action as a first principle of knowing, truth, science, philosophy and wisdom.

This essay heeds Redpath's warning and accepts his exhortation that it is indeed a de-formation of the metaphysics of the human person at the source of the crisis in Western culture. Redpath's etiology of the corruption of the human person and its disturbing effects are further elaborated by integrating the thoughts of Gabriel Marcel, a philosopher who Redpath acknowledges as possessing a "legitimately philosophical wisdom."[3] Following Redpath and Marcel, this essay details some of the effects of the crisis by showing how in current Catholicism, the traditional Christian metaphysics of the human person is being supplanted by an emerging progressive spirituality, particularly in the areas of socioeconomics and environmentalism.

This spirituality does not qualify as a metaphysic according to traditional terms but is indeed the result of the "missing person" in Catholic thought and teaching. It is a spirituality, more passion than intellect and reason, which can, most properly, be called a collectivist or holistic spirituality. It favors an abstract humanism that elides, if not denies, the person as an individual with free will immersed in the reality of concrete situations with other persons. It seeks to absorb the individual person into a collectivistic mass, a holistic spiritual oneness manifested in socioeconomics as utopian socialism or in environmentalism as an "integral ecology."[4]

Redpath and Marcel on the Lost Person in Utopian Socialisms

For Redpath, the crisis in Modern Western culture began to foment with Descartes and then exploded into an all-engulfing cultural phenomenon with Rousseau. Redpath argues that Descartes replaced the human soul with an incorporeal mind, which contained a collection of innate ideas. Descartes, moreover, primarily relocated truth, science and wisdom as acts of the will and not acts of the intellect or reason. Truth in all knowledge was thereby reduced to the strength of the will, i.e., the will's relation to the intellect and not to acts of the intellect themselves. A strong will leading the intellect is the source of truth, whereas a weak will allows the intellect to succumb to imagination, which is the source of error. In effect, Descartes transformed wisdom, science and philosophy into a type of disembodied willpower having no concrete individual as its principle of origin. His view, as Redpath sees it, was a disordered understanding of the human person as pure spirit.[6]

Rousseau, however, was much more progressive than Descartes, extending the Cartesian disembodied intellect to an abstract collectivist reason, which was without any understanding

of real human relationships, of individual, free rational or loving acts. For Redpath, with Rousseau there is some universal
feeling, a sort of neo-Averroistic socialist intellect shared by
tolerant people. Such tolerant people communicate the General Will of the body politic: a social will. Truth, then, is established by some fully inclusive social feeling, a socialist intellect
shared by tolerant people collectively.[7]

Rousseau's collectivism burst into Modern utopian scientific socialism. Socialism's tendency to deny individual freedom
and individual intellect are akin, as Redpath observes, to Aver-
roes's denial of knowledge, science and freedom to the individual mind, and the denial of the existence of the individual
soul after death, the eschatology of personal immortality. Utopian socialism, not the human person, becomes the new metaphysical foundation with its emphasis on the power of the
General Will and its collectivist theory of truth.[8] Tolerance became the 'voice of conscience' whose message is an inclusive
socialist feeling for love of humanity and a willingness to in-
corporate all human differences into a higher moral status of
socialistic collective conscience.[9]

The free, concrete, individual human person is, however,
lost in this undifferentiated abstract collective consciousness
and tolerant conscience. The feeling for the love of humanity,
an abstract humanism, is disconnected from the concrete loving relationships of individual human persons. At the expense
of the individual human person, the collective feeling of love
for humanity drives the General Will of this abstract humanism
toward its utopian ideal, namely, an enlightened collective of
humanity in which truth is established by the collective will of
the tolerant conscience.

Of course, with such a collectivist utopian humanism, there
cannot be factional political leadership and disputes over truth.

There must be a collective government, an imperious centralized bureaucracy which arbitrates the General Will to determine truth.[10] Consequently, science, including scientific education and economics, must be directed by the centralized government to ensure that their 'truths' properly serve the tolerant
love of humanity and the utopian desideratum. Science,
thereby, becomes dependent on the socialist state for its foundation and purposes, and the state itself substitutes for any real
metaphysical first principles, including the metaphysics of the
human person.

Marcel was no less alarmed than Redpath about the crisis
afflicting the Modern West. Although Marcel did not specifically use the term "utopian socialism" as a driver of the crisis,
he did consistently and strongly emphasize that socialism is
causally integral to the crisis. Marcel believed that the crisis
emerges from the "very depths of man's being,"[11] because
"Man is in his death throes."[12] This dire condition results from
the degradation of man, particularly the degradation of freedom for the individual human person. As he expressed the situation, "But what we have to ask ourselves first is the following
question: what becomes of freedom in a world in which man,
or at least man at a certain level of awareness, is forced to recognize that he has entered his death throes?"[13]

In a blunt self-identification of his political stance, Marcel
once confessed that he is a classical "liberal," though one "who
has become more and more painfully aware of the limits of
liberalism but who at the same time has remained convinced
of the absolutely maleficent character of totalitarian regimes of
any sort."[14] He believed in and defended the concrete reality of
the free, individual human person, but rejected the distortions
of individualism, the painful limits of liberalism that lead to a

hyper-competitive society of atomic individuals.[15] He also condemned all collectivisms because they lead to a totalitarian mass society wherein the mass, an abstractly aggregated humanity, is taken as more concrete and real than any human person individually.[16]

The convulsing tensions of individualism vs. collectivism are, for Marcel, precisely the death throes which are enervating the freedom of the individual human person and are the source of the "present universal crisis"[17] in Western politics and society. He framed his approach for confronting this crisis by asking, "how to get people out of the false dilemma between an imaginary individualism and a collectivism that denies the human personality."[18]

The opposition between individualism and collectivism is false because both distort and degrade the human person. Collectivism, which includes socialism, erases the individual personality and stifles personal freedom. It subsumes individual persons into a faceless and de-personalized abstract mass. It advances an abstract humanism wherein tolerant egalitarianism is the supreme moral value, at the expense of allowing the concrete individual person's free pursuit of truth, of loving personal relationships within a community, and a better quality of life.[19] Marcel explicitly warns that the collective, socialistic state denies the interdependence between truth and freedom because "freedom can survive only in a climate of truth . . . and truth can be worthily pursued only where no external constraint (particularly from the state) is used against it."[20] When the socialist state supplants the human person as the metaphysical foundation for truth, knowledge and community, the free, individual human person is lost because socialism manages "to subordinate personal initiative in every field to state control."[21]

The individualism that opposes collectivism is, for Marcel, "imaginary" because it is a distortion of the human person's essential relationships with other persons within community. Although he stresses that undermining the person as a free individual is a major factor in the crisis engulfing the West, Marcel is not a libertarian of any sort. Moreover, with his rejection of collectivist socialism, Marcel's "liberal" self-identification should not be understood as endorsing the progressive liberalism that advances "big government" solutions to social problems and promotes a high-tax statist economy of redistributed wealth in order to finance government's social agenda of egalitarian tolerance. Marcel maintains that any person's concrete situation is within community and the relationships one has with others are vital for flourishing as a person

John Smith clearly describes Marcel's views: "Community is essential for personality, because the intersubjectivity, or relation to the other, on which it is based, provides us with a means of discovering ourselves and finding our bearings in the world."[22] Freely recognizing and choosing to act with such moral values as charity, hope and fidelity open persons to each other, "which unlike the self-assertive spirit of equality, means having a concern for the other."[23] In this way community also "makes freedom possible because it is a form of life in which persons recognize each other as persons who are to be but who are not to be manipulated."[24]

In sum, for Marcel, and Redpath would certainly agree, persons cannot flourish, cannot develop a genuine moral character unless they freely choose to relate morally with others in community. An imperious socialist state mandating the morality of egalitarian tolerance based on a love of an abstract collective humanity eliminates the possibility for concrete, individual persons to develop authentic community. In addition, a libertarian individualism that atomizes individuals occludes if not eliminates the moral possibilities for engaging with others in relationships of community that are recognized as essential for a person's flourishing. This is the alarming crisis in the West, for without a metaphysic of the human person, as developed in traditional Christian philosophy, man's "death throes" become more and more critical.

The dreams of a utopian socialism combined with a vehement rejection of individualism degrade the human person by ignoring the basic metaphysical principle that persons are free individuals within community. The confused thinking is that the concrete metaphysical reality of persons as free individuals cannot be affirmed without conceding to morally corrupt self-centered individualism, so only an abstract collectivism can be hailed as truth. Traditional Christian metaphysics of the person is lost and what is emerging is not a philosophical metaphysics, but a passionate spirituality, a spirituality driven by a nebulous feeling for the abstract unity of the whole of humanity and, indeed, all of creation. This holistic spirituality is becoming a new metaphysics, the foundation for determining the truth of how we ought to understand ourselves as persons and what our moral responsibilities are. Furthermore, as indicated earlier in this essay, this spirituality is becoming especially prevalent in the areas of Catholic approaches to socioeconomics and environmentalism.

The Spirituality of Catholic Economic Collectivism

Catholic commentators are swirling in the tensions between economic individualism and collectivism. Economic and social justice is perhaps the issue today for Catholic thought, though views founded on traditional metaphysics of the human person are eclipsed by the impassioned collectivist spirituality. One traditional commentator, Andrew Hertzog, argues, not unlike Marcel, that both individualism and collectivism are dangerous and morally wrong.[25] Both advance a humanism that distorts the human person. Collectivism erases the person's individuality in seeking to establish its egalitarian society, "the equality of all people politically, economically, and socially."[26] Individualism styles itself as a humanism since it is centered on the subjective goals and values of each individual, though it claims that the individual has no necessary obligation to be responsible to the community.[27]

Daren Jonescu is forcefully critical of the Church's "general trend" toward progressive collectivism.[28] He denounces the trend as valuing an "irrational authoritarianism," that advances state control and as having a pronounced "anti-individual streak."[29] Jonescu warns that this general trend is too often not recognized because it does not honestly identify itself. The Catholic Church has officially condemned the collectivisms of socialism and communism, consequently those speaking for the Church or representing their views as within the Church do not explicitly self-identify as socialist or communist. Their moralistic spirituality of progressive collectivism is cloaked but nevertheless detectable.[30]

A prime example of a zealous, but masked, progressive spirituality is with the commentator Victor Gaetan.[31] Gaetan interpretively reports on Pope Francis's visit to South America in July/August 2015. Because of the interpretations, it is uncertain whether the Holy Father said, meant and did what Gaetan claims. What is certain, however, is that Gaetan's spirituality is boldly collectivist, though he does not self-identify as a socialist.

In his rendition, Gaetan claims that a principal theme of the Pope's visit was the social "inclusion" accomplished by egalitarian tolerance. For instance, Gaetan describes an incident when leftist Bolivian President Evo Morales gave Pope Francis a Soviet-style hammer-and-sickle crucifix, and Gaetan notes that Francis was not offended because he interpreted it as an artistic expression. Also in Bolivia, Gaetan characterizes the Holy Father's message in an address to the second World Meeting of Popular Movements as "a scathing rebuke of socioeconomic systems prioritizing individualism and capital." He continues by insisting that Pope Francis' vision "can be seen as largely at odds with characteristics of the United States – as a capitalist and military powerhouse with global reach, and engine of consumerism and individualism."

Gaetan further explains the Pope's rebuke of the United States by indicating that the "Church criticizes both capitalism and socialism for allowing government control to displace individual and local decision-making." This criticism for Gaetan, however, was apparently merely tactical since "while communism was a world threat for most of the 20th century, it wasn't common for the Catholic Church to vocally confront capitalism, because such confrontation could be interpreted as benefiting the atheistic powers allied with the Soviet Union." In other words, for Gaetan and his socialist ilk, the Church denounced communism and socialism only because of the atheism of the Soviets and other major communist powers, and not at all because of the ways such authoritarian socioeconomics degraded the free individual human person. In fact, with Gaetan's passionate spirituality, it seems that socialism actually fortifies the Catholic teaching of subsidiarity, "which prioritizes the smallest, local decision-making body that can solve a problem over big answers that don't acknowledge individual preferences." Without a rational metaphysics of the person, zealous "true believers" like Gaetan can convince themselves that in a socialist utopia the subsidiarity of free individual preferences and decisions can be preserved, protected and enhanced, although in economics and even morality that possibility is fundamentally contrary to the ideology, actual practice and history of socialist governments.

As a final observation on Gaetan's 'report,' it is telling that he references Laudato Si and alludes to its concept of an "integral ecology."[32] In describing the altar for a mass Pope Francis said in Paraguay, Gaetan notes that it was made from edible materials, e.g., corn, gourds, pumpkins, seeds, etc. He says that this "proved the creativity of believers responding to the idea of recycling as well as respect for Mother Earth, as people in the Andes do." In Gaetan's holistic spirituality, economic collectivism is inclusive of aggressive environmentalism, since individualism and capitalism threaten our home, the Earth. Consequently, his spirituality of integral ecology apparently even allows for a sort of eco-paganism that will acknowledge a type of 'Gaean goddess,' Mother Earth.

The Spirituality of Catholic Environmentalism

In 1995 the Catholic Bishops of the USA's Appalachia region issued a pastoral letter, "At Home in the Web of Life, A Pastoral Message on Sustainable Community Appalachia from the Catholic Bishops of the Region." Brian O'Donnell describes this letter as a "green version" of the 1975 letter, "This Land is Home to Me, a Pastoral Letter on Powerlessness in Appalachia by the Catholic Bishops of the Region."[33] Both letters express in poetic fashion a holistic spirituality and emphatically convey its utopianism. As O'Donnell notes, the 1995 letter "ends with an echo of the close of the 1975 letter: Dear sisters and brothers, we urge all of you not to stop living, to be a part of the rebirth of utopia, to recover and defend the struggling dream of Appalachia itself."[34] These letters also prefigure the integration of human ecology with natural ecology within the utopian socialist spirituality of progressive integral ecology.

Maureen Mullarkey, a traditionalist commentator, recognizes the emergence of utopian "eco-spirituality," warning that Catholicism could be sliding into "nature mysticism" and that a sort of "messianic environmentalism" could assume the "status of dogma."[35] She describes 'save the planet' spiritual ardor as being integral to some Catholics' religious belief that is founded upon eliminating and reversing anthropogenic global warming (AGW). Citing the words of atmospheric physicist John Reid, she indicates that AGW is "the central tenet of this new belief system in much the same way that the Resurrection is the central tenet of Christianity . . . My skepticism about AGW arises from the fact that, as a physicist who has worked in closely related areas, I know how poor the underlying science is. In effect, the scientific method has been abandoned in this field."[36]

As eco-spirituality has it, AGW is mainly the result of Western economic growth and voracious consumerism which must be rejected in favor of a spiritual conversion that finds God dwelling in all things, the union of creation and Creator. Mullarkey describes such belief as a "nature mysticism" that aims at sacralizing the natural world, a nature piety that evokes an eco-paganism motivated by anti-capitalist fervor. Mullarkey further recognizes that like Marxism, which used 'science' to demonstrate the 'truths' of its utopian aims, eco-spirituality seeks authoritarian controls in economics and subordinates "science to the advocacy needs of politics."[37]

Ghanaian Cardinal Peter Turkson, head of the Pontifical Council for Peace and Justice, delivered the opening address at a four-day conference on climate change at Boston College. Turkson exhorted the USA to lead a global effort to combat climate change. As Brian Roewe reports, Turkson urged that "Today, American support for the United Nations and American international leadership are more needed than ever, specifically to help solve the crisis of climate change. This may well be the most important challenge of the 21st century. It calls for global dialogue and leadership. It is a moral issue of the highest order. No country can tackle this problem alone, nor can the poorer ones without much help."[38]

Clearly Turkson's eco-spirituality is animated by a messianic zeal. He believes strongly that "America can marshal its best resources to solve the climate challenge and protect our common home . . ."[39] The real practical and scientific question of whether it is possible literally to control and alter the condition of climate in order to save the planet from disastrous climate change is not even broached by Turkson and the eco-spirituality zealots. What is definitely possible to change, however, as Turkson advocates, is socioeconomics. Turkson calls for a massive global redistribution of wealth based on the belief that capitalism, which is in effect synonymous with "individualism," is the cause of the climate change problem. He insists that "When many act on private self-interest, it endangers the common home. The roots of the problem are the bondage of individualism and putting short-term gain above longer-term sustainability."[40] What Turkson means, in the words of Roewe, is that practical judgments must be made and authoritatively executed, "such as repaying the 'ecological debt' of the global north to the global south; placing the global common good above national interest; avoiding a profit-first ideology; and replacing 'without delay' highly polluting fossil fuels."[41]

Turkson's "integral ecology" is messianic not only to save the planet from climate change but also from capitalist economic development which is devastating our common home. Turkson apparently wants a new global economic order, a morally superior global socialism that is as collectivistic as his eco-spirituality. It is a spirituality that, as his Catholic ilk believes, transcends traditional Christian metaphysics and reorders what it means to be an individual human person so that the free individual person is subsumed into the greater collective world order.

Final Remarks

Redpath's and Marcel's warnings of a crisis in the West are not mere abstruse philosophical clamor. The crisis is degrading the free individual human person. With the opposition to socioeconomic individualism as a foil, perhaps even a straw man pretext, socialistic collectivism ascends as a utopian solution for socioeconomic inequality and the apocalyptic threat of climate change. The free individual person, however, goes missing with this solution, as well as the person's capacity for knowing truth. Truth in science, economics and environmentalism becomes more and more dictated by the collective, which is ultimately authoritarian and politically advantageous. Moral truth is also subverted by the egalitarian tolerance that the collective imposes as requisite for achieving its promised utopia.

With the subversion of traditional metaphysics of the human person, the emerging Catholic spirituality of integral ecology certainly can be seen as born of the crisis. It is fixed on a messianic end of attaining a moral, socioeconomic and environmental utopia. It may be deeply heartfelt, but it is unfortunately headless because it does not understand rationally the damage being done to the human person. It aims to serve and even save 'global humanity' but does not comprehend that such a collectivist objective is nothing but an 'abstract humanism,' which as Redpath and Marcel caution is at the very source of the crisis. The concrete, free individual human person is truly missing in the Catholic spirituality of integral ecology.

References and Notes

1. Reprinted with permission from: "The Missing Person in Catholic Spirituality," in *Studia Gilsoniana: A Festschrift in Honor of Peter Redpath,* ed. Piotr Jaroszynski (Cromwell, CT: The International Etienne Gilson Society, 5:1, January–March 2016, Special Edition) pp. 163-177.

2. Peter Redpath, *A Not-So-Elementary Christian Metaphysics* (Manito Springs, CO: Socratic Press, 2012), 21. Hereafter cited as *NSECM.*

3. Peter Redpath, "Gabriel Marcel and the Recovery of Philosophy in Our Time," *American Catholic Philosophical Quarterly* 80, No. 3 (Summer 2006): 343-353, at343. Hereafter cited as, Redpath, ACPQ

4. This term is used in the Encyclical of Pope Francis, *Laudato Si*, May 2015, #11.

5. See *NSECM,* 7.

6. *Ibid.*

7. See *NSECM,* 18-19.

8. See *NSECM,* 23.

9. *Ibid.*

10. *Ibid.*

11. Gabriel Marcel, *Man Against Mass Society*, trans. G. S. Fraser (Chicago: Regnery, 1962) 37. Hereafter cited as *MAMS*.

12. See Redpath, *ACPQ*, 345-6.

13. *MAMS*, 15.

14. Gabriel Marcel, "An Autobiographical Essay," trans. Forrest Williams, in *The Philosophy of Gabriel Marcel*, ed. Paul Arthur Schilpp and Lewis Hahn (La Salle, Open Court, 1984) 1 – 68, at 62-3. Hereafter cited as, *A E*.

15. See John E. Smith, "The Individual, the Collective and the Community," in *The Philosophy of Gabriel Marcel*, 337-51, at 337.

16. See *MAMS*, 166. See also, Thomas Michaud, "Gabriel Marcel's Politics: Theory and Practice," *American Catholic Philosophical Quarterly* 80, No. 3 (Summer 2006): 435-451. This essay summarizes some of the much more extensive and detailed expositions of Marcel's political thought presented in my cited article in the "Gabriel Marcel" ACPQ Volume that I edited and introduced.

17. Gabriel Marcel, *Searchings*, ed. Wolfgang Ruf (New York: Newman Press, 1967) 88.

18. *Ibid.*

19. Marcel cautioned that our nature as human persons is to be "in a situation of some sort of other, and this is what a too abstract kind of humanism always runs the risk of forgetting." *MAMS*, 13.

20. Gabriel Marcel, *Tragic Wisdom and Beyond*, trans. Stephen Jolin and Peter McCormick (Evanston: Northwestern University Press, 1973) 43. Hereafter cited as *TWB*.

21. Gabriel Marcel, *Homo Viator*, trans. Emma Crawford (Gloucester, Mass.: Peter Smith, 1978) 74. Hereafter cited as *HV*.

22. Smith, "The Individual, the Collective, and the Community," 343.
23. *Ibid.*, 345.
24. *Ibid.*
25. Andrew Hertzog, (May 14, 2012). "What the Catholic Church Thinks about Individualism and Catholicism," para. 2. Retrieved from http://baronhertzog.hub-pages.com/hub/Does-the-Catholic-Church-Support-Collectivism-or-Individualism-Neither.
26. *Ibid.*, para. 1
27. See *ibid.*, para. 2
28. Daren Jonescu, (Dec, 3, 2013). "Catholics and Communists," *American Thinker*," para. 13. Retrieved from http://american/thinker.com/articles/2013/12/catholics_and_communists.html.
29. *Ibid.*, para. 1.
30. See *ibid.*, para. 20.
31. Victor Gaetan, (July 26 – Aug. 8, 2015 Issue). "Pope's South-American Visit Solidifies his Papal Vision," *National Catholic Register.* Retrieved from http://www.ncregister.com/site/print_article/45949/. All of the following quotes in this section are from this Gaetan article.
32. See above note #3.
33. Fr. Brian O'Donnell, S. J. (Sept. 18, 2015). "Our 'Common Home' and 'God's Sacred Appalachia'," *The Catholic Spirit*, 6-7, at 6.
34. *Ibid.*, 6. Both the 1975 and 1995 letters can be accessed at: www.catholicconferencewv.org
35. Maureen Mullarkey, (May 28, 2015). "Is the Catholic Church Drifting into Eco-Spirituality?" Retrieved from: http://the   federalist.com/2015/05/28/is-the-catholic-

church-drifting-into-eco-spirituality/. Much of what follows paraphrases and directly quotes Mullarkey's article.

36. *Ibid.*, para. 5.

37. *Ibid.*, para. 18.

38. Brian Roewe, (October 2, 2015). "At Boston College, Turkson maps 'Laudato Si' path to Paris climate agreement, *"National Catholic Reporter.* Retrieved from: http://naronline.org/print/blogs/eco-catholic/boston-college-turkson-maps-lavdato-si-path-paris-climate-agreement

39. *Ibid.* This is a quote from Cardinal Turkson as reported by Roewe.

40. *Ibid.* Roewe's report of the words of Cardinal Turkson.

41. *Ibid.* Another Roewe report of a Cardinal Turkson statement.

Section III

Leadership Formation

Section Introduction

In the early 2000s I became involved with the academic area of Leadership Studies. At the University where I was teaching at the time, I was asked to contribute to developing a Master's program in organizational leadership. Since the late 1980s, I had been involved in designing and delivering Ethics and Leadership training seminars for corporations, professional associations, government agencies, non-profit organizations and university programs. For ten years (1996-2006), I also wrote a monthly column on Business Ethics for <u>The West Virginia State Journal</u>, West Virginia's business newspaper. Those columns and other lectures and exercises from my seminars were collected and published as a course text, <u>The Virtues of Business Ethics: Through Common Sense to Virtuous Common Decency</u> (Acton, Massachusetts: Copely Custom Textbooks, 2010, Third Edition).

As I became more conversant with academic leadership studies, I realized that like so many other areas of academic pursuit, Progressivism was also influencing leadership studies and by extension the practices of leadership in for-profit and non-profit organizations. Approaches such as servant leadership and transformational leadership that were and are being taught in academic programs across the USA are clearly Progressive in their ideological bent.

The three selections in this Section are representative of a realistic approach to leadership. The first is a lecture that in variations I have given many times; it is very basic. The second is also a lecture that I gave in Poland; it is a spin-off from an article that has been published as: "Leadership: Idealism vs. Realism," *Studia Philosophiae Christianae,* September 30, 2019, Vol. 55, No. 3 (UKSW Scientific Printing House) pp. 81-103. Available https://czasopisma.uksw.edu.pl/index.php/spch/issue/view/557. The third selection is a philosophical essay that argues for the importance of teaching traditional rhetoric in leadership education, especially since leaders today are so often confronted by WOKE colleagues, subordinates, employees and government regulatory agencies.

Six Essential Traits of Leadership
June 2018

1. **Leadership is much more than management. Management skills are a subset of leadership competencies.**

    a. All effective leaders must be effective managers, but not all effective managers are effective leaders.
    b. Leaders have the vision to know where to go and their management skills are vital for actually getting there.
    c. Leaders who want nothing to do with management are those who do not execute well their intentions.
    d. Management is necessary for leadership, but leadership is more than management because leadership, for one very important reason, is rooted in and emerges from the character of the leader.

2. **Leaders strive to become a steward of the organization.**

    a. Leader-stewards are caretakers of the organization; the overall purpose in all of their work is the **common good** of what is truly best for their followers, their peers, their superiors and for the organization at large.
    b. No man will make a great leader who wants to do it all himself or get all the credit for doing it. – Andrew Carnegie

3. **Leaders strive to develop a habit of enterprise wherein their work and character are integrated**

    a. Their work is an extension of themselves for the sake of their followers, peers, superiors and organization.
    b. When we work, we are proud of what we do, of where we work, and of those with whom and for whom we work. – Thomas Michaud

4. **Leaders base their actions on the attitude that they are self-employed.**

    a. They act as if they are playing a critical role in an organization, wherein they are at risk of losing money/esteem/clients/funding but also receiving profit/etc.
    b. Leaders accept profoundly that they are **accountable** for their work, their decisions, their followers and their organization.
    c. A real leader faces the music, even when he doesn't like the tune. – *Anonymous*

5.   **Leaders view each problem or mistake situation as if it were significant** rather than a matter that will be solved or neutralized by the normal functioning of the organization.

    a.   As soon as problems or mistakes show up, leaders begin looking for solutions. To find solutions, leaders must possess a **smart confidence** that is not arrogant, but listens to, learns and values input from followers, peers and superiors.

    b.   One of the true tests of leadership is the ability to recognize a problem before it becomes an emergency. – *Arnold H. Glasgow*

    c.   He who has never learned to obey cannot be a good [leader]. – *Aristotle*

    d.   The best leaders are the best note-takers, best askers, and best learners – They are shameless thieves. – *Tom Peters*

    e.   Leadership and learning are indispensable to each other. - *John Fitzgerald Kennedy*

6.   **Leaders are models of decorum.**

    a.   They show pride in the language they use, how they dress, how they keep up their workplace, and in what they expect from themselves, followers, peers and superiors.

    b.   Shabby decorum is corrosive to good leadership; without decorum, uncivil conduct and an unkempt workplace can result which can threaten safety, undermine morale and damage the productivity of the organization.

Leadership Idealism vs Realism[1]
June 2018

If it is stipulated that a measure of the merit of a civilization is the substance of its predominate philosophies, then a civilization's philosophies of leadership are essential to assessing its merit. Leadership philosophies can contribute to orienting, developing and even largely defining a civilization. They can turn a civilization toward oppressive totalitarianism or toward humane freedom; they can engender a democratic republic that values the individual person, or a depersonalizing social-economic collectivism led by elitist despots. It is crucial, then, that leadership philosophies be explicated and critiqued in order that their tendencies in shaping civilizations can be exposed. A valuable conceptual framework for doing so is the contrasts between leadership realism and elitist leadership idealism.

There are many types of elites, ranging from business through the political to the media and even the ethnic, religious and educational. What all of these types have in common, as implied by the lexical definition of "elite," is the "social superiority" of a particular individual or group.[2] "Elitism," however, has a more specific definition, namely, "leadership or rule by an elite."[3] By merging these meanings, "elitism" can be interpreted as a type of leadership in which leaders, within any sort of organization, are regarded or conceive themselves as superior. Superiority, whether accorded to leaders by members of an organization or merely assumed by the leaders themselves, is, then, a distinguishing trait of elitist leadership. It is, moreover, important to emphasize that such elitist superiority can be characteristic of leadership in organizations of any scale or type: they can be corporations with their divisions and departments, non-profit NGO's, governmental organizations, or educational institutions; they can be local, regional, national or even global in the scope of their authority.

Before summarizing the contrasting tendencies of leadership idealism and realism, it must be indicated that the tendencies are not necessarily characteristic of every idealist or realist leadership philosophy. In other words, some tendencies may be characteristic of some idealist or realist approaches, and others may not. There are also greater or lesser degrees to which a particular tendency may be characteristic of a particular leader or philosophy. Finally, it is helpful to interpret the tendencies by thinking that the idealist or realist leadership philosophies tend to have at least some but not necessarily all of these characteristics.

It must be re-emphasized that although the descriptions of these tendencies are offered as generalities, they do have relevant application to particular leaders in organizations of almost any kind or size. The descriptions refer to leadership in general, but any particular person with leadership status in any sort of organization can manifest the idealist or realist tendencies in ways that are contextualized within the type of organization.

In idealist approaches, leadership capabilities are conceived as being innate within a person; there is an in-born leadership superiority such that the person's leadership status is viewed as a sort of destiny fulfillment. This is the basis of the elitism with idealism. Realist approaches, on the other hand, assert that leadership can be taught and learned, and leadership status must be earned by effective, successful performance: there is no innate leadership status and no claim of elitist superiority.

Idealist leaders are typically thoroughgoing visionaries, acting on their utopian vision for the "perfect" organization and aiming to construct their own organizational reality so that it conforms to their vision. In so doing, they invent their own standards, including ethics standards, for what is best and right for the organization. Realists, in contrast, maintain a concrete, down-to-earth perspective recognizing that leaders must act within the given parameters of an organization and conform their goals to the reality of the situation. To accomplish this, realists seek to discover conscientiously the best and right standards and ethics, conform to them and apply them within and among the structures and people of the organization

For idealists, hope is striving to instantiate the utopian vision the leader has constructed. Change is endeavoring to transform reality through any means to make it conform to the leader's vision. In the process of such hopeful change, the possible real consequences that challenge the leader's vision are ignored or de-emphasized. Realists' hope is respecting what is discovered about reality and trusting that conforming to the best and right standards will lead to what is good and successful. Their approach to change is endeavoring to actualize the best and right standards within the reality of the organization. Consequently, they accept that ideas have real consequences. Such consequences must be foreseen, as much as possible, and factored into assessing whether and how an idea should be implemented.

Finally, idealists treat followers as a collective entity, or entities, having a group identity based on, for example, race, ethnicity, gender, job position or class status. With this collectivist mentality, idealists assign these group identities to their followers enabling them to fabricate diversity according to the leader's projected group traits. The real individual identities of the followers are subsumed into the group identity the leader constitutes. Realists, however, aim to get to know, respect and treat the individual followers as who they are as real persons and not as mere instances of the collective identity the leader has projected upon them.

Transformational Leadership (TL) and Servant Leadership (SL) are two of the currently popular and widely implemented approaches that have definite idealist tendencies. TL aims at changing and transforming followers by leaders motivating and developing them. Transformational leaders are charismatic visionaries who reach their followers principally on the emotional level. In order to inspire the followers and influence them to accept moral transformation, transformational leaders convince followers to believe that the moral message empowers the followers beyond what they thought was possible. TL further differentiates between authentic and pseudo-transformational leadership basically claiming that any leadership which is not socialized leadership focused on the collective good is immoral because it is selfish and power hungry. Peter Northouse notes that TL can be "used to describe a wide range of leadership, from very specific attempts to influence followers on a one-to-one level, to very broad attempts to influence whole organizations and even entire cultures."[4]

TL is clearly an idealism that depicts authentic leaders as moral elites whose charisma is so potent that they can transform followers to trust fully in the leader's ideology, to have unquestioning acceptance of the leader, to express affection toward the leader and become emotionally involved in the leader's goals.[5] With TL, collectivism is overt in that it is not only the collective good which is pursued, but TL aims to bind the individual identities of the followers to the collective identity of the organization: the individual is subsumed into and effectively lost within the collective.

SL, which has been adopted and promoted by various influential organizations such as the Kettering and Kellogg

Foundations, has the morality of an explicit social justice orientation. Servant leaders 'lead from behind' in that they aim to empower the "have-nots" within communities or nations to engage the struggle against inequalities and injustices. In the ideal world that SL pursues, community and societal changes are targeted on an egalitarianism which will establish the utopia SL desires. SL in this way believes that the scope of a "community organizer" is not just a neighborhood or a limited group of "have nots," but can and even should be global in its influence.

TL and SL are just two current examples of elitist idealism. Their prominence has led to a global moralizing whose leadership in so many political, economic and religious areas has made socialistic collectivism not merely appealing but a moral standard that is displacing inferior, intolerant, and warped traditional morality. In what direction 21st century philosophies of leadership will evolve is a very serious question, since global civilization itself as one of despotic totalitarianism or humane freedom could be ultimately at stake.

References and Notes

1. This lecture was delivered at Cardinal Stefan Wyszynski University, Warsaw, Poland in June 2018. It is a version of my published article, "Leadership: Idealism vs. Realism," Studia Philosophiae Christianae, September 30, 2019, Vol. 55, No. 3 (UKSW Scientific Printing House) pp. 81-103. Available online at: https://czasopisma.uksw.edu.pl/ index.php/spch/issue/view/557

2. *Webster's New Collegiate Dictionary*, (Springfield, MA: G. & C. Merriam Co., 1980) p. 366.

3. *Ibid.*

4. Peter Northhouse, *Leadership: Theory and Practice*, Third Edition, (New Delhi: Sage Publications, 2013) p.186. Much of this paragraph's description of TL is based on Northouse, pp.185-187.
5. See Northouse, p. 189.

The Importance of Rhetoric in Leadership Formation[1]
April 2021

ABSTRACT

Contrary to much academic, public and businesspersons' opinion, education in rhetoric is definitely important for leadership formation. Leaders who are uneducated in the art of persuasive communications are severely handicapped. This article argues this claim 1) By defining what and who a leader is. 2) By describing the intrinsic relationship between leadership and rhetoric. 3) By identifying aspects of rhetoric that are central to practicing good leadership. 4) And, finally, by concluding with some observations on leadership, rhetoric and the current "cancel culture" movement.

The public relations consultant James Horton believes firmly that a solid education in rhetoric is crucial to the formation of successful business leaders.[2] Though his focus is on business, what Horton claims about leadership can be applied to any organization of any type or scale, such as universities, organizational departments and work teams, non-profits, government agencies and national governments themselves, religious organizations, etc. To paraphrase Horton: Because we live in an information age, persuasive communications, the art of rhetoric, are more important than ever. Leaders who avoid learning the art of persuasive communications handicap themselves severely. This is especially true with the top position of any organization. For every Steve Jobs, who could hold an audience in the palm of his hand, there are 10 CEOs, Presidents, Chairs or Exalted Clerics who read boringly from a teleprompter, stand rigidly behind a lectern, or give rambling informal remarks that lose an audience more quickly than winning it.

To continue paraphrasing, Horton relates a story about a CEO of one of the largest corporations in the world who said with chagrin that he hated the Organizational Behavior course in his business education because it dealt with the 'touchy-feely' stuff of leadership. But, now, the CEO realizes that he should have paid more attention because he spends most of his time on 'touchy-feely' stuff. Communication is frequently grouped as part of the 'touchy-feely' stuff of leadership, but as rhetoricians understand, it is one of the most important studies of all because one's life and livelihood can depend on it. One would think that modern leaders would understand this, but sadly, they don't.

Rhetoric is far too often viewed negatively as merely the manipulation of words, empty word play, or a weak substitute for real action. A dismissive expression of the sort, "Don't bother with it, its just rhetoric!" reveals the cultural scorn for rhetoric today. Nevertheless, Horton and many others are right in championing the crucial importance of appreciating and studying rhetoric in leadership formation. Why they are right can be concisely demonstrated: 1) By defining what and who a leader is. 2) By describing the intrinsic relationship between leadership and rhetoric. 3) By identifying aspects of rhetoric that are central to practicing good leadership. 4) And, finally, by concluding with some observations on leadership, rhetoric and the current "cancel culture" movement.

Understanding what and who a leader is begins with a basic proposition: Presuming certain educable aptitudes, intelligence and communication abilities, leaders are not born but made. Leadership is not given by nature, but is nurtured by proper education, training and experience. Still, the process of becoming a leader is essentially a process of character formation. This is much different from just acquiring a set of skills. This character formation is a matter of cultivating dispositional habits, or to use a current word for 'habits', competencies, which are rooted in a leader's character: "characterial competencies," to coin a term.

Leadership is unfortunately misunderstood as a higher grade or degree of management. In organizations today, someone is selected to be a leader because his or her management skills are superior. There is, however, a difference in kind between leadership and management such that all good (effective, successful) leaders must be good managers, but not all good managers are good leaders. Good management skills are a subset of well-formed leadership competencies, but leadership is not merely a species of management. Leaders have the vision to know where to go, and their management skills are vital for actually getting there. Leaders who want nothing to do with the so-called "details" of management are failures because they do not execute well their intentions for the organization. Good management is necessary for leadership, but leadership is indeed a different kind because leadership is embedded in and emerges from the character of the leader.

Among other goals, ethical integrity is a principal aim of the process of leadership character formation. Ethical integrity as a characterial competency means a wholeness of character. Within the leader's character there is no break, no fracture between what leaders know they ought to do and what they actually do. As Brian Tracy observed, "The glue that holds all relationships together, including the relationship between the leader and the led, is trust, and trust is based on integrity."[3] And, as Peter Drucker explains, "Management is doing things right; leadership is doing the right thing."[4]

There is an intrinsic connection between rhetoric and leadership because good rhetoric is a necessary characterial competency for good leadership. Warren Bennis believes that it is essential for good leaders to be able to translate their intentions into reality and sustain them.[5] Leaders must be able to persuade their followers for the sake of motivating, organizing and aligning them so that the leader's aims yield and sustain the intended results.

Rhetoric is a significant means by which this can and does happen. Such rhetoric, however, is not merely techniques with communication, manipulating the followers with the right buzzwords, telling them only what the leader thinks they might like to hear as a sophistic politician does. Aristotle teaches that persuasion is achieved when the leader's personal character is perceived as credible: "We believe good [people] more fully and more readily than others: this is true generally whatever the question is, and absolutely true where exact certainty is impossible and opinions are divided."[6] Aristotle continues his clear-eyed emphasis on character, virtue and credibility for effective rhetoric by stating that, "It is not true, as some writers assume in their treatises on rhetoric, that the personal goodness revealed by the speaker contributes nothing to his power of persuasion; on the contrary, his character may almost be called the most effective means of persuasion."[7]

One of the aspects of Classical Rhetoric that is central to the practice of good leadership is understanding the meanings of and the proper relationship between ethos, pathos and logos in rhetorical communication. Ethos, obviously, relates to the integrity of leaders since they must establish their credibility, authority and trust with their followers. Leaders must realize that persuasion is an action which is in the category of "moral acts" because the leader's rhetoric aims to persuasively convince followers that what is being communicated is true or probably true. In order to do so, leaders themselves must know and believe as much as possible it is true, because any deception, any lie, would violate the leaders' trust and credibility. With deception, leaders would be manipulating the followers and disrespecting their integrity as persons, and such would be unethical.

Logos involves an appeal to the audience's reasoning with well-constructed arguments using factual information, accurate data, and pithy and real (or realistic) examples. When issuing from authentic ethos, logos is the primary means by which leaders should aim to persuade followers of the truth or probable truth of their message. With logos, moreover, leaders should be open and prepared to engage rational objections to their arguments. In fact, leaders' logos should itself frame and offer logical rebuttals to expected counter-arguments in order to strengthen the persuasive truth of their message.

Pathos communicates emotional appeals to connect with an audience through their feelings, sentiments and passionate self-interests. With pathos, leaders can sympathize or empathize with their followers, creating an affective bond with them that can reinforce their ethos and contribute to followers more readily "taking to heart" the logos of the leaders' message. For example, honestly addressing the ways in which the message could positively or negatively affect the followers' morale and sense of organizational loyalty is a clear example of the proper use of pathos as bolstering and moderated by ethos and logos.

Pathos, however, is perhaps the most misused aspect of rhetoric. Aristotle warned against rhetoric that merely and only plays on emotions to persuade. He cautioned that, "…persuasion may come through the [audience], when the [message] stirs their emotions. Our judgments when we are pleased and friendly are not the same as when we are pained and hostile. It is towards producing these effects, as we maintain, that present-day writers on rhetoric direct the whole of their efforts."[8] Aristotle recognized that sophistic emotional rhetoric can be effective, but it is deceptive and disingenuous since it lacks ethos and is not as effectively persuasive as logos. As he states, "…persuasion is effected through the [rhetoric] itself when we have proved a truth or an apparent truth by means of persuasive arguments suitable to the case in question."[9] For Aristotle it was clear that logos fortified by ethos should be the primary means of persuasion.

The proper use of pathos in rhetoric can be further elaborated by analyzing Aristotle's views on catharsis in his Poetics. Richard Janko in his "Introduction" to his translation of the Poetics proposes a compelling case for what Aristotle actually meant by catharsis.[10] Janko contends that Aristotle's meaning of catharsis was deformed by the psycho-analytic school of therapy which viewed catharsis as a type of psychological healing. This healing is effected when audience members viewing, reading or hearing a stage-drama, film/TV show, speech, or any literary form, experience the arousal and then the release of pent-up undesirable emotions. Catharsis in this psycho-analytic sense is, then, the purgation of negative emotions: sort of a curative sweat-lodge for the psyche.

Janko, however, maintains that Aristotelian catharsis is not the purgation of undesirable emotions but the rectification of emotions. He indicates that catharsis makes the emotions tractable for education. For Janko, Aristotle saw emotions as essential to forming good character and making good judgments. Therefore, catharsis applies to errors or flaws in character and emotion, as well as to errors in moral judgment. As Janko interprets Aristotle, we should feel the right emotion, towards the right object, at the right time, to the right degree. In the formation of good character, it is important to develop the habit, the characterial competency, to feel emotions properly so we can make ethically and rationally correct decisions.

The pathos in leaders' rhetoric must be moderated by their ethos and logos, especially when their organization is distressed and facing morale challenges. In these circumstances, leaders whose persuasion is mainly arousing "happy" emotions with an abundance of feel-good promises of fatuous "new solutions" are merely pandering to their followers to assuage their discontent. Such leaders are just manipulating their followers' emotions, which cannot yield organizational recovery.

What good leaders should do is achieve a catharsis issuing from ethos tempered by the logos of a realistic recovery plan. The leaders must argue that the followers' anger of resentment or their indignant resistance to leadership cannot sustain the recovery plan. The leaders must empathize with followers and persuade them that only a collaborative effort based on a pathos of reasonable hope, mutual loyalty and mutual sacrifice can generate effective recovery. In doing so, the leaders would aim to rectify the negative emotions of the organization and accomplish recovery with a genuine Aristotelian catharsis.

As a concluding section of this presentation and perhaps as a bit of an excursus from the above material, it would be worthwhile to examine briefly the rhetoric of the cancel culture movement. Progressive leaders, namely social media influencers, mainstream media figures, academic intellectual elites and demagogic politicians, mainly prosecute the aggressive Kulturkampf of the movement. The targets of their "cancel rhetoric" range from the inane to the contemptuously profane, from cancelling Pepe Le Pew and Dr. Seuss to Saint Junipero Serra and Andrew Jackson. It is the resentful rhetoric of the self-proclaimed offended, which sadly transmits a contagious pathos that can debilitate organizations. Good leaders must recognize that their own organizational cultures can be sickened by this virulent "cancel pathos" and they should aim to keep their cultures safe by understanding, exposing and challenging the motivations and claims of this pathetic rhetoric.

In order to resist the Progressive cancellers, leaders must understand that the cancellers maintain as axiomatic that culture is downstream of politics. Traditionalists, however, generally accept the so-called "Breitbart Doctrine" named after the late conservative commentator Andrew Breitbart that posits, "Politics is downstream from culture."[11] According to Dan McLaughlin this dictum means that people tend to invest more of their hearts and free time into cultural pursuits than political ones. People are much more engaged with their families, churches, schools, civic groups, sports, hobbies, mass and social media, etc. than they are with the strategies and struggles of politics. Consequently, the beliefs and attitudes that pervade the larger spaces of their lives affect the smaller ones, not just in what they believe but whom they know and trust, as well. People's politics is, then, a smaller space, which is formed and developed by their lives within culture. So, effecting changes in politics, winning elections and securing political power requires influencing the people's culture. Cultural change and evolution

yield political change and evolution, which for the traditional-
ists/conservatives is a type of "socially organic" process; it is
the "natural" way in which culture lives and grows within a
society, or, on a larger scale, a civilization.

The Progressives differ strongly. Daniel Patrick Moynihan
once astutely claimed, "The central conservative truth is that it
is culture, not politics, that determines the success of a society.
The central liberal truth is that politics can change a culture and
save it from itself."[12] As Moynihan affirmed, Liberals/Progres-
sives believe that is it is politics that is the supreme engine of
cultural change: It takes cultural change to change society and
cultural change happens through politics; it happens through
winning elections, controlling the judiciary and the system of
jurisprudence, and dominating mass and social media with
their political aims.

The cancellers are ideological zealots whose tactics intend
to secure political power. Their political power grows with
their cancellations, and the more cancellations, the more they
exert the power not merely to change but to erase and wholly
dismantle existing culture. They reject that any type of culture
can or should be organically or naturally developed. The cancellers emotionally despise the organic growth of a culture because it does not necessarily conform to their political designs.
They hate any culture that is not engineered by their politics
because all of such cultures are offensive and oppressive. Their
emotional resentment teems within a vengeful retaliation,
which cannot be entirely assuaged since its actual object is to
suppress fully their political opposition. They cannot accept
political defeat on any scale. Their success must be total in order for their politics to fundamentally transform culture. They
feel convinced that their opposition will find their politicized
replacement culture so "naggingly" inhospitable that ultimately

the opposition will be worn down and accept it just to live in some peace.

For organizational leaders, maybe the most threatening tactic of the cancellers is when their rhetoric insists that their target must be cancelled because it embodies and propagates racism, misogyny, ethnic prejudice, or sexual orientation intolerance. The public spread of their offended pathos can eventually infect an organization's personnel so that they begin to splinter into antagonistic groups along the lines of the cancellers' assaults. Such balkanization creates serious morale problems and gravely disrupts the organizational culture.

To resist the cancellers, the leaders should communicate to their followers that the ethos of their organizational culture respects the integrity and equality of individuals. This respect does not subsume individuals into group identities but values the dignity of individual persons as such. They should emphasize, moreover, that followers should not be swept up by the politicized emotions of vengeful retaliation, since to be so manipulated is to become pawns in the political tactics of the cancellers, which again, is an assault on their individual dignity. Finally, the leaders need to exhort followers that their organizational culture is indeed theirs. If they acquiesce to cancellations and take on politicized group identities as what they are primarily, the cancellers will never be satisfied until their organizational culture is reduced to rubble and the emotionally unstable pathos of the offended is all that is left. It is indeed the very dignity of individual persons that is at stake, and unless leaders strive to resist the cancellers' attacks, individuals will become nothing more than collectivized drones engineered to carry out the angry politics of "woke" culture.

References and Notes

1. This paper was presented at the 20th International Conference on the Future of Western Civilization, Conference Theme - Exposing a Lie: The Controversy about the Place of Rhetoric in Culture, John Paul the Great Catholic University of Lublin, Poland, April 22, 2021.

2. The material from Horton's article has been paraphrased and rewritten in places though his ideas and points made have been maintained. James Horton, "Persuasion Principles: They Haven't Changed Much," http://www.online-pr.com/Holding/PersuasionPrinciples.com

3. This is a well-known quote from Brian Tracy. See: https://www.inspiringquotes.us/author/1007-brian-tracy/page:14.

4. This is a famous quote from Peter Drucker. See: https://quotefancy.com/quote/20738/Peter-F-Drucker-Management-is-doing-things-right-leadership-is-doing-the-right-things

5. W. Bennis, "The Artform of Leadership," in *The Leader's Companion,* ed. by J. Th. Wren, The Free Press., New York 1995, 377.

6. This quote (and the following quotes) from Aristotle is in J. Horton's article, "Persuasion Principles: They Haven't Changed Much" and is from: Aristotle *Rhetoric*, I.2,1356a 5-10, in *The Basic Works of Aristotle*, trans. by W Rhys Roberts and edited by Richard McKeon, Random House, New York: 1941, 1329.

7. Ibidem, *Rhet.* I.2, 1356a 10-15,

8. Ibidem, *Rhet.* I.2, 1356a 14-18, 1329-30

9. Ibidem, *Rhet.* I.2, 1356a 19-21, 1330

10. Richard Janko, "Introduction," Aristotle's *Poetics*, trans. Richard Janko, Indianapolis: Hackett, 1987, pp. ix-xxvi.
11. Dan McLaughlin, "Politics is Still Downstream of Culture," https://redstate.com/dan_mclaughlin/2016/05/04politics-still-downstream-from-culture-n58816. The following description of Breitbart's Doctrine paraphrases some of McLaughlin's points.
12. Daniel Patrick Moynihan, https://www.godreads.com/quotes/116754-the-central-conservative-truth-is-that-it-is-culture-not.

Bibliography

Aristotle. *Rhetoric* in *The Basic Works of Aristotle*. Translated by W. Rhys Roberts. Edited by Richard McKeon. New York: Random House, 1941. 1318-1451.

Bennis, Warren. "The Artform of Leadership," (1982) in *The Leader's Companion*. Edited by J. Th. Wren. New York: The Free Press, 1995. 377-378.

Horton, James. "Persuasion Principles: They Haven't Changed Much." http://www.online-pr.com/Holding/Persuasion-Principles

Janko, Richard. "Introduction," Aristotle's *Poetics*, Translated by Richard Janko. Indianapolis: Hackett, 1987.

McLaughlin, Dan. "Politics is Still Downstream of Culture." https://redstate.com/dan_mclaughlin/2016/05/04politics-still-downstream -from-culture-n58816

Section IV

Environmentalism and Realism

Section Introduction

The inclusion of the two essays in this Section may seem at first to be sort of random without any unifying complementarity. One might wonder, for instance, what does ecoterrorism have to do with realism and hope? The essays do however complement each other, with the "Realism" essay extending and further elaborating points made in the "Ecoterrorism" essay. Both of these essays, moreover, without explicitly mentioning Progressivism, expose the philosophical flaws in what is certainly the current prevailing Progressive environmental ideology, namely ecocentrism.

"On Beyond Going Green: Environmental Ecoterrorism" details the pernicious outcomes of adopting a radical ecocentric ideology. It also explains how a realistic ideology of conservationism is complemented and enriched by traditional teaching of the Catholic Church, especially in regard to the "animal rights" issue.

"Realism: The Way to Cross the Threshold of Hope" employs Pope John Paul II's concept of the Modern anthropocentric shift in which the subjectivism of a philosophy of consciousness replaced a realistic philosophy of existence. The essay argues that genuine hope is possible only on the basis of a realist metaphysics and not a subjectivist, anthropocentric metaphysics. This is one of the reasons why, for example, the Progressive environmentalists' animal rights issue suffers from hope-less Modern anthropocentrism. In addition, it is a reason why Progressivism will never be able to appreciate and steward the *opus gloriae* of God's creation

On Beyond Going Green:
Environmental Ecoterrorism[1]
August 2009

In 2005, the USA Federal Bureau of Investigation (FBI) declared ecoterrorism as America's No. 1 domestic terror threat. Since 2003 "ecotage" (a combination of "eco" with the word "sabotage") has wreaked hundreds of millions of dollars in property damage and destruction in the USA. Ecotage, however, is not confined to the USA. "Ecoteurs" (a wordplay on "saboteurs") are operative throughout the world, creating wrack and ruin wherever and whenever it serves their cause. International ecoterriorist groups like the Animal Liberation Front (ALF) and the Earth Liberation Front (ELF) have become some of the most active criminal extremist organizations in the world.

Leaders and supporters of ALF and ELF bluntly state their acceptance of ecotage. Alex Pacheco, co-founder of People for the Ethical Treatment of Animals (PETA), once claimed, "Arson, property destruction, burglary and theft are 'acceptable crimes' when used for the animal cause."[2] Jerry Vlask of the Animal Defense League urged ecoteurs to "Get arrested. Destroy the property of those who torture animals. Liberate those animals interred in the hellholes our society tolerates."[3] Tim Daley, a British ALF leader, insisted that "In a war you have to take up arms and people will get killed, and I can support that kind of action by petrol bombing and bombs under cars, and probably at a later stage the shooting of vivisectors on their doorsteps."[4]

In the global media, in schools, in churches, and certainly in governments and economic unions, a "culture of environmentalism" has been developing for many decades now. To be sure, this culture has had many positive effects. It has, for instance, heightened our awareness of the real dangers of pollution, deforestation, careless acquisition and consumption of energy resources, and abuse of living things. This culture, however, has also spawned an extremist fringe of the organized ecoteurs, and their ecoterrorism is indeed unconscionable. The FBI defines "ecoterrorism" as "the use or threatened use of violence of a criminal nature against innocent victims or property by an environmentally-oriented subnational groups for environmental-political reasons, or aimed at an audience beyond the target, often of a symbolic nature."[5]

The culture of environmentalism has been deformed by the ecoteurs. The real benefits of "going green," of environmentally sustainable building construction and commerce, and nature conservancy, have been warped by the radical ideology and resulting ecotage of the ecoteurs.[6] But what is the ideology that drives ecoterrorism? Perhaps if that ideology is rationally exposed and critiqued, it will be possible to distinguish between sound and distorted environmentalism, so that the culture of environmentalism can advance with a solid, beneficial philosophical foundation.

Understanding and critiquing the ecoterrorist ideology can be best achieved by first of all defining it as one of three basics, but clearly distinct, environmental ideologies. Secondly, a sound philosophical foundation for environmental ideology can be developed by integrating the traditional teachings of the Catholic Church, which offer a beneficial and rational alternative to the other problematic ideologies.

The three basic environmental ideologies are anthropocentrism, ecocentrism and conservationism. Anthropocentrism
maintains that human interests, human activities (including
economic development), and human beings have a value which
is greater than or equal to the things of the environment,
namely animals, plants and minerals. For anthropocentrism,
environmental things have no intrinsic value, moral or otherwise. Like the Ancient Sophist Protagoras, it holds that "man
is the measure of the value all things," and, consequently, the
value of environmental things is determined entirely by the
value humans assign to them. "Greenies" typically ascribe anthropocentrism to the mentality of businesses and "unenlightened" governments wherein the greenies charge that instru-
mentalism is the norm for the way nature is treated. Nature is
manipulated, changed, used and abused merely as an object of
human actions for fulfilling human needs and wants. Nature,
then, is an instrument in the hands of man, and its value is
defined only by its value for man.

Ecocentrism, in contrast, opposes treating nature as an instrument for human fulfillment. Ecocentrism claims that natural things have an intrinsic value, which includes moral value
that is equal to or greater than the value of human interests,
activities and even human beings themselves. Ecocentrism,
thereby, denies that man has a privileged status on earth and
rejects that nature is under the dominion of man. Simply stated,
for ecocentrics man has no greater value than any of the other
things of nature.

With such views, ecocentrism tends to blur the distinction
between human and non-human living things. As John Moore
observes, ecocentrics believe that there is an "intricate web of
connections among all Earth's residents, the human and the
non-human, the animate and inanimate" so that "humankind

is merely one of the many sorts of beings for whom earth is home." This constitutes an "Earth Community" in which humans and non-human things share the Earth and form a web of interdependency.[7]

With their version of the "Earth Community," ecocentrics do not effectively distinguish between human and non-human beings. The radical types actually hold that to claim humans have superior moral status to non-human beings is to be guilty of "speciesism." Such speciesism, they believe, is as heinously immoral as racism or sexism. Ingrid Newkirk, a national director of PETA once said that "Animal liberationists do not separate out the human animal, so there is no natural basis for saying that a human being has special rights. A rat is a pig is a dog is a boy. They are all mammals."[8] Newkirk also rejects the word "pet" because she thinks it is "speciesist language". She prefers the term "companion animals," and in PETA's "Statement on Companion Animals" it states that pets are "like slaves, even if well-kept slaves."[9]

Other extremist ecocentrics who espouse Newkirk-like views include Michael W. Fox, who as Vice-President of the US Humane Society stated that "The life of an ant and that of my child should be granted equal consideration."[10] In addition, the so-called "ethicists" Peter Singer and Tom Regan have some equally troubling views. Singer proposed that, "Surely there will be some non-human animals whose lives by any standards are more valuable than the lives of some human beings."[11] Regan illustrated what Singer meant by "some human beings" when Regan was asked which, a dog or a baby, he would save if a boat capsized in the ocean. He responded, "If it were a retarded baby and a bright dog, I'd save the dog."[12] For Regan, in the web of interdependency a retarded baby is obviously one of those human animals whose life is less morally valuable than the life of a smart dog.

The extremist dogmas of ecocentric ideology are, fortunately, challenged by the philosophical wisdom of conservationism. This wisdom, moreover, integrates with the teachings of the Catholic Church on environmentalism.

Conservationism both differs from and is similar to anthropocentricism and ecocentrism. Like ecocentrism, conservationism holds that natural things have intrinsic value, but like anthropocentrism, it maintains that human interests, human activities and human beings have a value, especially a moral value, greater than the things of the environment. Still, as beings who are interdependent with other humans and the environment, humans have an obligation to be virtuous stewards of the environment.

Conservationism does not subordinate human value to the value of environmental things. It stresses respect for and preservation of human value because out of all earthly things, humans are the most developed, the most capable, and the only species with reason and rational moral conscience. Conservationism, as indicated, does not deny that environmental things have intrinsic value, as anthropocentrism does, and conservationism obliges us to respect the value of environmental things as they are themselves and not merely as humans assign or define their value.

Even with its emphasis on human interdependency with environmental things, conservationism does not in any way blur the distinction between humans and non-human environmental things. It respects and preserves man's special status as a rational creature, different in kind and superior in value to all other environmental things. In this way, conservationism is enriched by the Church's environmentalism, which is further en-hanced by conservationism's emphasis on stewardship. Eco-centric views frequently criticize the Church's environmental-ism by insisting that the verse in Genesis wherein God gives humans dominion over all creation[13] leads to an environmental anthropocentrism, which justifies human license to exploit na-ture entirely for human benefit.

As the *Catechism of the Catholic Church* teaches, however, this dominion is not absolute or unconditional, especially in regard to ownership: (Quoting the *Catechism*) "Man's dominion over inanimate and other living beings granted by the Creator is not absolute . . . it requires a . . . respect for the integrity of crea-tion."[14] This dominion, when interpreted in accord with con-servationism's stewardship, means that humans are commis-sioned to, have a moral obligation to, protect and nurture all environmental things for two important reasons.

The first reason why humans have this obligation is because all things have an intrinsic value insofar as they are what they are. In the language of traditional Scholasticism, environmental things have their own essences, their "whatnesses," which de-fine them to be the kinds of things they are. Consequently, what a thing is and whatever value it has are ultimately integral to its essence, and to claim that the whatness and value of a thing are merely assigned by humans is to disrespect the integ-rity of the thing. Because of their essential integrity, environ-mental things are, then, intrinsically good as such, which reso-nates with the Church's teaching that they are intrinsically good since God declared them to be in Genesis.[15]

The second reason is based on conservationism's affirma-tion of man's essential interdependency with other men and environmental things, which establishes generational justice.

This is not an extremist "web" doctrine as with some ecocentrics, since as the *Compendium of the Social Doctrine of the Church*
indicates, "Responsibility for the environment, the common
heritage of mankind, extends not only to present needs but also
to those of the future . . . this is a responsibility that present
generations have towards those of the future, a responsibility
that also concerns individual States and the international community."[16] Both the Catholic Church and conservationism emphasize that the human obligation of stewardship is to preserve
and protect the goodness of environmental things so that they
can be cared for, enjoyed by, and be of use to future generations of people.

Because of these two reasons, conservationism's moral
norm of stewardship is enriched by what the Church's Catechism calls the solidarity among all creatures and the things of
God's creation.[17] The first reason is, again, the integrity of environmental things that conservationism affirms, and the second is generational justice, which conservationism bases on
human interdependency with other humans and the things of
the environment.

As explained above, ecocentric ideology principally shapes
the culture of environmentalism, which predominates today in
education, the media, and government. One of the most widespread and problematic aspects of this culture is the animal
rights dogma, which is for the most part accepted as a given
truism. Their refusal to differentiate clearly between human
and non-human creatures, leads them to denounce any claim
that humans have superior moral status to other non-human
creatures as immoral "speciesism."

In assessing ecocentrics' animal rights position, Rev. Paul
Fitzgerald, S.J., observes that it is based on the notion that animals "are capable of suffering and have an interest in leading

their own lives."[18] He rightly affirms that animals experience pain and suffering. He also rightly affirms that through acting from instinctual behavior patterns, some animal species can learn about their environments and even "use tools to alter their environment for their own better survival."[19]

Fitzgerald, however, questions the claim that animals have an "interest in leading their own lives."[20] He explains that the word "interest" is derived from the Latin inter, meaning "between," and esse, meaning "to be". In thought about civil matters, rights, and the law, "interest" connotes "participation in advantage and responsibility." He continues by indicating that "in other words, to enjoy certain concrete rights within a social system, a moral agent has certain duties towards others within that social system."[21] For instance, if one claims the right to free speech, "one is thereby duty bound to protect the freedom of speech for all others."[22]

An animal's "interest" to survive, however, has no accompanying obligations to others, since it is merely an interest based on instinctual survival of the fittest. Animals are not moral agents whose interest in survival includes any rationally conscious sense of responsibility for the rights of others in a social system. There are, therefore, no legitimate grounds to claim that animals have rights. Fitzgerald would no doubt agree that "animal rights" is a grossly oxymoronic term.

Still, in spite of such compelling arguments, PETA people like Newkirk insist that "We're looking for good lawsuits that will establish the interests of animals as a legitimate area of concern in law."[23] Their ecocentric animal rights ideology is not only confused in regard to what rights are and what they entail, but their dogmatic insistence on animal rights reflects their actual anthropocentrism. They aim to assign rights to animals to legitimize their belief that animals ought to be respected; but, by claiming that animals have rights they are actually disrespecting the animals qua animals. Their rights claim issues from nothing other than anthropocentric human chauvinism.

This is so because of their anthropocentric mentality that in order to legitimize respect for animals, they simply have to endow animals with human traits, such as rights. This would be like a male chauvinist's claim that men should endow women with rights only if women display male traits. Such chauvinism would certainly disrespect women as women, just as assigning rights to animals, merely through ideological will, disrespects the essential integrity of animals.

Unlike ecocentrism, conservationism does not slip into anthropocentric chauvinism because it does not succumb to the philosophically deformed dogma of animal rights. Conservationism holds that, for example, one should respect and care for a dog just because it is a dog. Animals ought to be respected for what they naturally are. They are not moral agents, they have no sense of social or civil responsibility, but they do have an essential integrity, which is intrinsic and value laden. Animals and all environmental things deserve our respect, which is reinforced by our responsibilities of stewardship and interdependence.

The ecocentric ideology with its ill-formed claims such as animal rights, must be challenged by the philosophical wisdom of conservationism. The more ecocentricism is critiqued, the more it is weakened and the less it is capable of spawning radical ecoterrorists. As the challenges to ecocentrism mount, moreover, conservationism with its integration of the Church's environmentalism will more fully emerge as the sound environmental philosophy. And, as conservationism continues to replace ecocentrism within the culture of environmentalism, we should pray as did His Holiness John Paul the Great: "It is my hope that the inspiration of St. Francis will help us to keep ever alive a sense of 'fraternity' with all those good and beautiful things, which Almighty God has created. And may he remind us of our serious obligation to respect and watch over them with care, in light of that greater and higher fraternity that exists within the human family[24]

References and Notes

1. This is a version of a paper that was presented at the Eighth International Congress of Philosophy on the Future of Western Civilization, Conference Theme: Terrorism, John Paul the Great Catholic University of Lublin, Poland, April 2009

2. Alex Pacheco, reported by Associated Press 1/3/89, http://www.activistcash.com

3. Jerry Vlask, Internet post to animal rights views list, 6/21/96, http://feldentertainment.com

4. Tim Daley, ibid.

5. James F. Jarbone, FBI Section Chief, Counterterrorism Division, Testimony Before the US House of Representatives Resources Subcommittee on Forests and Forest Health, 2/12/2002, www.fbi.gov/news/testimony/the-threat-of-eco-terrorism

6. For a comprehensive, current and alarming record of eco-terroist acts of ecotage and other environmentalists' political causes see, Andrew K. Dart, 2012, www.akdart.com/enviro5.html

7. John Moore, "Humankind has unique place in God's plan," http://www.catholicregister.org/content/view/1865/852

8. Ingrid Newkirk, quoted in *Vogue*, September 1989, from "Quotes Proving the Real Agenda of the Animal Rights Movement," http://www.feldentertainment.com/pr/aca/quotes.htm. (Hereafter cited as "Real Agenda Animal Rights").

9. Newkirk, "Real Agenda Animal Rights."

10. Michael W. Fox, "Real Agenda Animal Rights."

11. Peter Singer in *Animal Liberation*, 2nd edition, 1990, from "Real Agenda Animal Rights."

12. Tom Regan, Q & A session following a speech, Univ. of Wisconsin-Madison, Oct. 27, 1989, from "Real Agenda Animal Rights."

13. *Genesis* 1:26

14. The *Catechism of the Catholic Church*, Liguori Publications, English Translation, 1994, #2415.

15. God's declaration of the things He creates as "good" appears many times in *Genesis* 1.

16. From the *Compendium of the Social Doctrine of the Church* #467, http://www.vatican.va/roman_curia/pontifical_councils/justpeace/documentsrc_pc_justpeace_doc_20060526_comp_endio.d.t/-soc_en. See also, *Catechism of the Catholic Church* #2456.

17. See the *Catechism*, #344.

18. This PETA statement is quoted in Rev. Paul Fitzgerald, S.J., Do Animals Have Rights?, http://www.scu.edu./scm/exclusives/animals.cfm

19. Ibid.

20. Ibid.

21. Ibid.

22. Ibid.
23. Ingrid Newkirk, Animal Rights Quotes
24. John Paul II, Message for the Celebration of World Peace Day, 1 January, 1990, http://www.animalsvoice.com/sites/godandanimals/PAGES/edits/linzey/church9.html

Realism: The Way to Cross the Threshold of Hope[1]
July 2011

Only realists can truly hope! Only those who understand and live by the truths of metaphysical, epistemological and moral realism can develop the virtue of hope as a habitus of character. With the "great anthropocentric shift" in our modern era, however, realism and thereby hope have been replaced by subjectivism.[2] This subjectivism privileges a philosophy of consciousness over a realistic philosophy of existence so that thought supplants reality and only what conforms to human thought is deemed as true. Whether what is thought corresponds to what really exists, whether the thought is objectively true, are inconsequential issues, since only the thoughts and what conforms to them within subjective consciousness are the criteria of truth.

The subjectivist philosophy of consciousness precludes hope because hope is the humble deference to an order, to a design, to a truth of reality, which is greater than and beyond the subjective consciousness of one who hopes. To hope for, to place hope in, or to hope with, is essentially a self-transcending act. The virtue of hope engages us in truths of metaphysical reality, of epistemological objectivity, of moral life which are not of our own making. Hope lifts us out of our subjective consciousness. It disposes us to shift away from our anthropocentric and egocentric indulgence in the truth of our own thoughts or of our human-made reality. We defer to truths which are not mere constructs of our particular consciousness, or even of the human mind in general. In hope, we conform to the truth of what is real; we participate in the order of reality, an order we do not invent, but an order which hope helps us to discover.

Because of the fixation on subjective consciousness, there is not much hope in our modern times. There is much optimism and pessimism, but neither one is hope. Francois De la Rochefoucauld once observed that, "Hope and fear are inseparable."[3] Hope is bound to fear, but it is a loving fear, while optimism, or at its extreme, hubris, and pessimism, at its extreme, nihilism, are tied to servile fear.[4] The pessimist/nihilist laments, "Woe is me, the world, reality, is not what I want it to be and never will be." The pessimist/nihilist fears being subject to a world, to a reality, which does not conform to his wants, his will. The pessimist/nihilist fears being enslaved or subjugated by a reality which is beyond his control, because it resists his willful designs, his subjective thoughts and desires. The fear of the pessimist/nihilist is induced by his confrontation with the limits of his modern egocentrism; the order of reality is not of his or human making. Gripped by such servile fear, the pessimist/nihilist becomes mastered by the absurd: there is no way to make sense of existence, there is no purpose to life, there is no truth!

The modern optimist/"hubrist"[5] avers, "The world, reality, will be what I want. Things will be the way I will them to be." He will not allow himself to succumb to servile fear and he reacts with vehement arrogance. He is supremely confident that reality can be made to conform to his designs, especially given the power of his will, his reason, his science and technol-

ogy. Still, even with his arrogance, he remains mastered by servile fear, since it is precisely his fear of being powerless in the
face of reality which drives his optimism/hubris.

Vaclav Havel explained that "Hope is definitely not the
same thing as optimism. It is not the conviction that something
will turn out well, but the certainty that something makes sense,
regardless of how it turns out".[6] Hope trusts that the order of
reality makes sense. It trusts that the order is to some extent
rationally intelligible so that objective truths can be discovered.
Hope trusts that in reality the difference between moral and
immoral acts can be known. This is the wisdom which hope
inspires, but this wisdom is not without fear. It is the fear and
trembling before the awesome grandeur of the order of reality
which implicates a Majestic Designer, a Divine Creator. Still
this fear, which is the beginning of hope and wisdom, is not a
servile fear. It is a loving fear, a fear infused with the love of
the wisdom which trusts in the Creator and the Logos of His
design of the order of reality.

The modern anthropocentric shift is hope-less because it
rejects realism. It arrogantly proclaims that human-constituted
meaning defines what is real, what is true and what is moral.
This is why since the Enlightenment Encyclopediasts,[7] history,
human history, has become the "new" metaphysics. Human
meaning, human actions and events establish the order of reality, and history studies the course of that order. Given such
a "metaphysicalizing" of history, it is not hard to understand
why modern Legal Positivism rejects objective moral principles
as a foundation of law and jurisprudence in favor of exclusively
emphasizing the legal precedent as a basis for judgments. Precedents, human-made decisions, constitute the history of law,

and such history is regarded as metaphysically normative. Precedents define the order of the reality of law, and no universal, higher moral norms are respected.

There are, however, many other manifestations of the hope-less anthropocentric philosophy of consciousness in modern culture, politics and education. Discussing some of these should evidence strongly why a defense of realism is so timely and vital for invigorating hope in our modern world.

As a young college philosophy student in the early 1970s, I was a realist. In regard to epistemology, I believed that what I perceived and cognized, the objects of my knowledge, were the objects of reality. What I knew were not simply images or ideas of the objects in my mind, but the objects themselves. Moreover, I did not believe that I knew an object in exhaustive detail, or that every detail I knew about an object matched exactly what that object was in reality. I knew, obviously, that my senses were limited and subject to deception. Nevertheless, I was certain that my perceptions gave me a reliable cognition of objects in the world, though with reasonable limitations. I was, however, disabused of my epistemological realism through many debates I had with professors and through many philosophical works I studied, especially writings of Descartes, Hume and Kant. I particularly recall an instance when a professor during a spirited exchange insisted that I held a naïve realism. Since no college student wants to be naïve, I began to assess my realism, eventually adopting what philosophers would call a coherence theory of truth.

How I ultimately realized that my youthful realism was indeed more sound than the coherence theory I once favored is a story that would lead beyond the scope of this essay. What is more germane is what the label "naïve realism" implies within modern culture and politics. Looking back from my more mature perspective today, I recognize that even though my youthful realism was actually a "critical" rather than a "naïve" realism, it seems that modern thought tends to deprecate any epistemological realism as "naïve." The reason for this is perhaps more political than epistemological, more ideological than philosophical.

The more citizens can become convinced that reality itself is unknowable, the more they become susceptible to accepting the paradigms, models and constructs which a dominant regime wants them to accept as reality. If we believe that our perceptions and cognition can access what is true of reality, then we are threats to the hegemony of a regime which aims to expand the power of its ideological paradigms, models and constructs. The regime wants its ideology to be the real truth, and if citizens believe that real truths are accessible by all rational creatures, then the regime's power is jeopardized. Dismissing realism as "naïve," denigrates a realist as being unsophisticated, undereducated, a follower of a herd mentality. Consequently, we tend to abandon realism in order to become "sophisticated," a member of the elite, educated cognoscenti.

The regime's goal to make us conform to the "sophisticated" reality of its ideology is fundamentally anti-democratic and totalitarian. It is, however, genuinely democratic and pluralistic to maintain that the truths of reality are accessible to all persons, and no ideology has the Truth. Epistemological realism is, then, in this way a necessary condition for authentic democracy, and without such realism, democracy is stunted and hopeless.

A recurring experience I have had during my thirty-one years of teaching introductory Logic is a concrete example of how a regime of modern anthropocentrism corrupts students' education in epistemology and morality. For some decades now, educators have emphasized that logic should be taught as critical thinking, which, unfortunately, is usually taught as rank sophism. Logic is a necessary skill for good reasoning, an invaluable tool for discovering the truths of reality. Today, however, because of the regnant skepticism and relativism which anthropocentrism engenders, critical thinking is promoted as an end-in-itself. Similar to the old slogan of the 1960s, "Question Authority," critical thinking means, "Question Truth." But, without being animated by a truth-loving realistic epistemology, the tools of critical thinking become mere truth-deconstructing WMDs, "Weapons of Mass Distraction." They inculcate a vicious habit of truth-denial, which distracts students from loving truth and makes them vulnerable to modern power-based ideologies.

For instance, in teaching immediate inferences on the traditional square of opposition, I typically encounter students who insist that a True I proposition immediately entails a True O proposition, and vice-versa. My sense is that their addled assumption is premised on a sort of epistemological moral egalitarianism which bespeaks the "absolute tolerance" of modern anthropocentrism. If "Some S is P" is True, then "Some S is not P" must also be accepted as True since modern tolerance morally requires that anyone who has the opinion that an I proposition is True, must be open to accepting another's contrary opinion that the O proposition is also True. The students' ideological conviction is so strong that they don't even budge when challenged with the argument that what if the I asserts an obvious fact that is a universally True A proposition. For them, any claim of a True A proposition is suspect, since universal truths do not conform to their skepticism. Their anthropocentric view is that facts are just subjective interpretations.

As such, facts are opinions, and, of course, all opinions must be tolerated as equally true.[8] The students' ideological misology has been hardened by their education in the epistemology, morality and politics of modern anthropocentrism. Their scorn for truth has rendered them hope-less and easy prey for a regime which aims to increase the power of its "sophisticated," "morally progressive," paradigms, models and constructs.

Another current example of modern anthropocentrism is the "animal rights" issue. As is often the case with politicized issues, the terminology chosen to identify the issue can be biased about the issue itself. The term "animal rights" is not only biased in favor of attributing rights to animals, but it also presumes a mythic, unreal conception of rights. It is mythic because if the meaning of rights is correctly understood, "animal rights" does become recognized as an oxymoron.

Those who persistently use the oxymoron "animal rights" evidence that our modern culture is not sure about what rights are. They insist that animals have rights to legitimize their belief that animals should not be mistreated or abused and should be cared for and respected. Their claim, that animals ought to be respected because they have rights, is, however, actually disrespecting the animals qua animals.

The "animal rights" claim emerges from an anthropocentric attitude, a human chauvinism. The attitude is that in order to legitimize respect for animals, we humans have to endow them with human-like traits such as rights. We must give them the meaning, the value, of bearers of rights. We must anthropomorphize animals as rights-bearers in order to deem them as worthy of our respect. In a sense, such a mentality is like a male chauvinist's wrongheaded claim that in order for women to be respected, males must endow them with rights. Such a male chauvinistic attitude does not respect women as women, and similarly "animal rights" actually disrespects the animals as animals. Why, for instance, should we not respect and care for a dog simply because it is a dog? Does a dog not have meaning and value in itself which ought to be respected? For the anthropocentric mentality, however, meaning and value are human constructs, and therefore, the dog has meaning and value only with the "rights" we assign to it.

This assignment of rights to animals expresses, perhaps, an even more pernicious consequence of modern anthropocentrism, namely the modern confusion of what rights really are. There are two general classes of rights: natural (or human) rights and civil rights. Natural or human rights are most succinctly expressed as life, liberty and the pursuit of happiness. These rights are inalienable because they are inherent in us as humans; they are endowed by our Creator. Moreover, these rights carry with them the duty to respect them in all persons, and to contribute proactively to the common good of humanity by ensuring that these rights are preserved and protected.

There are two types of civil rights, positive and negative. Positive civil rights are those which specify what a citizen is due from society. For example, in the U.S. Constitution's Bill of Rights, due process under the law and no excessive bail are positive rights. Negative civil rights specify the limits of government interference in a citizen's life. For instance, in the Bill of Rights, the rights to free speech, free assembly, etc., are negative civil rights.

It is important to emphasize that the ultimate goal of civil rights is to preserve natural rights in specific ways, and, thereby, to ensure that free citizens can rationally understand and consciously act to fulfill their duties to the common good. What, however, are the natural or civic duties of animals? How do animals rationally understand and consciously act to fulfill their duties to the common good?

With the anthropocentric mind-set, it appears that with more insistence on animal rights, the more our understanding of rights becomes separated from an understanding of our duties. The result of this separation is the growing refusal of an objective moral order which defines our duties, our moral obligations to the common good of humanity, and indeed, of all creation. The "animal rights" issue is another sign of hope-less modern anthropocentrism.

Pope John Paul II taught that the *opus gloriae* of creation is "the fundamental destiny of every creature, and above all man, who was created in order to become, in Christ, the priest, prophet and king of all earthly creatures."[9] Creation was given and entrusted to humankind as a duty, the duty to perfect creation. This entails that humans have a duty to be caretakers, stewards, of creation. As steward "priests" of creation we have the duty to respect all creatures, in fact all things of creation, living and non-living, because they have meaning and value in themselves according to the Creator's design. No matter what modern anthropocentric attitudes claim, animals do not have rights, neither natural nor civil. Humans, however, have a duty to respect them simply because they are animals. In doing so, we carry out our God-given duty to perfect creation and nurture its *opus gloriae*. Only a realism, which affirms an objective moral order in creation and the moral objectivity of human duties as inseparable from rights, can truly hope and dutifully act to foster the *opus gloriae* of creation.

Realism is necessary for authentic hope. Realism grows hope and enables our participation in the order and design of reality. The subjectivism of modern anthropocentrism oc-

cludes hope. Without hope, modern epistemology and morality are stunted by a servile fear. Such servile fear precludes the
wisdom which is inspired by a loving fear that trembles before
the Logos of creation. The defense of realism is the way to
reinvigorate hope in our hope-less modern world. Realism,
graced with hope and the living fear which engenders wisdom,
can help us to: Be not afraid. Have no servile fear. His creation
is before us in all of its grandeur and majesty.

References and Notes

1. This paper is printed with permission from: "Realism: The
    Way to Cross the Threshold of Hope" ("*Realizm: jedyna
    droga przekroczenia progu nadziei*"), trans. by Rafael Lizut in
    Man in Culture: In Defense of Realism, 19/2007 (*Człowiek
    w Kulturze: W Obronie Realizmu*), ed. Imelda Chlodna, et al.
    (Lublin, Poland: Lublin School of Philosophy Foundation,
    2007), pp. 277-286.
2. The following description of the "great anthropocentric
    shift" follows Pope John Paul II, *Crossing the Threshold of
    Hope* (New York: Alfred Knopf, Inc., 1994) 30–31. Here-
    after cited as CTH.
3. See, www.great-quotes.com
4. This discussion of hope and fear was stimulated by and is
    loosely based on CTH 115–16.
5. Please allow this use of "hubrist" although it is not lexical.
6. See, www.great-quotes.com
7. I must acknowledge my numerous discussions with my
    colleague and friend, Peter Redpath, for this insight into
    history as the "new metaphysics."
8. This topic of late modern, sometimes labeled as "post-
    modern," pluralism and tolerance is treated in detail in my

essay, "The Problematic Politics of Postmodern Pluralism," ("Problematyczna Polityka Postmodernisty-cznego
Pluralismu") in *Politics and Religion* (*Polityka a Religia*) (Lublin, Poland: Fundacja Lubelska Szkola Filozofii Chresci-
janskiej, 2007) 47–56.
9. CTH 12.

Section V

Critiques of Progressive Politics, Pluralism, Political Economy and Revolution

Section Introduction

The five essays in this Section offer together a comprehensive yet detailed philosophical evaluation the facets of Progressivism. The essays, "The Problematic Politics of Postmodern Pluralism" and "Diversity within the United States' Culture and Politics" address the same basic theme, pluralism/diversity. The first essay does so in the context of Progressivism's derivative form of Postmodernism and the second essay offers a brief history of ideal diversity, which was a chief Progressive objective in the U.S.A. during the early twentieth century and beyond.

Progressivism has typically shunned or flatly denounced religion as vital to the maintenance of a democratic republic. The essay, "Democracy Needs Religion," relies on the thought of Alexis de Tocqueville and Michael Novak to argue that religion is in fact necessary for sustaining and advancing a democratic republic in that religion establishes foundational grounds for moral judgements, it provides bases for personal convictions such as freedom so the people are not prey to totalitarian regimes, and religion curbs the temptations to slip into materialistic hedonism and greed, types of selfishness which can inhibit all people from flourishing within the republic.

"Blasts from the Preclassical Past: Why Contemporary Economics Education Should Listen to Preclassical Thought" is an analysis of Progressive political economy as it is rendered currently by millennials with their quickly growing support of socialism and its related social justice morality. Basic economic principles from the Preclassical era of economic thought are identified and explained in regard to presenting a moral defense of free-market economics. In addition, Michael Novak's articulation of the moral responsibilities that are inherent to business corporations themselves and necessary for their own success establishes that businesses do not absolutely need to be heavily controlled by the government in order to be moral and just.

The final essay, "Anatomy of the Progressive Revolution," critiques current Progressivism as a revolution and not merely a reformist movement. When Progressives insist that they are seeking a fundamental transformation of American society, this is a revolutionary cry and not just a reformist agenda item. The overall strategy of the revolution is articulated, showing how and why Progressivism's basic tactic is to interrupt the organic development of a society through religion and culture by installing politics and economics based on social justice morality as the principal drivers of cultural transformation.

The Problematic Politics of Postmodern Pluralism[1]
April 2006

The POMO passion for pluralism is a piece of pernicious prestidigitation. It is a clever slight-of-hand trick to fool us into accepting its supreme value of absolute tolerance. In accepting such tolerance, we, in turn, are rendered vulnerable to the POMO political platform, and the POMO pursuit of power progresses.

We are told that if we do not respect pluralism with a disposition of absolute tolerance, then we are guilty of fanatic bigotry, or, at least, suffer from some sort of irrational fear: a phobia like xenophobia (fear of strangers), allodoxaphobia (fear of opinions), anthropophobia (fear of people or society), homophobia (fear of homosexuality) or europhobia (fear of European Union).[2] We do not want to be dysfunctional; we are afraid of having irrational fears, which according to the official list of current phobias is labeled as "phobophobia," so we are inclined to acquiesce to some degree to POMO tolerance. Once we do, however, we become enablers, contributors to propagating POMO's political power.

Ryszard Legutko recognizes that the supreme value of POMO politics is tolerance, and that intolerance is more to be feared than all traditional sins.[3] Legutko distinguishes between negative and positive toleration. Negative toleration is a virtue of individual character. It is a habit of temperance which involves self-governance and humility, and it helps people to live together and cooperate in society. This tolerance is not a substitute for other moral and political qualities such as justice or equality. This tolerance, as a habit of character, cannot make any positive claims, such as that a certain category of persons should be given certain political or social positions, certain privileges or "special rights," specifically on the grounds of toleration.

It is an aggressive positive toleration that POMO politics promotes. This tolerance is pitched as socially and politically normative. It is not indifferent to contests between opposing views, since in a partisan way it condemns any view, it perceives as coercive, authoritarian, domineering or repressive. The moral norm it prizes is made in its own image, namely, "We ought to make the world safe for toleration." The practical principle this imperative implies is that, "We must liquidate all cultural bases of intolerance."

This is the culture war which POMO wages. POMO's total commitment to the cause of positive tolerance entirely excludes negative tolerance, since negative tolerance preaches only self-control and humility, and POMO believes it can allow for intolerance. POMO, unfortunately, does not understand the principal merit of negative tolerance, namely that Catholics, Protestants, Jews, Moslems, capitalists, socialists, etc. are not compelled to renounce their beliefs, but only to be humbly temperate in espousing or acting on them in society. POMO's positive tolerance campaign, however, aims for a fundamental transformation of our worldviews, if POMO deems them as socially or politically offensive.

What for POMO is the criterion for a worldview being offensive? It is whether the worldview makes a claim to truth. In the POMO mind, truth itself is responsible for intolerance because it marginalizes people. Truth alienates those who disagree as heretics, subversives or misfits. Truth spawns prejudice, which leads to persecution. So, in order to secure tolerance and eliminate prejudice and persecution, we must abandon all traditional criteria of truth, which means specifically, traditional realist metaphysics, epistemology and morality.

This is the platform of POMO politics, for with the assault on truth, it is power which substitutes. As Michel Foucault believed, truth is a regime, nothing but an ensemble of conventional rules, which establish the difference between the true and the false and attach power to the true. The truth is not powerful because it corresponds to what is real, but truth is the power to define or create what is real.

What are the strategies of POMO's political agenda? How is it accomplishing its pursuit of power? There are at least three strategies which together are targeted at gaining control of educational institutions and/or the media as the bases of power. The first is the politics of anti-realism, the second, the politics of absolute alterity, and the third, the politics of hyper-reality. Through educational systems and the media, these strategies combine to disconnect us from reality, to seduce us to embrace absolute positive tolerance and become party to POMO's power trip.

The politics of anti-realism are clearly manifest in Richard Rorty's axiom: democracy is prior to philosophy.[4] Rorty emphasizes that maintaining harmony within a pluralized democratic society, what for him is genuine solidarity, supersedes serious philosophical pursuit of objective truth. In fact, for Rorty all philosophical claims of objective truth are empty, since all truth is relative to the society in which we participate. Rorty, therefore, views truth merely as social consensus, and objectivity is reduced to solidarity. The only types of "truths" he supports are those values which conform to his version of solidarity, and of course for him, the highest value is absolute tolerance.

Rorty would agree that for the sake of solidarity, we must respect others' beliefs as if they were our own. This respect, moreover, must be absolute, so no matter how different from or even contradictory to our beliefs another's beliefs might be, they are not to be challenged in any way. This is Rorty's so-called "democratic" value of egalitarianism. All beliefs must be respected as equal in truth-merit to our own beliefs. Hence, for the sake of harmonious solidarity we must acknowledge that everyone's opinions of truth, everyone's views of reality are as respectable as ours. For Rorty, solidarity is not built on truth, solidarity does not defer to reality, but solidarity builds truth and manufactures reality.

As promoted through educational institutions and the media, Rorty's brand of egalitarian solidarity is not really democratic at all. Students are taught in schools and the media transmits the message that all lifestyles, all moral choices, all religious preferences are equally valuable, except, of course, those that commit intolerance. No belief has any special access to the truth, and no belief can claim any special correspondence with what is real.

The traditional view of democracy is, however, founded on realism. As rational creatures, all persons, regardless of class, gender, ethnicity or culture, are equally capable of knowing truths which correspond to reality. Accessing reality and knowing truths is sometimes not easy; among other things, it often requires a virtuous disposition of prudence, temperance, courage and justice. All persons do not necessarily know the truths of reality to the same degree, but all are capable to some degree of becoming truth-knowers. Rorty's egalitarian solidarity with its consensual theory of truth is not merely anti-realist, but it is anti-democratic as well. It perpetuates the POMO power of education and the media to impose on us their versions of the truths of reality. The more we are convinced that we cannot discover the truths of reality ourselves, the more we are rendered powerless, and the more our beliefs, our moral choices and our very lives become invented by our schools and the media.

The politics of absolute alterity are based on the POMO claim that any other person is absolutely other. Realists object that others are not absolutely other, since we do, even cross-culturally, communicate with others, exchange our thoughts, know each other's feelings and experience mutual love. Still, a POMO pundit like Jacques Derrida insists on the radical otherness of the other. This leads him to put community under erasure. For Derrida, a community which shares virtues, which engages in a common effort to discover the truths of reality, which values interpersonal communication and love, is a useless fiction. Derridian otherness, thereby, entails the difference of extreme pluralism and irreconcilable diversity.

As with Rorty's egalitarianism, Derrida's otherness fortifies POMO's agenda of absolute tolerance, since it is only such tolerance that can preserve harmony in the face of radical diversity. Diversity, the differences between people, is not affirmed as a means for strengthening the pursuit of truth. Realist truth-seekers accept that their purposes are invigorated by understanding and evaluating diverse and even competing truth-claims. With absolute alterity, diversity becomes autotelic: it becomes its own purpose, in that whatever can be said to be true is only whatever affirms diversity itself. Consequently, in education, POMO curricula impose gender studies, multiculturalism, and assorted ethnologies. Theology becomes "Religious Studies," in which zealous ecumaniacs typically promote an indiscriminate ecumenism. The aim, again, is not to teach about diverse views to support our search for truth. The aim is to teach us that diversity is itself absolute, and that objective common truths which can reconcile differences are nowhere to be found. Absolute positive tolerance is, therefore, our only option and we must yield to POMO power.

As the term itself suggests, the POMO politics of "hyper-reality" are designed to replace our connection to the real with a world of phantasmic meanings. The origins of such hyper-reality are in, among other sources, Ferdinand de Saussure's semiology. He claims that the meaning of any action or object is never fixed or finite but is founded on a socially fluid system of shared convention.[5] Meaning is, thereby, a process of signification which binds together the signifier and the signified to produce the sign. A sign is a relation which has no meaning outside the continuously evolving social process of signification. The signified, moreover, refers only to the image or concept and not to the thing itself in reality. Therefore, the meanings we know and what those meanings represent are merely the outcomes of a social process of learning, and they do not represent or refer to anything definite, stable or certain in reality.

The French sociologist, Jean Baudrillard, extends Saussure's semiology to claim that all of the meanings we know, all of the contents of our thoughts, intensify within our imaginations so that the images breed incestuously with each other without reference to reality.[6] This is hyper-reality wherein the sign becomes a simulacrum of and a substitute for reality. The distinction between representation and reality, between signs and what they refer to, breaks down. Images merge into one another and their hybrid significations become the meanings of our reality. For instance, the image of "The Madonna" breeds with the pop-diva Madonna's image so that the meaning "Queen of Heaven," the perfect female role model, becomes subsumed within the MTV role model of the "Queen of All Material Girls Living in a Material World."

The politics of POMO hyper-reality should be apparent: those who implant the images in us, those who teach us the preferred politically correct language, those who establish the social conventions for the system of signification do, to various degrees, construct our hyper-reality and thereby control what reality means for us. Overloaded with the incessant intercourse of diverse images, we become confused and weakened. We are rendered docile, willing to accept that only the image of a reality harmonized by absolute tolerance can make sense of, can unify, our inchoate hyper-reality. We allow ourselves, then, to become "imago POMI."

POMO political power is indeed pervasive globally. It thrives on perpetuating absolute tolerance as the moral means for respecting pluralism. As has been discussed, however, POMO's absolute tolerance is nothing but a political device to expand its power. Pluralism and absolute tolerance are used as techniques to undermine what it perceives as the threat of traditional metaphysical, epistemological and moral realism. What, though, can or should be a response to POMO's tactics?

Aristotle once offered words to the effect that: Courage is the virtue which makes all of the other virtues possible. POMO's politics can be opposed with the courage to discover and appreciate what is truly real. It takes courage to judge prudently what ought to be the real and true qualities of a person's moral life. It takes courage to act with the real tolerance of a humble temperance in a pluralistic society and world. It is courage which can sustain those who hunger and thirst for real justice and do not impose on people the indignity of ideological egalitarianism. And, finally, with the grace of the Holy Spirit, courage can help us to be gifted with the faith, hope and charity which are the real and true bases of a solidarity that can challenge and resist POMO's political power.

References and Notes

1. Reprinted with permission from: "The Problematic Politics of Postmodern Pluralism" *("Problematczna politikya postmodernistycznego pluralizmu")*, trans. by Agnieska Lekka-Kowalik in <u>Politics and Religion</u> *(Politikya a Religia)*, ed. Piotr Jaroszynski et al. (Lublin, Poland: Katedra Filozfi

Kultury KUL, 2007) pp. 47-55. Presented at the <u>Fifth International Congress of Philosophy on the Future of Western Civilization</u>, Conference Theme: Politics and Religion, Catholic University of Lublin, Poland, April 2006.

2. For an expansive list of current phobias see: *www.aboutphobias.com/phobialist.html*

3. This paragraph and the four paragraphs which follow paraphrase statements, and summarize and interpret points in Ryszard Legutko's "The Trouble with Toleration" in *A Free Society Reader*, edited by Michael Novak, William Brailsford and Cornelius Heesters (Lanham, MD: Lexington Books, 2000) 166-178.

4. See Richard Rorty's "The Priority of Democracy to Philosophy," in *Objectivity, Relativism and Truth* (Cambridge: Cambridge University Press, 1991).

5. This brief rendition of Ferdinand de Saussure's semiology is based on: Richard Appignanesi and Chris Garrat, *Introducing Postmodernism* (Thirplow, Cambridge,UK: Totem Books, 2005) 58-60

6. See *Introducing Postmodernism*, 54-55.

Democracy Needs Religion[1]
Spring 2008

According to the United States Constitution (Article II, Section, I, Clause 8), an oath or affirmation of office is mandatory for a President upon beginning a term of office. The Constitution prescribes the wording of the oath as:

I do solemnly swear that I will faithfully execute the Office of the President of the United States, and will,

to the best of my ability, preserve, protect, and defend
the Constitution of the United States.

Although there is debate among historians as to whether
George Washington added the phrase "So help me God" to
the oath, and whether all of the Presidents between Washing-
ton and Herbert Hoover used the phrase, it is certain that since
Franklin Roosevelt, all Presidents have added, "So help me
God."[2]

Although twenty-four US state constitutions explicitly prohibit the use of a religious test to qualify as a witness or juror
in court, a test such as an oath that in some way mentions God,
the other twenty-six states do require a "religious" oath. Those
oaths are typically versions of the common oath: I swear to tell
the truth, the whole truth and nothing but the truth. So help
me God.[3]

What does such "So help me God" oath-taking mean philosophically in regard to religion and democracy? The US President takes an oath which concludes with an expression of humility before and in deference to the Highest Authority. The
so-called "Leader of the Free World" affirms that his political
leadership is subordinate to a Transcendent Omnipotence, a
power greater than any which man can develop or wield with
his politics. The court oath is an invocation by which the om-
niscient God of Truth is called upon as a witness. It is, furthermore, a supplication through which He, as an all-just and all-
powerful Being, is asked to punish perjury.

Both types of oaths acknowledge God as an objective
standard of righteousness. In doing so, they imply that the politics, leadership and jurisprudence of a democratic republic can
not and should not rely exclusively on man-made laws, political

policies, and judicial decisions in order to establish truth, justice, and morality. God, the Word of Truth, the Ultimate Lawgiver and the Author of Morality, is faithfully recognized as the origin and ground of the democratic republic. Without Him, the republic lacks an objective standard: truth becomes merely the consensus of the citizens or the will of the dominant majority, justice becomes merely what is imposed by judicial fiat, and morality becomes mere custom and habit, or what is useful for political advantage. Without Him, democracy devolves into anthropocentric subjectivism wherein truth, justice, and morality are simply the products of human desire and volition; also, the people's government, which includes jurisprudence, becomes not only the arbiter but the creator of truth, justice, and morality. Democracy needs religion, or more specifically, needs God, because without Him the democratic state becomes entirely autonomous, subject to no authority, no standard, beyond itself; it thereby becomes easily victimized, enervated, by its political iniquities, its moral vicissitudes, and ideological contests to define and enact justice.

If democracy needs God, however, how can there ever be a "wall of separation" between church and state? Is not such a wall necessary to protect the religious or even anti-religious freedoms of citizens? If the state subordinates itself to a Transcendent Deity, would this not be a sort of state-established religion and a violation of the First Amendment of the US Constitution?[4] Would not such a violation engender intolerance and the oppression of citizens whose religious or atheistic beliefs do not conform to the state's religion?

The remainder of this essay will address and answer these important questions, and then to buttress these answers, some of the philosophical positions of Alexis de Tocqueville will be explained. His work, <u>Democracy in America</u>, details many reasons why democracy needs religion, and they will be interpretively applied to show why religion is indeed a necessary condition for a healthy, sustainable democratic republic.

To return now to the above questions, it is worthwhile to examine the historical origin and philosophical meaning of the "wall of separation." This metaphor was penned by Thomas Jefferson in an 1802 letter to the Danbury (Connecticut) Baptist Association, and became popular when cited by US Supreme Court Justice Hugo Black in the landmark Everson v. Board of Education case in 1947. Black's decision in that case was that public (i.e., government) schools must be kept free of any religion, religious references, and religious curricula, and the wall of separation must be kept "high and impregnable."[5] As Supreme Court Justice Rehnquist observed in 1985, however, the wall of separation is "a metaphor based on bad history, a metaphor which has proved useless as a guide to judging. It should be frankly and explicitly abandoned."[6]

Rehnquist's words are profoundly instructive. As a matter of history, Daniel Driesbach has shown that Jefferson's "wall" aimed to "separate the federal regime on one side from states' governments and church authorities on the other,"[7] so that federal authority did not extend to what states and church authorities within states decided for themselves. Still, because the wall is such an ambiguous metaphor, it has led to two pernicious mis-conceptualizations. First, because it emphasizes separation and not non-establishment and free exercise of religion, it is interpreted as separating religious influences from public life and policy. Second, since a wall is a bilateral barrier, it inhibits the activities of both the civil government and religion, whereas the First Amendment imposes restrictions on civil government only. The bilateral wall is then used:

to deprive religious citizens of the civil liberty to participate in politics armed with ideas informed by their
spiritual beliefs, and infringes on the right of religious
communities and institutions to extend their ministries
into the public square...[It] has been used to silence
the religious voice in the public marketplace of ideas
and to segregate faith communities behind a restrictive
barrier.[8]

As an oft-repeated adage indicates, the wall is not aimed to
establish freedom from religion in the public square, but to
protect freedom of religion in the public square, and in the private lives of citizens.[9] The First Amendment prohibits government from establishing a state religion, but it does not prohibit
government policies and institutions from being open to religious influences, and from even acknowledging the importance of religious beliefs for the health of the democracy.
In other words, the government cannot endorse, promote, or
impose any particular religion, but it can and should allow for
the free exercise of religion in regard to citizens' efforts to influence government policies, laws, and jurisprudence. In this
way, religious tolerance is genuinely preserved, since it does not
involve the intolerance of excluding all religious input on public policies and institutions. In short, the view that anything
governmental must be pristinely secular and thereby free from
all religious content, including a non-sectarian affirmation of
God as the Word of Truth, Ultimate Lawgiver, and Author of
Morality, is not what the Constitution and the wall of separation require.

Perhaps as a way of explaining the heavy emphasis he
placed upon religion in his masterful study, Democracy in
America, Alexis de Tocqueville states unequivocally that, "On

my arrival in the United States the religious aspect of the country was the first thing that struck my attention; and the longer I stayed there, the more I perceived the great political consequences resulting from this new state of things."[10] Stressing the significance of religion for maintaining a strong and vigorous democracy, he, moreover, states that "Religion in America takes no direct part in the government of society; but it must be regarded as the first of their political institutions..."[11] Religion should have such prominence because, for Tocqueville, beliefs about freedom (liberty), equality and morality are necessary for the maintenance of a democratic republic, and religion offers a foundation for such beliefs.

In a brief article, Michael Novak interprets Tocqueville's views on why democracy needs religion. Novak condenses Tocqueville's thesis in this way: "The premises of secular materialism do not sustain democracy, but undermine it, while the premises of Judaism and Christianity include and by inductive experience lead to democracy, uplift it, carry it over its inherent weaknesses and sustain it."[12] Although Tocqueville endorses the separation of church and state that he found to be commonly accepted in 19c America, he affirmed that certain Judeo-Christian "premises," as Novak calls them, are critical for a viable democracy. In fact, Tocqueville believed that the "separation" was a strength of democracy, since clergy do not generally hold "public posts" and they distance themselves from partisan politics but do promote principles and practices of faith that are essential to the health of the democratic republic.[13]

Novak identifies belief in the immortal soul as the major religious premise that Tocqueville develops. The soul is the foundation for affirming the inherent dignity of each person, for the freedom that translates into civil liberty, and for the universal equality of all persons in the sight of God, despite any natural inequalities that may exist.

Universal equality, even as rooted in the soul, can, however, have a downside, which is why it must be kept in the "sight of God." Tocqueville saw that those who live in social conditions of equality tend not to place authority to which they must submit outside of or above humanity because:

> It is in themselves or in those like themselves that they
> ordinarily seek the sources of truth democratic peoples
> will want the principal arbiter of their beliefs within the
> limits of humanity, not beyond it.[14]

But if there is no standard of truth beyond humanity itself, then how can cases of competing truth-claims, especially about moral issues, ever be finally decided? The inertia of universal equality leads to unhealthy ends, namely the aforementioned anthropocentric subjectivism,[15] if not held in check by religious beliefs. If God, the Word of Truth, is not believed in, then it is hard to believe that the people themselves could ever judge for themselves the truth of grave moral issues. The people tend to believe that since all people are equal, so too are all of their moral opinions equally true. So, it is difficult, if not impossible, to finally resolve conflicts between moral views, and people must accept a type of general "pro-choice" morality, wherein what is good or evil depends on what one chooses to be so, and one's choice is equal in veracity to all others' choices, even if they disagree.

In addition to the basic, founding premises of dignity, equality and liberty, Novak articulates other advantages which religion, especially the Judeo-Christian tradition, brings to a democratic republic.[16] First of all, religion strengthens morals and manners. In a free society, laws can be enacted to allow people to do almost anything, but religious moral norms prohibit people from doing or even thinking about doing so many depraved things. As Tocqueville states, "...at the same time that the law permits the American people to do everything, religion prevents them from conceiving everything and forbids them to dare everything."[17]

Second, religion provides defined ideas about God and human nature that are vital for the conduct of daily life, but the demands of daily life prevent most people from having the time to figure out these ideas. Tocqueville describes these defined ideas as solutions to "primordial questions," which are "clear, precise, intelligible to the crowd, and very lasting."[18] To interpret his intent, such solutions would answer questions like: Does God exist? What is my purpose in life? Do I have an immortal soul? Is there an afterlife? Am I truly free as a human being? Can I know the difference between good and evil? Without defined ideas as answers to such questions, doubt, as Tocqueville warns, can "take hold of the highest portions of the intellect" and paralyze them. When this happens, people become accustomed to having confused and changing ideas about primordial questions. As a further result, they are unable to defend successfully their opinions about the questions, "and as one despairs of being able to resolve by oneself the greatest problems that human destiny presents, one is reduced, like a coward, to not thinking about them at all." This condition enervates people, weakening their will and preparing them for a servitude in which they either readily give over their freedom or easily allow it to be taken from them.[19] To interpret Tocqueville's intent with this second advantage of religion: he believes that without a philosophical anthropology and metaphysics ultimately grounded in authoritative, definite religious answers to "primordial questions" that are understandable by the people, the people are weakened in their personal and political resolve. They can fall prey to a totalitarian political regime, which usurps their freedom and imposes its solutions to primordial questions on the people.[20]

Third, Novak focuses on democracy's tendency to induce a taste for physical pleasures and material enjoyments, and thusly tends to lower tastes, which "weakens most people in their commitment to the high and difficult principles on which democratic life depends."[21] Religious beliefs, however, consistently expose the dangers of hedonistic materialism and consumerism, and demand that people draw back from them and attend to fundamental things. Belief in the soul's immortality, moreover, "prods people to aspire upwards, and to aim for further moral progress along the line of their own dignity and self-government."

Tocqueville's expressions of this third advantage are distinct. He cautions that people within democratic equality open "their souls excessively to the love of material enjoyments," while "religion inspires wholly contrary instincts."[22] He continues by stating matter-of-factly that, "There is no religion that does not place man's desires beyond and above earthly goods and that does not raise his soul towards regions much superior to those of the senses."[23]

Tocqueville, however, does not disparage people's honest work and the drive for wealth and material progress to improve their well-being; he does fear that this drive can become all-consuming, and that by working to improve themselves and everything around them, they can lose the use of their "most sublime faculties and finally degrade themselves."[24] Consequently, Tocqueville encourages leaders of all sorts in democracies to "unite and in concert make continuous efforts to spread a taste for the infinite, a sentiment of greatness, and a love of immaterial pleasures."[25] To restate Tocqueville's view: a democratic republic whose people sink into hedonistic materialism and consumerism, loses consciousness of and commitment to the basic traits of the immortal soul, dignity, freedom and equality, and since those traits are fundamental to the maintenance of the democracy, the democracy itself is imperiled.

By way of concluding this essay, it is worthwhile to offer summations of its principal arguments for why, as the essay's title claims, democracy needs religion. The oaths of office and US courts are expressions of some of the reasons why democracy needs religion in that the oaths invoke an all-knowing, all-powerful God as a needed standard of truth, justice, and morality that is transcendent to the republic. Religion is necessary, but the state should not establish a religion, though the people's belief in the immortal soul, since it is the root of all-important notions of human dignity, freedom, and equality, should be supported by the state. Finally, there are three more pressing reasons for why democracy needs religion in order to flourish. First, without religious grounds, there would be no foundational truth upon which to base grave moral decisions, and without sound moral decisions, all people would not be able to pursue life, liberty, and happiness as they should. Second, religion defines ideas that help people remain firm in their personal and political resolve so that they do not fall prey to a totalitarian regime. Lastly, religion helps curb the actions of materialistic greed and hedonism that inhibit all people from flourishing in a true democracy. Democracy needs religion, for an entirely secular democratic republic is without necessary foundations and liable to decompose into the dust of history.

References and Notes

1. Reprinted with permission from: "Democracy Needs Religion" (*"Demokracja potrzebuje religii"*), trans. by Pawel Tarasiewicz Man in Culture: Contemporary Challenges to Democracy, 20/2008 (*Człowiek w Kulturze: Wyzania wspolczesnej demokracji*), ed. Piotr Jaroszynski et al. (Lublin, Poland: Lublin School of Philosophy Foundation, 2008) pp. 101 – 111.

2. This historical information on the President's oath of office is from: Wikipedia/Online Encyclopedia. http://en.wikipedia.org/wiki/OathofofficeofthePresidentoftheUnitedStates #cite_note-1 It is worthwhile to note, moreover, that all elected members of the U.S. Congress, the Vice President, members of the President's Cabinet, all other civil and military officers and federal employees, and all Supreme Court justices and district court judges, must take an oath of office which includes "So help me God." See: "Oath of office of the President of the United States," http://www.state.com/id/1006398

3. Background on and explanations of the court oath are from: Gabrielle Banks, Pittsburgh Post-Gazette, "Truthfully, our court oath is elaborate" (8-10-06), http://www.post-gazette.com/pg/06222/712484-85.stm

4. The first clause of the US Constitution's First Amendment is: "Congress shall make no law respecting an establishment of religion, or prohibiting the free exercise thereof."

5. This information is from, Joseph A.P. DeFeo, "Thomas Jeffferson and the Wall of Separation between Church and State." http://www.catholicleague.org/research/dreisbach.html

6. Ibid.

7. Daniel L. Driesbach, "Thomas Jefferson and the 'Wall of Separation,'" http://www.jeffersonlegacy.org/newsletter.html Much of this paragraph closely follows the language of and points made in Dreisbach's article.

8. Ibid.

9. The "public square" is a figurative reference to the *agora*, a place of public assembly in Ancient Greece, which was a commercial marketplace, as well as a marketplace of ideas that involved discussions and debates about political, juridical, religious, and moral issues. "Public square" in this context retains that Ancient Greek meaning, but emphasizes the connotation that the "public square" includes all of the places where public life and discourse about public affairs take place.

10. Alexis de Tocqueville, *Democracy in America,* translated, edited and introduction by Harvey Mansfield and Debra Winthrop, (Chicago: University of Chicago Press, 2000), 280.

11. Ibid., 282.

12. Michael Novak, "Democracy and Religion in America," http://www.nationalreview.com

13. See Tocqueville, 283. It is also interesting to note that Tocqueville believed that the Islamic faith does not maintain the separation of church and state. In the *Koran*, not only are religious doctrines believed to be "descended from Heaven", but so are "political maxims, civil and criminal laws, and scientific theories" (419). Because Islamic faith is so specific about politics and jurisprudence, Tocqueville believes it cannot "dominate for long in enlightened and democratic times" (419). On the other hand, the "Gospels speak of the general relations of men to God and among themselves. Outside of that they teach nothing and oblige

nothing to be believed" (419-420). Consequently, the Gospels are much more suited to a democratic.

14. Tocqueville, 408

15. See p. 2 above regarding the problems with anthropocentric subjectivism.

16. The following discussion of these advantages follows but elaborates on the points made by Novak in "Democracy and Religion in America" (see above, Footnote #11). It is also noteworthy that Tocqueville himself averred "...I am so convinced that one must maintain Christianity within the new democracies at all cost..." (521).

17. Tocqueville, 280.

18. Tocqueville, 418.

19. This paragraph's quotes and paraphrased lines are from: Tocqueville, 418.

20. This point relates to the regime of the former Soviet Union in that the Soviets not only imposed their ideas of political economy on the people, but also imposed their atheism, scientific naturalism and determinism in regard to religion, metaphysics and philosophical anthropology. One could argue that some nations' peoples were easy victims of such oppression because the skepticism, anti-authoritarianism, and aggressive secularism of the Modern era weakened their personal and political resolve.

21. This paragraph quotes from, paraphrases and interprets Novak's discussion of the third advantage that religion provides democracy.

22. Tocqueville, 419.

23. Ibid.

24. Tocqueville, 518.

25. Tocqueville, 518-519.

Diversity within United States' Culture and Politics[1]
May 2011

An appropriate subtitle for this paper is a re-expression of one of the US's revered mottos, "E Pluribus Unum" to "E Pluribus Plures", ("From Many [We Are] One" to "From Many [We Are] Many More"). This re-expression captures the mentality of US Progressivism, an ideology which drives most of the US's political and cultural approaches to immigration and its moral ethos, diversity.

Before Progressivism gained ascendancy in politics and culture, especially educational culture, the "Unum" of our revered motto was characterized as a "melting pot". Immigrants of diverse racial, ethnic and religious backgrounds came to the US. Within the foundational principles of our Constitutional Republic, our democratic capitalism, and our ordered freedom, diverse immigrants, as well as Native Americans and liberated African slaves, united to form a national identity. To be sure, this identity was and is a fluid and, too often, tumultuous medium. Ethnic prejudices, religious intolerance, racial strife, and full-out war, such as with the Indians and American Civil War, kept the "melting pot" simmering if not tempestuously boiling over.

Within this churning pot our national identity, nevertheless, did congeal, though only as a kind of base substratum, which melded together diverse peoples and beliefs due to the agency of our foundational principles. This identity was not a complete homogeneous mixture, since, in accord with our foundational principles, particularly as configured in our Constitution, differences between peoples and beliefs were preserved. Assimilation according to the rule of law, which protected individual identity and property, as well as racial and ethnic differences, did not require an oppressive conformity but merely a common belief in and existential realization of our foundational principles.

Progressivism, however, replaced the "melting pot" with the image of a "mosaic".[2] Progressives claim that the peoples of the US do not and should not blend together so that they have to conform to a so-called foundational national identity. For Progressives the diversity of the various peoples must be maintained, and for the US to compromise their diversity in any way, by rule of law or socio-cultural pressure, would be a morally egregious act of nationalistic intolerance.

The image of the 'mosaic' which Progressives advance is itself telling. Consider that each piece in a mosaic is in a way separate from all of the other pieces. If we examine a mosaic close-up, we can see that its pieces are indeed atomistically diverse, and the more closely we scrutinize them, the more the pieces are disconnected from the entire tableau. The unity of the mosaic's representation is perceivable only if we stand back from it to view it in its entirety. In this way a mosaic's unity is just a perceived unity: a phenomenal unity, a Gestalt, which is a kind of illusion, merely an image and not, in a sense, real.

For Progressives, a substratum of national identity is, like the mosaic, an illusory unity: hence their dedication to Plures over any real Unum. Their promotion of diversity, especially through "immigration reform," as the present US regime calls it, is bound to their aims to transcend nations in efforts to realize a new world order. In fact, before he was elected President, Barack Obama stated in a speech to a crowd of thousands in Berlin, Germany on July 24, 2008, that although he is a "proud American citizen," he is also a "citizen of the world".

Which citizenship is primary for him remains an open question.

Obama's self-described "world citizenship" has been echoed by Progressives throughout the US and especially in the fields of education. For example, Fr. Jeffery von Arx, S.J., the current President of Fairfield University in Connecticut, a Jesuit University and my undergraduate alma mater, proclaimed in a letter to alumni, ". . . we believe at Fairfield that the purpose of our educational mission is to form 'global citizens'". He further claimed that this purpose is "consistent with St. Ignatius' vision," namely forming "global citizens" who will "act as transformative agents in the world".[3]

What is a "citizen of the world" or a "global citizen"? Is such a citizen really nothing more than "A Man without a Country", to evoke the title of a classic 19ᶜ American short story by Edward Everett Hale? What are the foundational principles of global citizenship? Are there no substrata of national identities? And, if the maintenance of diversity is the moral rule, as it appears to be for Progressives, what could be the basis of unity for nations, and indeed, for a new world order itself? Is such an order just another illusion, a utopian fantasia, which is self-negated by the diversity it champions as a moral imperative?

This paper will continue to address these issues of diversity, immigration and Progressivism in the US with three more topics. First of all, it will offer a brief sketch of the intellectual history of Progressivism in the US focusing on the theme of cultural pluralism. The next part will critique the ways in which the Progressive dedication to diversity actually engenders extreme entitlement-thinking and occludes solidarity among persons within a community, nation, or a so-called new world order. And finally, some closing suggestive remarks will be offered about how recovering an appreciation of the nature of person can offer a sound alternative to Progressive views of diversity.

Progressivism, in general, has its roots in Modern Rationalism and Positivism. To express it in "broad strokes," its origins are with thinkers and works such as Marquis de Condorcet's Outlines of an Historical View of the Progress of the Human Mind (1795), August Comte's Course on Positive Philosophy (six volumes, 1830-1842) and System of a Positive Polity or Treatise on Sociology and Instituting the Religion of Humanity (1851-1854), and Comte's friend John Stewart Mill in the later editions of his Principles of Political Economy and Some of the Applications on Social Philosophy (original edition 1840, "Chapters on Socialism", 1874). Despite certain differences, all of these works have in common the view that scientific principles can engineer a much better, perhaps even utopian, society: one which is egalitarian, yet pluralistic, with a version of a socialist economy.

US Progressivism emerged in the early 20^c adapting European views such as those mentioned above. There were, however, distinct differences in the approaches of the Progressive thinkers. Progressive pragmatists like William James and John Dewey, rejected rationalism and positivistic science, although both, but especially Dewey, did advocate a reformist social agenda that located "cultural pluralism" at its center. Their pluralism sought a cultural unity without uniformity, and they both, therefore, disavowed a melting pot model, which idealized the final homogenizing fusion of all of the United States' diverse peoples and cultures. Dewey, in fact, once remarked that the "theory of the melting pot" gave him "rather a pang".[4]

They both, nonetheless, heeded the Progressive politician Theodore Roosevelt's warning that "the one absolutely certain way of bringing this nation to ruin, of preventing all possibility of its continuing to be a nation at all, would be to permit it to become a tangle of squabbling nationalities".[5]

Realizing that America's racial and ethnic diversity could degenerate into atomized contesting political interest groups, James and Dewey placed emphasis on the democratic process as the way in which differences could be integrated. James would have agreed that "there is a balance to be sought between the unity of the country and the diversity of its constituent social and political elements or units. This balance is reasonably sought in the intellectual and moral roots of American federalism and pluralism, as these have been contrasted with American nationalism."[6] Dewey, likewise, emphasized democratic interaction and mutual influence among diverse cultural groups to create a unity "by drawing out and composing into a harmonious whole the best, the most characteristic which each contributing race and people has to offer".[7]

Despite the balanced approach of James and Dewey, other thinkers of the times, particularly the social scientists, advocated more radicalized views of cultural pluralism. Perhaps because of the inherent philosophical weaknesses in Progressive pragmatism itself, such as its prioritizing a democratic process over substance, namely a substantial metaphysical foundation, the radical views have become what Progressivism is today.

Randolph Bourne, a contemporary of James and Dewey, published in 1916 a landmark essay, "Trans-National America," which has become a standard for current Progressive views on American multiculturalism.[8] It is likely that the term "postmodern" occurred for the first time in his essay, which

envisioned America as a "trans-national" entity holding together a variety of ethnic communities lead by the lofty democratic goal that the equality of individuals should be paralleled
by the equality of ethnic communities.[9] The essay abounds with
a utopian egalitarianism in its call for the US to become a "cosmopolitan federation of national colonies, of foreign cultures,
from whom the sting of devastating competition has been re-
moved"[10]. "America", Bourne wrote, "is already the world-fed-
eration in miniature, the continent where for the first time in
history has been achieved that miracle of hope, the peaceful
living side by side, with character substantially preserved, of the
most heterogeneous peoples under the sun . . . It is for the
American of the younger generation to accept this cosmopoli-
tanism, and carry it along with self-conscious and fruitful purpose".[11]

Bourne's utopian "hope and change" rhetoric captivated
the Progressive psyche, especially his proclamation that by accepting the cosmopolitan enterprise he promotes, "Only the
American . . . has the chance to become a citizen of the
world"[12]. Like utopian fantasias in general, however, Bourne's
ideal image was simply disconnected from reality because Progressivism today yields a US which is a "tangle of squabbling
nationalities", a balkanized society in which ethnic, racial and
religious groups have become atomized competing political
factions.

At the core of Progressive balkanization is the mentality
that diversity is an end-in-itself. In hyphenated America, the
ethnic identity takes precedence over the American identity:
consider, French-American, Irish-American, African-American, Hispanic-American, etc. The "American" part merely lo-
cates a geographical place, since what one is, is principally de-

fined by one's diversity index. This index, moreover, has become the basis for claiming one's civil rights because one's group identity, which today also includes gender and sexual-lifestyle identity, entitles one to special rights and privileges.

This entitlement-thinking argues its claims in a rather simplistic fashion: Progressive multiculturalism affirms that we are entitled to our diversity. Because we are so entitled, our diversity is then an end-in-itself. As such an end-in-itself, our diversity, in turn, entitles us to rights and privileges to which others who do not share, or are not equal to, our diversity are not entitled. Separatism, tribalism, and political factionalism are the results of this entitlement-thinking.

Progressive diversity is indomitable, only spawning greater diversity: E Pluribus Plures. And, thereby, immigration reform, which currently proposes legalizing undocumented aliens and virtually opening national borders, is considered to be a morally good means because it tolerantly promotes the hallowed end of diversity. The Progressive demagogues of diversity with their view of the US as a "Star Trek-like" federation of equal but separate cultures have indeed balkanized the US and have disintegrated even the most meager substratum of a national identity based on foundational principles.

A fruitful alternative to Progressive diversity is, however, possible, and this alternative is rooted in an understanding of the nature of the person. Still, regardless of the merit of this alternative, its conceptualization of personhood is not likely to displace Progressivism in the US because the influence Progressivism has is a matter of practical politics. Progressivism will hold sway as long as its ideological proponents, its politicians, judges, educators, financiers, media spokespeople, etc., continue to have their way at the ballot boxes.

All human beings are individuals, and as such are different. We are truly diverse, but not in any absolute way, as Progressivism appears to hold. All humans share a fundamental nature in common with all other humans. "Human nature" is not, however, a philosophical view accepted by Progressives, including the pragmatists, and accordingly, Progressives have no interest in understanding the nature of the person.

Individuals are naturally oriented to mature into persons. In becoming persons, individuals fulfill aspects of their human nature. A chief virtue of this process of becoming persons is solidarity. We, as individuals, mature as persons by developing relationships with others. In solidarity with, for and among others, we transcend the differences between ourselves and others. For example, when we develop a genuine friendship with another, that friendship is a bond of solidarity which transcends the differences, including ethnicity and gender, we might have with our friend. The solidarity of friendship transcends but does not negate differences. The friendship, which helps to nurture the growth of the individual friends into persons, is strong enough to preserve and even love the other, not in spite of but precisely for the other's differences.

Why, then, is maintaining at least a substratum of national identity vital to the process of becoming a person? Why, for instance, should my national identity and cultural background as a US citizen make any difference in regard to developing solidarity relationships and growing into a person? In fact, why should anyone's national identity, whether it be as a Polish citizen, a Japanese citizen, or whatever citizenship, make any difference?

Progressives apparently believe that their indomitable diversity can be somewhat mitigated if one abandons national identity to leap into becoming global citizens, or at least by becoming citizens of some transnational union. What Progressives do not understand, however, is that the process of becoming persons is and ought to be guided by subsidiarity. Our national and cultural identities, if they are indeed morally sound, are vital to our growth as persons. We do and should initiate our growth as persons by developing solidarity relationships with those who share features of our identities, those who are closest to us, and then extend ourselves to larger communities: such as from family and friends, to neighborhood, to city, state, nation and finally, globally. With their utopian fantasies, Progressives believe that diverse individuals can simply abandon their identities, but maintain their diversity, while jumping into the union of a new world order. Of course, Progressives further believe that a world government, based on their version of socialistic economics, can scientifically engineer this visionary utopia.

According to subsidiarity, the process by which we as individuals mature as persons is a gradual one. Our identities help us to strive, through subsidiarity, toward fulfilling aspects of our human nature and grow from individuals into persons. Our identities are integral to the process of realizing solidarity with others. No trans-national ideology, no government, no Progressive economic union can catapult individuals into a new order of federated diversities, no matter how scientific their engineering might be.

The engineered mosaic is nothing but an illusion, which, sadly, only disintegrates our national and cultural identities, erases subsidiarity as the guide to realizing solidarity, and, finally, stifles our growth into persons. We should not sacrifice our identities at the altar of Progressive global citizenship. As human nature demands, we must persist in our efforts to become the persons we ought to be.

References and Notes

1. Reprinted with permission from: "Diversity within United States' Culture and Politics" (,,*Roznorodnosc w kulturze i polityce Stanow Zjednczonych* "), trans. by Joanna Kieres-Lach in <u>Man in Culture: Immigration and Civilization</u>, 23 (2013) (*Czlowiek w Kulturze: Emigracja i cywilizacje*), ed. Piotr Jaroszynski et al. (Lublin, Poland: Lublin School of Philosophy Foundation, 2013) pp. 63-73. This paper was also presented at the <u>Tenth International Congress of Philosophy on the Future of Western Civilization</u>, Theme: Immigration and Civilization, John Paul II Catholic University of Lublin, Poland, May 2011

2. Some US Progressive politicians have communicated the rejection of the melting pot quite bluntly. Former US President Jimmy Carter stated, "We become not a melting pot but a beautiful mosaic. Different people, different beliefs, different yearnings, different hopes, different dreams." Former US Vice-President Hubert H. Humphrey. once stated, "Fortunately, the time has long passed when people liked to regard the US as some kind of melting pot, taking men and women from every part of the world and converting them into standardized Americans. We are, I think, much more mature and wise today. Just as we welcome a world of diversity, so we glory in an America of diversity – an America all the richer for the many distinctive standards of which it is woven." – Quote Cosmos/Multiculturalism, http://www.quitecosmos.com/subjects/792/Multiculturalism.

3. Jeffrey von Arx, S.J., "Letter from the President", Fairfield University Magazine, Spring 2011, p. 4.
4. Quoted in H. G. Callaway, "Pragmatic Pluralism and American Democracy, p. 4 – http://www.espeirce.com/menu/library/aboutcsp/callaway/plural.html. From John Dewey (1917) "The Principle of Nationality", originally published in the *Menorah Journal*, reprinted in Dewey, *The Middle Works*, vol. 10, Carbondale, S. Illinois U., pp. 285-291.
5. Calloway, p.3. Quoted in Arthur Schlesinger (1991) *The Disuniting of America, Reflections on a Multicultural Society*, New York and London: W.W. Norton, p. 118.
6. Calloway, p.3.
7. Quoted in Calloway, p.7. From John Dewey (1916) "Nationalizing Education", originally published in Journal of Education 84, pp. 425-28, reprinted in Dewey, *The Middle Works*, vol. 10, pp. 201-210.
8. Randolph Bourne, "Transnational America", from the Atlantic Monthly, 118 (July 1916), 86-97. www.swarthmore.edu/SocSci/rbannis1/AIH19th/Bourne.html
9. Paraphrased from Marius Jucan, "Cultural Pluralism and the Issue of American Identity in Randolph Bourne's 'Trans-national America'", originally published in the *Journal for the Study of Religions and Ideologies*, July 1, 2010, p. 1 (Abstract) – http://www.faqs.org/periodicals/201007/2078379061.html
10. Bourne, p. 6.
11. Bourne, p. 6.
12. Bourne, p. 9.

Blasts from the Preclassical Past:
Why Contemporary Economics Education Should Listen to Preclassical Thought[1]
Fall 2019

ABSTRACT

Contemporary economics is dominated by logical positivism, a methodology that emphasizes empirical validation of theories but excludes normative evaluation. Preclassical economics was premised on normative analysis. With the growing socialist movement in the USA, especially among the millennials, who are fixated on moral issues of justice and equality, positive economics is alienated from addressing the normative challenges of socialism. There are, however, basic normative principles from Preclassical thought which can be used to contest socialist moral claims, particularly in economics education.

Introduction: The Rise of Socialism in the USA

It is beyond dispute that support for socialism is growing in the USA, especially among the millennial generation.[2] Among many poll results, a late 2017 YouGov poll reported that 44% of millennials would prefer to live in a socialist country.[3] An August 2018 Gallup Poll found that 51% of respondents aged 18 to 29 have positive feelings about socialism, compared to just 45% for capitalism. The poll further showed that the support for capitalism plunged 12 percentage points in only two years.[4] Why is there such a growing millennial enthrallment with the dirigisme of socialism and such disdain for a capitalist free-market economy?

There are a number of possible reasons for this trend. One is that for more than the past 20 years there has been a distinct socialist progressive bias in millennials' education that begins in high school and continues through college.[5] Another, perhaps more profound reason is that millennials are fixated on social economic moral issues and believe that in socialism, it is the government's duty to legislate economic justice and fairness. Capitalism creates the injustice and unfairness, so socialist dirigisme must rectify the immorality capitalism has wrought.

The millennials' moral stance against capitalism tends to be indomitable, thereby, as fostered through their schooling, they are under- or simply un-educated in market-based economics. Their moral claims, moreover, bespeak a hapless confusion buttressed by an absolutist righteous indignation that market economies are the agents of moral turpitude. As an anecdotal sign of such confusion and indignation, I have many times in my courses on business/organizational ethics encountered millennials who adamantly proclaim that the federal government has a moral obligation to raise the minimum wage to $15.00 per hour because it is a much-needed act of charity. Discussions concerning actual consequences of the raise are dismissed. They simply ignore facts that a $15 minimum wage has already led to wage workers having their hours severely cut or being terminated so that a business can mitigate its labor expenses and stay in business.[6] It is apparent that the millennial mentality is willing to accept serious economic collateral damage as long as their "high-ground" morality is actualized.

Given the growth of socialism and millennials' bias against market economics, the field of economics faces daunting chal-

lenges particularly in education. These challenges emerge because orthodox economics, dominated as it is by logical positivism, has excluded normative, moral, analysis as unscientific
speculation. Consequently, economics educators are alienated
from addressing the socialist moral claims of their millennial
students and their science becomes irrelevant to what most
concerns the millennials. Preclassical economics, however, was
marked by a robust, principled normative orientation and there
is much that contemporary economics educators could learn
from Preclassical thought in order to meet effectively the socialist moral challenges.

By explicating some Preclassical principles and perspectives
germane to contesting socialist moral claims, this paper will offer a foundation for economics education to become relevant.
It argues that economics education can communicate a "moral
conscience" and can expose socialist moral claims as mis-
guided and ill-formed. This exposition will proceed through
the following topics: 1) the normative limitations of economics; 2) the morality of private property; 3) the morality of the
just price; 4) Michael Novak's Preclassical approach to business corporations; and 5) entrepreneurship and the morality of
new wealth creation. A final section will prescribe some possible directions for integrating a moral conscience into economics education.

The Normative Limitations of Economics

At least since the early twentieth century, logical positivism
has been the methodological orientation of economics such
that positivism is accepted as orthodoxy in most areas of economics, including economics education. Positive economics

studies the mechanisms that govern economic activity, developing theories which can be empirically tested, verified or falsified. With its emphasis on empirical testing, normative discussions that range into the philosophically speculative and unverifiable were purged from economic science. For instance, it is rare that an introductory college-level economics textbook includes any substantive treatment of normative issues.[7]

Positive economics' focus on the forces governing economic activity deals with the problem of relative scarcity that arises because individuals consume more goods and services than are available. Individual wants exceed the resources that could satisfy them, so there must be social mechanisms for allocating limited resources. Positive economic theory maintains that the free market is the primary allocation mechanism. The reality of scarcity, however, requires that some wants are unmet, which engenders issues of equity, justice and fairness: the proverbial "haves vs. the have-nots."[8]

Normative issues, then, are embedded in the problem of scarcity. Nevertheless, modern economics focuses exclusively on how the self-regulating marketplace serves to mediate the problems of scarcity. The irony here is that with the rise of socialism, which supports government control of resource allocation, the self-regulating, free market is actually more and more rejected. The very subject of its study, the free marketplace, is what positive economics would lose if it continues to ignore normative claims and lets socialism continue to grow. In short, if there aren't free, self-regulating markets, then economics, according to its current orthodoxy, has nothing to study.

From the perspective of positive economics, the Preclassical thinkers were unable to grasp the central importance of the self-regulating marketplace. In Ancient and Medieval times, markets had not reached the stage of development which could yield socially efficient resource allocation. There were limited-participation markets which could not protect consumers by the law of large numbers and rigorous competition. Consequently, Preclassical thinkers became involved in normative issues to offer consumer protection, to propose moral norms that would contribute to the quality and justice of life.[10]

The normative Preclassical orientation did not engage in broad abstractions. For Preclassicals, the marketplace, for example, was an actual physical space and not an artificial conceptual construct. The marketplace was where real people traded, bought and sold goods and services with other people. The normative effort was to provide moral prescriptions for virtuous, honest and just marketplace commerce.[11] It is this morally realistic orientation of Preclassical thought that can most effectively benefit today's economics education. The Preclassical approach to many fundamental moral issues which occupy the millennial socialists can be expressed in a concrete, down-to-earth fashion which can better educate them in the morality of free-market economics.

The Morality of Private Property

The first principle of capitalist economics is the respect for and protection of private property. Though this claim may appear to be an overstatement since it might seem that social freedom, liberty, is more fundamental than private property, such is not the case. It is possible even in an autocratic communist state to have capitalist markets, although the extent and growth of those markets may indeed be restricted by government control. Nonetheless, as long as there are buyers and sellers engaged in commerce, albeit limited, private property is a necessary condition. Liberty is, in fact, a necessary condition for wealth generation and economic growth. Liberty enables commerce, based on private property, to develop and thrive as free-market economies.[12]

A typical claim of millennial socialists is that private property is basically immoral in that it is the source of greedy selfishness which leads to the "haves" exploiting the "have-nots." As a result, the socialists aver that communal ownership of property is what is truly moral. Although this normative issue is most often neglected by positive economics, some Preclassical thinkers showed clearly and persuasively that private property is truly what is right and moral.

Thomas Aquinas offered solid, practical arguments in defense of private property.[13] Aquinas indicated that private property engenders good stewardship because individuals take more trouble to care for something that is their sole responsibility than what is held in common. With communal ownership, individuals shirk the work and leave the responsibility to someone else. As an illustration of this point, Andrew Spencer observes that:

> "In the 1980s, the Soviets were buying American grain, though the USSR had as much arable land dedicated to grain production as the United States. Farmers who had once owned their own farms and built wealth through their efforts were now deprived of the work of their lands because any profit from their hard work was granted to the collective. If the Soviet farmers had owned the land and the produce from it, their productivity levels would most likely have increased."[14]

Aquinas further asserts that private ownership supports order in society and helps maintain peace in communities. This is so because human affairs are more efficiently organized if individuals have their own responsibility to discharge; while if everybody had to care for everything, there would be confusion and chaos. Peace among individuals is, moreover, more likely when each has his or her own belongings and decides on their use. With communal property, quarrels and discontent often arise because no one is sure who has or can have use of the property or why they can have the use.[15]

Beyond Aquinas other Preclassical thinkers offered trenchant insights on the morality of private property. Such Scholastics as San Bernardino of Siena (1380 – 1444) and Sant'Antonio of Florence (1389 – 1459) supported private property because of the efficiency it affords to society and its benefits to the common welfare of a community as compared to communalism. They realized that communal societies would be plagued by inefficiency, face insuperable managerial difficulties and suffer from perennial anarchy.[16] A number of the sixteenth and seventeenth century Scholastics of the School of Salamanca affirmed the morality of private property. A prime example was the Jesuit Luis de Molina (1535 – 1601) who believed, like Aquinas, that when property is held in common, it will not be taken care of and people will fight to possess it. Communal property does not really advance the common good because when property is not owned by individuals, the strong people in the group will take advantage of the weak by monopolizing and consuming the most resources. Molina also recognized that common ownership of property would guarantee the end of liberality and charity since people would not have their own resources to give.[17]

The socialist contention that private property is fundamentally and intrinsically immoral can be contested by educators by applying some of the normative propositions of the Preclassicals. Private, as opposed to communal, property is morally sound and not necessarily a source of selfish greed because it engenders: better care for resources, individual responsibility for work, more efficient order and organization in society, greater social stability and peace, and opportunities for individuals' liberality and charitable giving. To be sure, with private property there might be greedy misers without a virtuous moral conscience who exploit others for selfish gain. Still, in contrast to communalism, private property does indeed best serve the overall economic welfare and common good of society, and thereby, it is morally superior to communalism.

The Morality of the Just Price

Positive economics identifies the Preclassical occupation with the normative issue of just price as a "vague and imprecise idea unsuited to an operational theory of a purely scientific nature." Positivists maintain that the market price is simply the "objective result of impersonal forces."[18] Regardless of the positivists' position, millennial socialists insist that the federal government regulation of prices must be done to counter the immoral exploitative business practices. And, although, the positivists dismiss normative analyses, there is much that economics educators could glean from the Preclassicals in order to support a market-based norm of the just price.

In very basic and realistic terms, which economic educators could employ to enlighten socialist millennials, the Medieval Scholastics offered a morally sound version of market-driven just price which rejected government price-fixing. The esteemed commentator on the works of Aquinas, Cardinal Cajetan (1468-1534), maintained that for Aquinas and himself the just price is the price, which at a given time, a seller can obtain from buyers, assuming common knowledge and no fraud or coercion.[19] Cajetan's proposition morally qualifies the price, establishing it as just because it presumes that: 1) the buyer and seller have common knowledge of the market price; 2) there are no hidden problems with what is being purchased (no fraud); 3) what is being sold is what the seller purports it to be (again, no fraud); and 4) there is no coercion in that the buyer or seller is not being forced to buy or sell at the price (such as due to price-fixing or a monopoly).

Murray Rothbard further clarified the morality of the Medieval just price by referencing David Herlihy's observations. Rothbard notes that in the Italian city states of the twelfth and thirteenth centuries, the market price, the "common estimate" of buyers and sellers, was considered just because it was true and real, "if it was established or utilized without deceit or fraud."[20] Rothbard cites a probative passage from Herlihy in this regard: For the Scholastics, the just price of an object is its "true value as determined by one of two ways: for objects that were unique, by honest negotiation between seller and purchaser; for staple commodities by the consensus of the market place established in the absence of fraud or conspiracy."[21]

The Medieval Scholastics' approach to the just price issue emphatically specified normative qualifications that must be operative. To be just, market commerce must be free from fraud (deceit, dishonesty) and coercion (monopolies and conspiracy). Some Scholastics believed that a just price must also be free from government price control, which for them was a type of coercive price fixing, and thereby, immoral. For instance, Molina and Martin de Azpilcueta Navarro (1493-1576) believed that price controls are unnecessary in times of plenty and ineffective or positively harmful in times of scarcity.[22] In other words, if the supply of the object is abundant, then seller competition will determine a just market price. If the supply is scarce, and the government was to set a price like what it was when supply was abundant, then sellers might discontinue selling the object, since they would not be able to profit from it given what they had to pay for it.

Contrary to socialists' complaints, it is possible to achieve a just price in free markets without price fixing. Impersonal objective forces, like competition, are certainly significant factors, but as the Preclassicals taught, such impersonal forces are not all that is necessary. The personal moral consciences of buyers and sellers are also an important factor so that commerce is not adulterated by fraud, deceit, conspiracy, monopolies and price fixing of any sort. These immoralities can and should be regulated by civil and criminal law, as they are today in most developed free market economies, so that just prices can be ensured, and consumers protected.

Michael Novak's Preclassical Approach to Business Corporations

With his well-formed and prodigious intellectual background in Scholastic philosophy and theology, the contemporary thinker, Michael Novak (1933-2017), approached economics as if he were a Medieval Scholastic himself. He undertook a normative evaluation of many of the issues that rile millennial socialists. One of the most fundamental was the claim that business corporations are generally immoral, motivated by selfish greed and obsessively worried only about fattening the "bottom line." Corporations must be, the socialists insist, heavily regulated or even fully controlled by the government. In a landmark article, "Seven Plus Seven: The Responsibilities of Business Corporations,"[23] Novak refutes the socialists' accusations. In plain, understandable language he offers a reasoned evaluation of corporations, from which economics educators can learn an accurate and effective moral defense of corporations.

Novak's article identifies seven corporate responsibilities but detailing just the first and second ones should impart a solid foundation for corporate morality. Novak introduces his corporate responsibilities by explaining that contrary to socialist claims, a business corporation is not "morally naked" unless it is dressed in government regulations and control. He argues that there are moral responsibilities that are inherent to business itself. These are responsibilities that are not imposed from without but are intrinsic to becoming a successful business in a free, democratic society.

The primary responsibility is to satisfy customers with goods and services of real value. It is self-evident that unless its customers are served to their satisfaction, no business can survive. The second responsibility is to make a reasonable return on investors' funding. Although critics often charge that enriching the investors by exploiting the customers is primary for avaricious corporations, Novak explains that unless customers are truly satisfied, investors will not receive any reasonable returns on their investments.

The other five responsibilities that Novak delineates reinforce the inherent morality of businesses that can become successful only by putting the customer first. In order to remain successful in an economy, businesses must endeavor to: create new wealth and jobs, enable upward economic mobility and fairly reward hard work, promote invention and ingenuity, and diversify the economy. When businesses fulfill their inherent responsibilities for success, they not only satisfy customers, but contribute to the health and growth of the economy which, of course, morally serves the common good of society. As many of the Medieval Scholastics recognized in their era, no socialist dirigisme can accomplish what successful free-market businesses can do to engender moral economic outcomes.

Entrepreneurship and the Morality of New Wealth Creation

In regard to his third responsibility of business, to create new wealth, Novak poses a key question: If businesses do not create new wealth, then who can? Novak's question exposes the socialists' fundamental misunderstanding of wealth creation and a basic reason why socialist economies are doomed to failure. New wealth creation is absolutely vital for the health and growth of an economy. Without new wealth for research and development, for charitable donations, for job creation, and for improving standards of living, the economy falters, stagnates, and ultimately collapses. No government, no matter how just and fair it claims to be, can directly create new wealth, since it merely redistributes wealth collected in taxes, fees, fines, etc.

Where the socialists go wrong with their understanding of new wealth creation is with their failure to grasp that the government cannot directly create new wealth. The government can indirectly contribute to new wealth creation, but its indirect contributions are also funded by collected revenue, which is

the only source of financial capital the government has. Socialists argue that, for instance, government funded infrastructure
(such as roads, bridges, and their maintenance) and public education (at all levels) are contributions to new wealth creation.
But, again, it is ultimately the taxpayers who are the funding
source for such government contributions. Through its legislative policies, its agencies, its projects, and enforcement of
regulations, government contributions to new wealth creation
are ineluctably indirect, and often tenuously so because a government "contribution" can become more of an inhibitor than
a facilitator of new wealth creation such as with excessive taxation, irresponsible government largesse, and burdensome,
even job-killing, regulations.

Still, it is important to acknowledge that the government's
indirect contributions when operating efficiently and effectively can and do enable new wealth creation. Nevertheless, the
very best contribution the government can make in a free-market economy is to protect and serve the liberty of its citizens.
Private property is the foundational principle of a capitalist
economy, but liberty is a necessary condition for growing the
economy. The freedom for an individual or for a business corporation to initiate new ways of commerce, new types of goods
and services, are the opportunities that create new wealth and
foster economic growth.

The Medieval Scholastic, San Bernardino of Siena, apparently sensed the limitations for economic growth when a tax-
revenue government is in control. He extolled the rare qualities
and virtues of successful entrepreneurs with their contributions to advancing the economy. Entrepreneurial ability includes attention to detail, diligence, knowledge of the market,
and the willingness to assume and capacity to calculate risks,
with profit on invested capital justifiable for the risk and effort

of the entrepreneur. In addition, to be successful the entrepreneur must have a moral character so that the conduct of business is rational and orderly, by acting with integrity and promptly settling all accounts.[24]

San Bernardino clearly realized that entrepreneurs: 1) are freely acting private sector agents whose new wealth creation is vital for economic health and growth; 2) are exceptional people with uncommon abilities; 3) and they are successful only if they act with a moral conscience. These are some important lessons that economics educators can learn from San Bernardino which can effectively challenge the socialists' anti-capitalist biases.

Concluding Remarks: Pedagogical Prescriptions

If academic economics in secondary and higher education persists with its positivist orthodoxy, it runs the risk of becoming practically irrelevant. Millennials' demands for economic moral justice will continue to push them toward socialist dirigisme as the panacea for correcting the inherent injustice of capitalist free-market economics. Economics proclaimed scientific aversion to engaging normative issues of justice generate an ever-strengthening inertia which propels millennials to reject free-markets. Free-markets, however, are the very object of study upon which economics pedagogy and the science itself are based. So, in order to save itself, economic education must develop and teach its moral foundations in ways that can dispel the millennial inertia toward socialism.

The normative propositions of the Preclassicals should be integrated into economics pedagogy as prescriptions, as moral first principles of capitalist economics. As Preclassical thinkers and perspectives maintained, the morality of private property, the morality of the just price, the inherent moral responsibilities of successful businesses, and the morality of new wealth creation and entrepreneurial enterprise are foundations of capitalism. These normative first principles do indeed establish the moral conscience, the justice, of capitalism which much better serves the common good of a society than socialist dirigisme.

References and Notes

1. In the field of economics, Preclassical Thought is identified as spanning the historical periods from Antiquity to 1771. 1776 marks the beginning of the period of Classical Economic Thought since Adam Smith's *Wealth of Nations* was published that year. Also in the economics field, "Preclassical" is the standard spelling for the period. See, Harry Landreth and David Colander, *History of Economic Thought* (hereafter *HET*), Third Edition (Boston: Houghton Miflin, 1994). This paper is reprinted with permission from: "Blasts from the Preclassical Past: Why Contemporary Economics Education Should Listen to Preclassical Thought," Studia Gilsoniana: A Journal in Classical Philosophy, Oct.-Dec. 2019, Vol. 8, No. 4, 839 – 855. Volume topic: A Return to Pre-Modern Principles of Economic Science. Available online at: http://gilsonsociety.com/?8-4-(october-december-2019),149.

2. The exact dates which bracket the millennial generation are somewhat fluid and debatable, however, those born between 1982-2004 are common benchmarks. These dates were stipulated by William Strauss and Neil Howe. See: Kurt Cagle, "Rethinking Millennials and Generations Beyond" (August 22, 2018), https://.forbes.com/sites/cog-

nitiveworld/2018/08/22/rethinking-millennials-and-generations-beyond/#3f95bcb91893. The age range of millennials is, then, from 15-37. Since this range overlaps with what is called GenZ, 1995-2015, ages 4-24, this paper includes GenZ within the millennial generation.

3. Reported by Nate, "Communism is Gaining Ground: The Rise of Socialism in America Comes in Generational Waves," *The Christian Journal* (2/22/2018), https://christianjournal.net/turning-point/academia/communism-is-gaining-ground-the-rise-of-socialism-in-america-comes-in-generational-waves/.

4. Reported in *Investor's Business Daily* (8/24/18), https://www.investors.com/editorials/millennials-socialism/.

5. See: Charlie Kirk, "Liberal Bias Starts with High School Economics Textbooks" (April 26, 2012), *Breitbart.com.*, https://www.breitbart.com/politics/2012/04/26/liberal-bias-starts-in-high-school-economics/.

6. See: Jack Kelly, "The Unintended Consequences of Raising Minimum Wage to $15," https://www.forbes.com/sites/jackkelly/2019/07/10/the-unintended-consequences-of-the-15-minimum-wage/#b619ffee4a7c Other detrimental effects of the $15 minimum wage are indicated in the Congressional Budget Office Report released July 2019 entitled, "The Effects on Employment and Family Income of Increasing the Federal Minimum Wage," https://www.cbo.gov/publication/55410.

7. See *HET*, p. 11. Regarding the dominance of positivism in economics, *HET* states, "According to most economic textbooks, the reigning methodology in economics is still logical positivism . . ." *HET,* p. 15.

8. The description of positive economics and the problem of scarcity is largely based on *HET*, pp. 1-3.

9. See, Robert Eklund and Robert Herbert, *A History of Economic Theory and Method* (hereafter *HETM*), Fourth Edition (New York: McGraw Hill, 1997), p. 28.

10. See, *HET*, p. 25.

11. See, *HET*, pp. 25-26.

12. For further development of these points about private property and liberty, see the section below, Entrepreneurship and New Wealth Generation.

13. The following discussion of Aquinas' position on private property closely follows: Andrew Spencer, "Five Insights About Private Property from Aquinas," *Institute for Faith, Work and Economics* (September 2013), https://tifwe.org/five-insights-about-private-property-from-aquinas/. Spencer's insights are based on: Thomas Aquinas, *Summa Theologica* 2a2ae. Q66. A1&2.

14. Andrew Spencer, "Five Insights About Private Property from Aquinas," Point #2.

15. Aquinas does not maintain that private property is an inviolable right. With his theological ethics, he does believe that those things that we can and should own are ultimately owned communally in that as God's stewards, we hold them in trust for God, so we can use our resources for His glory (see Spencer, Point #5). For instance, in an extreme case, if someone had a water supply, he did not want to sell or give to others while an area was stricken with a devastating drought, it would be acceptable for Aquinas if people came together and appropriated from the water-owner the water they needed to survive. Nevertheless, Aquinas's

555

defenses of private property do offer foundational arguments that can contest socialist morality claims except perhaps in some extreme situations.

16. Chris Fleming, David Rigamer and Walter Block, "The Jesuits: From Markets to Marxism; From Property Protection to Social Progressivism" *Romanian Economic and Business Review*, Vol. 7, No. 2 (Summer 2012) pp. 7-22. This rendition of San Bernardino's and Sant'Antonino's views is based on p. 17 of this article.

17. Lew Rockwell, "The True Founders of Economics: The School of Salamanca" (May 1, 2018) *Mises Institute Canada*, https://austrian.economicblogs.org/mises-canada/2018/rockwell-founders-economics-school-salamanca/

18. *HETM*, pp. 27-28.

19. Murray N. Rothbard, "New Light on the Prehistory of the Austrian School," *Mises Institute: Mises Daily Articles* (November 11, 2006): p.8. https://mises.org/library/new-light-prehistory-austrian-school. This passage is Rothbard's rendition of an interpretation of Cajetan from Raymond de Roover, "The Concept of the Just Price: Theory and Economic Policy," *Journal of Economic History* 18 (December 1958): 422-23.

20. Ibid., p. 9. Rothbard references an interpretation from David Herlihy, "The Concept of the Just Price: Discussion," *Journal of Economic History* 18 (December 1958): 437.

21. Ibid., p. 9. Rothbard once again references Herlihy's article.

22. Ibid., p. 9. Rothbard's description of the views of Molina and Azpilcueta is based on the abovementioned de Roover article, "The Concept of the Just Price: Theory and Economic Policy."

23. Michael Novak, "Public Arguments: Seven Plus Seven – The Responsibilities of Business Corporations," *Crisis Magazine* (July 1, 1994), https://www.crisismagazine.com/1994/public-arguments-seven-plus-seven-the-responsibilities-of-business-corporations. The following discussion paraphrases and interprets Novak's article.

24. This discussion of San Bernardino on entrepreneurship is based on Murray Rothbard, "*New Light on the Prehistory of the Austrian School*" (See above, Note #19). Rothbard's views interpret Raymond de Roover's article, "*The Concept of the just Price: Theory and Economic Policy* (See above Note #19), and de Roover's booklet, *San Bernardino of Siena and Sant'Antonino of Florence: Two Great Economic Thinkers of the Middle Ages* (Boston: Kress Library of Business and Economics, 1967).

Bibliography

Cagle, Kurt. "Rethinking Millennials and Generations Beyond" (August 22, 2018). https://forbes.com/sites/cognitive%20world/2018/08/22/rethinking-millennials-and-generations-beyond/#3f95bcb91893.

Eklund, Robert and Herbert, Robert. *A History of Economic Theory and Method*. Fourth Edition. New York: McGraw Hill, 1997.

Investor's Business Daily. (August 24, 2018). https://www.investors.com/editorials/millennials-socialism/.

Kelly, Jack. "The Unintended Consequences of Raising Minimum Wage to $15" (July 10, 2019). https://www.forbes.com/sites/jackkelly/2019/07/10/the-unintended-consequences-of-the-15-minimum-wage/#b19ffee4a7c.

Kirk, Charlie. "The Liberal Bias Starts in High School Economics Textbooks" (April 26, 2012). *Breitbart.com*.: https://liberal-bias-starts-in-high-school-economics/.

Landreth, Harry and Colander, David. *History of Economic Thought*, Third Edition. Boston: Houghton Miflin, 1994.

Nate. "Communism is Gaining Ground: The Rise of Socialism in America Comes in Generational Waves." *The Christian Journal* (February 22, 2018). https://christianjournal.net/ turning-point/academia/ communism-is-gaining-ground-the-rise-of-socialism-in-america-comes-in-generational-waves/.

Novak, Michael. "Public Arguments: Seven Plus Seven – The Responsibilities of Business Corporations." *Crisis Magazine* (July 1, 1994). https://www.crisismagazine.com/1994/ public-arguments-seven-plus-seven-theresponsibilities-of-business-corporations.

Rigamen, David, Fleming, Chris and Block, Walter. "The Jesuits: From Markets to Marxism; From Property Protection to Social Progressivism." *Romanian Economic and Business Review*, 7.2 (Summer 2012) 7-22.

Rockwell, Lew. "The True Founders of Economics: The School of Salamanca" (May 1, 2018). *Mises Institute Canada*. https://austrian.economicsblogs.org/mises.canada/2018/ rockwell-founders-economics-school-salamanca/.

Rothband, Murray. "New Light on the Prehistory of the Austrian School" (November 11, 2006). *Mises Institute: Mises Daily Articles*. https://mises.org/library/new-light-prehistory-austrian-school.

Spencer, Andrew. "Five Insights About Private Property from Aquinas." *Institute for Faith, Works and Economics* (September 2013). https://tifwe.org/five-insights-about-private-property-from-aquinas/.

Anatomy of the Progressive Revolution[1]
Fall 2021

ABSTRACT

A cultural infrastructure of shared morality is necessary for the success of market economics. Traditional views maintain that religion is the nurturing source of the morality, which grows in the culture. The Progressive revolution aims to overturn Traditional morality and impose its social justice morality on culture. This article dissects and critiques the multifaceted Progressive revolution in the USA, while contrasting it with the Traditional view. It argues that the ultimate aim of the revolution is to redefine the human person through identity politics as a collective entity, which essentially liquidates the individual, conforms the person to social justice morality, and establishes socialistic economics.

The degree to which market economies are grounded on moral norms that are affirmed as metaphysically objective and universal, is the degree to which the market economies can flourish. Without such normative grounds, moral turpitude can corrupt a market economy, ultimately resulting in the economy's collapse. The actors in the economy lose trust in each other; there is no mutual respect and honesty among them. Without moral norms, market commerce degenerates into gang war types of vicious "combat zones" wherein success means eliminating the competition, both economically and literally.

Throughout history market morality has been due typically to the influence of religion on culture. The moral norms of religion establish a cultural infrastructure for trust, honesty, fair dealing and moral accountability among persons acting in the market.

There is also an historical non-religious source of market "morality." This is not a morality that is based on principles of honesty and mutual respect for the value and dignity of others. It is the "morality" of the dictates of a government authority exercising a "command and control" economy, which, in current times in the United States, is manifest in Progressive collectivist economics of socialism. The authoritarian collectivist government aims to establish, regulate and enforce what is "right" for commerce. Morality, in such collectivism, does not grow organically through the influence of religion, but is imposed on culture according to the ideological aims of the governing authority. As history has shown, however, command and control collectivist economies are not as long-lived or beneficial to persons as market economies that grow organically within the religiously nurtured morality of their culture.

The first two sections of this article will describe and contrast the Traditional view of religion as the source of cultural morality that influences politics and economics with the Progressive revolutionary aims to transform culture by imposing their ideological "social justice" morality of a collectivist political economy. The vicissitudes of the Progressive revolutionary agenda will be analyzed and critiqued in detail. The third section will expose a worrisome, fundamental philosophical problem with the Progressive agenda, namely the Progressive De-Personalization. This article will then finish with some remarks regarding what is at stake for the future of market-based USA political economy.

The Traditional View

Along with many other Traditionals, the late politico Andrew Breitbart believed that politics is downstream from culture, and culture is downstream from religion.[2] To expand on Breitbart's proposition, culture, especially morality, flows from religion, and politics and economics flow from culture.

Breitbart's Traditional view of the relationship between religion, culture, politics and economics has a profound heritage including some of the United States' founders. In his Farewell Address, George Washington, for example, stated,

> "Of all the dispositions which lead to political prosperity, religion and morality are indispensable supports these [are the] great pillars of human happiness. [Where] is the security for prosperity, for reputation, for life, if the sense of religious obligation deserts the oaths, which are the instruments of investigation in courts of justice? ... [Let] us with caution indulge the supposition that morality can be maintained without religion. Whatever may be conceded to the influence of refined education on minds of a peculiar structure, reason and experience both forbid us to expect that national morality can prevail in exclusion of religious principle. It is substantially true that virtue or morality is a necessary spring of popular government. The rule indeed extends with more or less force to every species of free government."[3]

Washington could not be more explicit with his belief that morality flows from religion, and since morality is necessary for a free "popular," democratic republic government, so too is religion necessary. His mentions of prosperity, property and happiness reveal his firm understanding that a free-market economy that allows for the pursuit of happiness does require a religiously based morality. His reference to religiously based oaths, such as swearing to "tell the truth, so help you God," further reinforces the need for religious morality to maintain honesty and justice in, and the security of, a free nation.[4]

Following Washington, John Adams recognized that the republic, freedom and prosperity depend on preserving a moral citizenry. Adams affirmed that, "It is religion and morality alone which can establish the principles upon which freedom can securely stand."[5]

Like Breitbart, Washington and Adams, the late Richard John Neuhaus, a 21st century culture commentator, observed that, "Politics is chiefly a function of culture, at the heart of culture is morality and at the heart of morality is religion."[6] To encapsulate these views, the traditional position can be represented as:

RELIGION spawns MORALITY which influences CULTURE which influences POLITICS and ECONOMICS

In the Traditional view, morality, norms/standards for what constitutes a good or bad action, flows from religion and grows organically in culture. It is ultimately from religion and morality that persons develop their beliefs as to virtue vs. vice, what is the good/happy life, the importance of the family, the sense of individual accountability, and the personal responsibility for earning and stewarding wealth. The interrelationship between politics and economics is influenced by the culture, which, for Traditionals, results in a political economy that values free enterprise, market commerce, individual achievement, a limited government and individual autonomy. Traditionals highly value citizens as free individual persons whose liberty to pursue happiness and personal flourishing should respect morally all other persons and should be protected, and unabridged by their democratic republic. This Traditional appreciation of the individual person is precisely a main Progressive target for fundamental change as will be explained in the following anatomy of the Progressive revolution

The Progressive View

The late U.S. Senator Daniel Patrick Moynihan analyzed the difference between Traditionalism (conservatism) and Progressivism (liberalism) as such, "The central conservative truth is that it is culture, not politics that determines the success of a society. The central liberal truth is that politics can change a culture and save it from itself."[7] Moynihan recognized that in the conservative, Traditional, view culture is the driver of social success. He also recognized that for liberals, politics rule so that a culture that is not driven by their Progressive politics is damned and must be reformed to save it from its own backwardness. His insight illumines a basic conviction of the Progressive revolutionary strategy that politics can change culture and make it conform to the ideological ideals for an enlightened, "woke" society. The full Progressive agenda can be represented with the following summation.

POLITICS spawns ECONOMICS. Both spawn CULTURE (MORALITY) which in turn influences EDUCATION, the JUSTICE SYSTEM, and the MEDIA

This summation can be best explicated by offering a series of points that describe briefly its facets and the relationships among them.

- For Progressives, collectivist politics is the prime mover for gaining power and control over society with their revolutionary agenda. Progressives' devotion to their ideology is a type of religious zeal. They are indeed zealots, uncompromising ideologues who are convinced that their position has all of the answers even before questions arise. And if their political answers, solutions, do fail or do not yield immediate results, they tend to blame it on the backward Traditionals, the unsophisticated and obstinate religious right, or some constructed "force" beyond their control like climate change or a pandemic.

- Progressive politics and their agenda itself are devoid of religion. In the name of their supreme value of social justice, religion must be excluded. No influential moral force greater than their ideology can be admitted. The unenlightened morality of Traditional religions must be deconstructed and substituted with their politically constructed "woke" morality: a social justice morality that serves their vision of collective unity.

- Progressive politics wages its revolution with the weapon of economics. Through socialist dirigisme, economic policies create antagonisms between classes, races, ethnicities and genders. Progressives' favored groups are those who are oppressed victims by past economic inequalities and inequities. They are given or promised privileged status through various government policies and programs. These groups' allegiance to the Progressive agenda is fortified by such privileges.

- Progressive economics secures their politics and engenders the change in culture they seek. They contend that without the social justice morality they promise, the nation will be overwhelmed by the many crises it faces. Only their political economic ideology will ensure true social justice. Janet Yellen, White House Cabinet Secretary for the Dept. of Treasury has bluntly stated this alarming warning, "The country is also facing a climate crisis, a crisis of systemic racism, and an economic crisis that has been building for fifty years...I believe economic policy can be a potent tool to improve society. We can -and should- use it to address inequality, racism, and climate change."[8]

- As indicated, it is social justice morality that Progressives strive to establish as a substitute for Traditional morality in economics and in culture at large. Their social justice morality emphasizes compensatory and distributive justice. Compensatory justice aims to correct the past and present injustices to oppressed groups. They promote government "compensations" such as, reparations - financial and otherwise, affirmative action programs, and selective applications of criminal justice in regard, for instance, to rioting, property destruction, and looting. Distributive justice aims to correct inequalities and inequities suffered by oppressed groups in regard to earning and accumulating wealth. Again, government managed and, if need be, enforced examples include free college tuition, guaranteed basic income, universal medical care, housing, food/meal programs, childcare, and "tax the rich" progressive income taxation.[9]

- Progressive politics implemented by their socialistic economics according to their social justice morality, and the interaction of these factors generates revolutionary changes in culture. These changes are spurred on and spread by facets of culture led by Progressive activists. Public education, and much of private education, adhere to and inject Progressive ideology into their curricula and organizational leadership. The revolutionaries want education at all levels, but especially higher education, to be "government education" which promotes the Progressive agenda. For them, education, happily, is indoctrination, since educators and educational contents that oppose "The Agenda" are summarily cancelled.[10]

- Progressives believe that the justice system has been systemically unjust and must be reformed and saved by their social justice morality. The system must be repopulated with Progressive ideologues in such positions as police leadership, government prosecutors, and judges, especially in the higher courts including the US Supreme Court. With the moral standards of social justice, the legal system must be used, when possible, to reform economic issues, as well as criminal law, while advocating for and ruling in favor of the oppressed.

- Education, the Justice System and the Media interact to form a collective unity that strengthens and advances the Progressive agenda. Their unified collective efforts are indefatigable; they seize every opportunity

Progressive politicians create for them in order to sustain a "permanent revolution" that simply does not retreat. The media are an integral factor in the unceasing propagation of the revolution. They spread the message of the Agenda, so that the facets of culture maintain a collective focus. "Media" in this context has a broad meaning. It includes print media, social media, mainstream TV news, and entertainment media, such as streaming TV services (e.g., Netflix, Hulu, Prime, Amazon, and HBO), sports shows (ESPN, CBSSN and FS1), and movie studios. TV series (comedies and dramas) and movies are filled with Progressive propaganda. In fact, if a series offers an alternative, more Traditional perspective, it risks cancellation. The Progressive scions of social media are uninhibited lords of their fiefdoms. "Un-woke" posts and individuals are cancelled if they communicate unenlightened views. The media's collective prosecution of the "cancel culture" movement has indeed become a potent force in executing the permanent revolution.

- The concept of "permanent revolution" is fundamental to the Progressive agenda. This Marxist notion was adopted and adapted by Leon Trotsky in the early 20ᶜ. Trotsky's words can be paraphrased to express the Progressive aims: The Progressive <u>permanent revolution</u> accepts <u>no compromise</u>. The revolution <u>can end only with the complete liquidation of</u> Traditional culture. The <u>permanent revolution is not a leap by the</u> Progressives <u>but the reconstruction of the nation under the dictatorship of the</u> Progressives.[11] Chairman Mao had similar ideas with his notion of Continuous

Revolution, which was the guiding thrust of his Cultural Revolution.[12] The Progressives' revolution is not new to history. Collectivist/socialistic morality, economics and culture have happened before, but never have they entirely succeeded. They have not succeeded in the Soviet Union, not in Cuba, and not even in China, which is refashioning its communism in certain ways to expand its sphere of influence by engaging the global market economy.

The Progressive Depersonalization

The political is the personal and the personal is the political.[13] This maxim was a slogan of the late 1960s feminist and student movements. It also expresses axiomatically the Progressives' "identity politics" which can be defined as, "Politics in which groups of people having a particular racial, ethnic, social, gender or cultural identity tend to promote their own specific interests or concerns…"[14] Identity politics "is a kind of cultural politics. It relies on the development of a culture that is able to create new and affirmative conceptions of the self, to articulate collective identities, and to forge a sense of group loyalty. Identity politics requires the development of rigid definitions of the boundaries between those who have particular collective identities and those who do not."[15] To offer some additional traits, identity politics is a politic of cultural change. The identity groups develop tribal boundaries, which may intersect with other identity groups that have suffered injustice and oppression, but boundaries absolutely exclude any group of non-victims, the oppressors. The identities define the self within the cultural collective. To self-identify with a collective requires group loyalty, typically a loyalty that replaces any Traditional aspect of culture, such as religious loyalty or patriotic commitment to one's nation.

The wicked irony of "the personal is the political" axiom is, however, that it is precisely the personal, the sense of oneself as an individual, which the Progressive revolution aims to cancel. A society's culture without a strong sense of the individual as essential to the person is bereft of crucial values like individual/personal autonomy and moral responsibility, self-reliance, individual/personal achievement and reward, and individual/personal property and wealth. These values are of baseline importance to Traditional culture but erasing and substituting them with ideologically charged collective identities enables the cultural transformation that Progressives desire.

The individual is a locus of rights and responsibilities. Our personal identity is who and what we become as individual persons. We become persons insofar as we respect those rights for others and ourselves, and fulfill those responsibilities. Individuals grow and mature to become persons. Persons retain their individuality while realizing their responsibilities to themselves, families, communities and nation. Our freedom, self-determination, liberty, ambitions and aspirations are most perfectly fulfilled in the process of becoming persons.

The Progressive personal identity effectively liquidates the individual. The individual is not something real, the core of our self, but merely an epiphenomenon of our collective group identity.[16] The collective group is the locus of rights and responsibilities. Our right to self-determination is nothing more than acting with and for the social justice's sake of the collective. Our prime responsibility is to oppose the social injustice that our group and all of the other groups with which we intersect have suffered and are suffering. With the cancellation of the individual person, the Progressive revolution is able to employ strategically its social justice morality to provide opportunity, cover for establishing its socialist economics, and fundamentally transform the culture of the USA to create a new nation that has disposed of its Traditional history. The Progressives' permanent revolution can abide no other outcome.

Final Remarks

The advancement of the Progressive revolution hinges on redefining the human person. Just as successful market economies need Traditional morality rooted in their culture, Progressives plant their ideological social justice morality in culture and nurture it with identity politics. Identity politics excises the individual and reduces the person to a collective entity, which then can be more easily manipulated by social justice morality and directed by the Progressive state. Socialist economics is a means for Progressive politics to command and control the culture and generate total cultural change. Full transformation of the culture requires widespread acceptance of the Progressive collective view of human nature.

The Progressive revolution aims to change the way in which people understand themselves, understand their very humanity as collective beings. If their revolution ultimately succeeds, it will have ongoing permanence since it will have to correct continuously lingering cultural issues. For instance, criminal guilt must become understood as the fault of some sort of injustice suffered by the perpetrator's collective. Any beliefs in and efforts to earn private wealth and property would have to be rectified by the state. Moreover, even eschatological beliefs in personal immortality, an individual afterlife, would have to be challenged, probably suppressed, by the state.

The Progressive revolution against Traditional society is fomenting a civil war in the USA, albeit a cold war, but a war nonetheless. Effective resistance begins with understanding the revolution's anatomy, recognizing and rejecting Progressive "woke" political strategies and leaders as abetted by educational institutions, the justice system and the media. Progressives will not abandon their permanent revolution, though resistance can weaken it, perhaps even to the extent that it becomes nothing more than an annoying facet of the cultural fringe.

References and Notes

1. Reprinted with permission from: "Anatomy of the Progressive Revolution," in *Studia Gilsoniana* 10, no.5 (special issue 2021) 1107-1120.

2. This Traditional view of Andrew Breitbart is referenced in Christopher Chantrill, "An American Manifesto," October 2017, 2010shttps://americanmanifestobook.blogspot.com/2017/10/politics-is-downstream-from-culture-is.html. Dan McLaughlin, "Politics is Still Downstream of Culture," May 2016, https://redstate.com/dan_mclaughlin/2016/ 05/04/politics-still-downstream-culture-n58816.

3. George Washington, *Farewell Address,* https://www.senate.gov/artandhistory/history/resources/pdf/Washingtons-Farewell-Address.pdf., pp. 16-17.

4. The significance of religiously based oaths, the so-called "wall of separation" between the public and private

realms concerning religion, and other issues pertaining to the importance of religion in a democratic republic are discussed at length in: Thomas Michaud, "Democracy Needs Religion" (*"Demokracja potrzebuje religii"*), trans. by Pawel Tarasiewicz in Man in Culture: Contemporary Challenges to Democracy, 20/2008 (*Człowiek w Kulturze: Wyzania wspolczesnej demokracji*), ed. Piotr Jaroszynski et al. (Lublin, Poland: Lublin School of Philosophy Foundation, 2008), pp. 101 – 111.

5. John Adams, *Letter to Zabdiel Adams, 21 June 1776.* https://founders.archives.gov/documents/Adams/04-02-0011.

6. This well-known quote from Richard John Neuhaus is often cited in "quotable quotes" sorts of sites, https://www.goodreads.com/author/quotes/8122. Richard John Neuhaus. Neuhaus, the founder of the journal *First Things*, also said that: "The first thing to say about politics is that politics is not the first thing." https://www.azquotes.com/author/10752-Richard_John_Neuhaus. The Traditional Neuhaus clearly did not believe that politics has or should have a greater influential force on society than religion, morality and culture, unlike the Progressives who maintain that politics is and should be the principal influential force on society.

7. The citation for this frequently referenced quote from Daniel Moynihan is: https://www.goodreads.com/quotes/116754-the-central-conservative-truth-is-that-it-is-culture-not.

8. Janet Yellen, Quoted in *Catalyst, Journal of the Catholic League for Religious and Civil Rights*, Vol. 48, No. 5, June 2021, p. 8.

9. For a thorough critique of Progressive social justice see: Thomas Michaud, "Critiquing 'Politically Correct' Justice" ("Krytyka sprawiedliwosci 'poprawnej politycznie'"), trans. by Rafael Lizut in Justice: Theories and Reality (Sprawiedliwosc – idée a rzeczywistosc), ed. Piotr Jaroszynski et al. (Lublin, Poland: Katedra Filozfi Kultury, 2009) pp. 37-44.

10. For more analysis of the Progressive impact on education see: Thomas Michaud, "Postmodern Challenges to Catholic Higher Education" (*"Postmodernistyczne wyzania dla katolickiego ksztalania na poziomie wxzszym"*), trans. by Agnieska Lekka-Kowalik in Philosophy and Education (*Filozofi i Edukacja*), ed. Piotr Jarosynski et al. (Lublin, Poland: *Katedra Filozofi Kultury* KUL, 2005) pp. 45-53.

11. The underlined words in this paragraph are from Leon Trotsky's "The Permanent Revolution," 1929, https://www.marxists.org/archive/trotsky/1931/tpr/. The word "Progressive" has been substituted for "Proletariat."

12. For more on Mao's notions of Continuous Revolution and Cultural Revolution see: https://en.wikipedia.org/wiki/Continuous_revolution_theory

13. For more on the background of this revolutionary slogan see: https://www.britannica.com/topic/the-personal-is-political and https://www.thoughtco.com/the-personal-is-political-slogan-origin-3528952

14. This is a paraphrase of the "identity politics" definition from: https://www.merriam-webster.com/dictionary/identity%20politics

15. Jeffrey Escofier, quoted in, Joan Mandle, "How Political is Personal: Identity, Politics and Social Change",

https://userpages.umbc.edu/~korenman/wmst/iden-
tity_pol.html
16. I must acknowledge my colleague and friend, Curtis Hancock, who used the term "epiphenomenon" to describe
the individual in our conversation about the Progressives'
fundamental change of the nature of the human person.

Bibliography

Adams, John. *Letter to Zabdiel Adams, 21 June1776.* Available
https://founders.archives.gov/documents/Adams/04-
02-0011.

Chantrill, Christopher. *"An American Manifesto."* October 2017.
Available   americanmanifestobook.blogspot.com/2017/
10/politics-is-downstream

Mandel, Joan. *"How Political is Personal: Identity, Politics and Social
Change."* Available https://userpages.umbc.edu/ ~koren-
man/wmst/identity_pol.html

McLaughlin, Dan. "Politics is Still Downstream of Culture."
Available   https://redstate.com/dan_mclaughlin/2016/
05/04/politics-still-downstream-culture-n58816

Trotsky, Leon. *"The Permanent Revolution,* 1929." Available
online   at: https://www.marxists.org/archive/trotsky/
1931/tpr/

Washington, George. Farewell Address. Available www.sen-
ate.gov./artandhistory/history/resource/Washingtons-
Farewell-Address pp. 17-19.

Yellen, Janet. Quoted in *"Biden Admin Claims America Is Racist."*
Catalyst: Journal of The Catholic League for Religious and
Civil Rights. Editor, William Donohue. Vol. 48, No.5, June
2021. p. 8.

Section VI

Progressivism's Challenges to Education and Millennials' Happiness

Section Introduction

Many of the congresses and conferences at which I presented in Poland had a "Catholic Education" theme. I believe this was so because after the collapse of Soviet hegemony, Catholic academics were free to recover their faith tradition within their universities. There seemed to be a certain urgency among them that it was imperative to invigorate the Catholic intellectual tradition so that it could and would be transmitted to the younger generation of professors and teachers. The energy of their efforts was infectious and enlivening, especially for American scholars because Catholic higher education in the U.S.A. was becoming derailed; it was losing its tradition and identity to the currents of Progressivism.

The first essay, "Postmodern Challenges to Catholic Higher Education," was the first paper I presented in Poland, Spring 2004. This essay offers a summative account of the Postmodern (POMO) movement's effects on higher education. As noted earlier in this volume, POMO is a derivative form of Progressivism, consequently it has many Progressive traits. The essay relies on Fr. James Schall's criticisms of POMO's confused ethics of "absolute tolerance" as a lead-in to an extensive discussion of Michael Novak's rejection of the claim that POMO's morality of social justice, which is so prominent in Catholic education, does not really treat it as a virtue but as a regulative principle of social order imposed by POMO ideologues and demagogues.

The next essay, "The Identity Crisis in U.S. Catholic Higher Education," shows specifically that Progressive social justice has become the core of so many Catholic universities' so-called Catholic identity. The Catholic intellectual tradition has been supplanted by social justice service centers and projects. And, with the growth of service and experiential learning, a type of civil religion emerges that displaces a personal God as the Author of all that is.

The third and fourth essays, "Philosophical Reflections of the 'New Progressivism' in Education" and "Progressive Higher Education: Through Homogeneity to Ideal Diversity" together offer a theoretical analysis coupled with anecdotal illustrations. "Philosophical Reflections..." begins with an account of the history of Progressivism in education, explains what is "new" about current Progressivism and then identifies and exemplifies four main principles of the "new" Progressivism. They are: 1. Collectivism Triumphs over Individuals. 2. Utopianism and the Limitless Perfectibility of Humanity. 3. Nature is a Construct. 4. Moral and Epistemological Relativism. "Progressive Higher Education..." argues that "diversity" at U.S. universities is really nothing but an ideal of homogeneity wherein whatever opposes the Progressive ideology is scorned and expelled. Many examples of Progressives' "diversity disturbances" after the 2016 Presidential election are cited.

The final essay, "Happiness Lost: The Ravages of Nihilism," takes a slightly different course. Despite Progressives' control of most institutions of higher learning in the U.S.A., millennial students in general are suffering from mental health problems in large, unprecedented numbers. They feel depressed, anxious, hopeless and unhappy in serious degrees. In fact, basic "Happiness" courses are becoming the most popular courses on campuses nation-wide. Why is this happening? These students are afflicted with an existential dread which causes a type of nihilism. Their dread is an anxiety at the core of their lives; it is an inarticulate fear and trembling about what is truly real. They have been barraged by Progressive constructs which has alienated them from the real. They simply cannot find true durable happiness in the ideologically driven constructs they have been educated to accept as "reality."

Postmodern Challenges to Catholic Higher Education[1]
April 2004

In the Fall of 1997, I received an invitation to attend a major conference on "After Postmodernism" at the University of Chicago. While citing postmodernism's so-called "achievements," such as exposing the hegemonic tendencies in Western "objectivity," the provocative notice delivered a somber eulogy for postmodernism. It's postmortem bemoaned postmodernism's relativistic historicism which resulted in "arbitrariness, stoppage, and an inability to think further," and then in apparent desperation, questioned, "What comes after postmodernism?" The notice, not surprisingly, offered no clear direction for philosophy after POMO, though frustration and a passionate uncertainty seemed to cry out from the notice's confusing, and lengthy conference agenda.

After more or less twenty-five years of rule in higher education, the postmodern movement, if it ever really was a philosophical "movement," was O.P.D. (Officially Pronounced Dead) in the late 1990's. However, is it really finished? The simple answer is, "No!" Aspects of POMO have not merely insinuated themselves into the academic mind-set, but they have actually become institutionalized with professors, administrators, curricula, academic disciplines, and university policies and governance. What POMO spawned is alive and thriving in higher education, including Catholic universities. The challenges it poses to Catholic higher education are nothing but daunting.

This exposition of POMO's challenges will develop in a two-fold manner. First of all, the philosophical roots and character of POMO will be described in light of their differences with the "perennial philosophy." Secondly, a number of specific concrete ways in which the effects of POMO remain and even dominate in Catholic higher education will be cited and critiqued.

POMO vs. the Perennial Philosophy

In his <u>Crossing the Threshold of Hope</u>, The Holy Father John Paul II distinguishes between the philosophy of existence and the philosophy of consciousness. He argues that Descartes' dictum which began the Modern era, Cogito ergo sum, inaugurated a great "anthropocentric shift" wherein philosophical emphasis changed from being on the external world, the world of really existing things, to the internal data of consciousness.[2] Subjective consciousness took center stage, and the reality of extra-mental existence was relegated to the role of an ignored understudy confined to the wings.[3]

With this Modern shift, subjective consciousness became absolutized as the autonomous origin of all meaning and truth, and the "perennial philosophy" was subverted. Succinctly stated, the perennial philosophy is a comprehensive realism in the metaphysical, epistemological and moral senses. It affirms the reality and intelligibility of extramental existence as God-designed ordered being and accepts truth as the correspondence between what is and what is known. Moreover, with such true knowledge, one can comprehend universal scientific laws, philosophical principles and moral norms.[4]

With the shift, however, Modern thought grew a Janus-like physiognomy. On one side, with the Rationalists and Positivists, autonomous rationality was proclaimed as the self-sufficient means for solving any and all philosophical, scientific and even social/ethical problems. Indubitable, apodictic epistemological foundations supported this rationality and made possible its veritable omnipotence at problem-solving and system-building.[5] Nevertheless, on the other side, looking away from and perhaps askance at such zealous rationalism, some post-Enlightenment moderns of a Humean or Nietzschean countenance proclaimed a thorough-going antinomianism, which rejected all types of universal laws, philosophical principles and moral norms. Their reactionary ardor insisted that because the quest for absolute foundations is doomed to failure, all rational knowledge is perforce impossible. Accordingly, they elevated feeling above rationality so that rationality became a mere epiphenomenon of feelings. Rationality was considered as an unreal faculty and was ineffective at articulating any objective truth since it was determined by the entirely subjective caprice of feelings.

It is this antinomian face of Modernity that postmoderns like Michel Foucault, Jacques Derrida, Richard Rorty, Stanley Fish and various others, radicalized and then donned. They were not, therefore, truly POST-modern but merely more philosophically extreme descendants of their post-Enlightenment ancestors. They absolutized their skeptical heritage to ensure that no vestige of Modem rationalism would survive their de-construction. They expanded the Baconian axiom, "Know-ledge is power ... " with the conjunct "and power is truth," so that any moral values, scientific laws and philosophical princi-ples have "truth" only insofar as they are fabricated and en-forced by the most willful. An anarchic voluntarism appeared as the only outcome of their rebellion. They offered no positive alternative to Modern rationalism except to champion their fa-vored political ideologies. But since "power is truth," and power is the achievement of a personal will exerting itself over others in society, the "personal is political." Consequently, ide-ologies devolved into demagoguery where personal politics be-came the origin and end of all intellectual inquiry.[6]

Postmodernism was, quite simply, a politic and its wake washed-up a mass of political ideologues and demagogues in higher education. Whether as a professor or administrator, an ideologue is one who absolutizes THE position, THE agenda, so he or she has all of the answers even before the questions arise. Ideologues are intolerant of broad-minded, truth-loving philosophical inquiry which authentically seeks an answer but does not know what that answer is except that it must corre-spond to the truth. Ideologues cannot think nor do political inquiry without promoting politicized causes, and in the ex-treme, a politicized regime. Ideologues are supremely confi-dent that their agenda captures and invincibly holds the high moral ground, and as such, they believe their agenda is self-justifying and can accomplish "enlightened" social engineering. As a servant of THE position, ideologues ignore fruitful com-munity-building to aver that solidarity is really nothing but ide-ological conformism.

Ideologues can devolve into demagogues who become THE position or agenda. Demagogues are "political cult gurus" as their very personalities are politicized and they style themselves as avatars of political truth. They claim to be embodiments of THE position because of their politicized creeds, gender, sexual lifestyle, ethnicity, race, class or whatever. They demand, "Believe and follow me because I am the truth." For demagogues, any philosophical challenge to their beliefs is construed as an ad hominem assault. So, for them, philosophical debates necessarily degenerate into clashes of Nietzschean "wills to power" wherein they try to overpower their opponent by insisting on something like, "My self is more politically meaningful, true or moral than yours!"

All of higher education, but particularly the humanities and social/behavioral sciences, is rife with POMO-spawned ideologues and demagogues. Academic disciplines, pedagogy and governance are becoming mere means for politicized indoctrination and activism. Marxists, Marxist feminists, post-colonial globalists and cultural materialists are just some of POMO's progeny. In Catholic institutions, the realism of the perennial philosophy, especially its moral realism, is being assailed as an illusory God-infested Meta-narrative which for centuries has oppressed multicultural diversity, women and the behaviors of those with alternative sexual lifestyles. The POMO-born zealots' scorn for the perennial philosophy is eroding the very foundations of Catholic higher education. Whether the perennial philosophy and Catholic higher education will survive depends, at least in part, on exposing the POMO-politicos as being in-power but not in-truth.

The Impact of POMO Politics on Catholic Higher Education

Among the numerous ways in which Catholic higher education is being accosted by POMO-offspring are three serious and concrete threats, namely absolute tolerance, power-based social justice and politicized literature. Each of the challenges cuts to the very core of the perennial philosophy.

The ideologues' pretension that their position holds the "high moral ground," and the demagogues' insistence that their politicized identities ought to be affirmed regardless of differing beliefs both stem in part from their invocation of "tolerance." With egalitarian fervor they demand that epistemological and moral pluralism morally mandate that all truth-claims are equal. Therefore, to claim a universal truth or universal moral norm is for them an act of vicious intolerance since such a claim discriminates against others' competing claims.

In *Fides et Ratio*, The Holy Father teaches that, "To believe it is possible to know a universally valid truth is in no way to encourage intolerance; on the contrary, it is the essential condition for a sincere and authentic dialogue between persons".[7] In commenting on this passage, Fr. James Schall, S.J., exposes the deficiencies in the principle of absolute tolerance. Schall recognizes that such tolerance is not and should not be the first principle of an epistemology, of an ethic or of a political philosophy. If tolerance is so construed, it must brand the claim of "universally valid truth" as fanatic and not worthy of consideration, although "it is itself intolerant to refuse to examine a philosophy that claims to be true." Following The Holy Father's teaching, Schall prescribes that genuine tolerance is a practical principle of virtue which allows the "highest things" to be examined through "sincere and authentic dialogue between persons."[9]

Because of their "absolute tolerance," the ideologues and demagogues who populate Catholic institutions all too frequently refuse to enter into sincere and authentic dialogue with "fanatics" who espouse the perennial philosophy. However, without curricula, pedagogies and governance, which engage the higher things in dialogue, can Catholic education long endure?

The missions of many, if not most, Catholic institutions are framed with an emphatic social justice purpose. As Michael Novak observes, however, with social justice the main focus is usually not on virtue but on power.[10] Novak, through referencing Friedrich Hayek, points out that most who use the term "social justice" designate it as a moral virtue. Nevertheless, they ascribe it not to the reflective and deliberate acts of individual persons, but to impersonal social systems and states of affairs, such as inequality of incomes.[11] If social justice is not ascribed to persons, then it is not really a virtue but merely a regulative principle of social order. It is not something that "emerges organically and spontaneously from the rule-abiding behavior of free individuals, but rather from an abstract ideal"[12] imposed by the coercive power of the ideological and demagogical elites.

A virtue is a practical moral habitus which in the perennial philosophy has soteriological import for individual persons. Persons acting together with the habitus of social justice develop solidarity, which the perennial philosophy would describe as an authentic community formed for the greater glory of God. Catholic institutions which define social justice merely as power, view it as a utopian goal toward which all social systems and structures should be made to conform by political coercion. With this orientation, Catholic institutions lose any higher, transcendent, consummatory purpose in their missions because they are not ultimately concerned with educating souls toward the Truth, but with the instantiation of their ideological version of a utopian "heaven on earth." The wicked irony here is that their secular, power-driven social justice missions will inevitably undermine the sacred, transcendent purposes to which Catholic higher education ought to be dedicated. And, without such sacred purposes, can Catholic higher education be truly Catholic?

In the <u>Poetics</u> Aristotle maintains that literature is one of the primary media through which one can become educated in the universally valid moral virtues. The characters, stories and themes in literature can help us understand how we can and should avoid evil and vice and dispose ourselves to develop habits of virtue.[13] Aristotle's realization of this role of literature has been a vital part of the perennial philosophy and a pedagogical norm within the tradition of Catholic liberal arts education. Now, however, POMO-produced poetics are de-constructing this tradition.

A typical example of the means for this deconstruction is the widely influential and academically bestselling book by Terry Eagleton, *Literary Theory*. This text is presently almost standard issue in literature graduate programs and is virtually a staple for reading in undergraduate courses in literary criticism. In the work, Eagleton proclaims the end of literary theory because literature itself is dead.[14] By his extreme claims, Eagleton, a nominalist and self-identified Marxist, means that literature is not and never was a medium for transmitting universal values (or virtues), since such values are non-existent. For Eagleton, "literature is an ideology" and has intimate relations to questions of social power because all of our values are ideological and reflect the social power conditions of our times.[15] Great works of literature are not great because their stories have some intrinsic universal value which they communicate, but because historical conditions of power cause various critics, readers and authors to extol them as great. As ideology, literature is merely a political instrument for such purposes as indoctrination, oppression, inciting rebellion, fomenting class struggles, liberating victims of social marginalization, or even maintaining the status quo.

The extent to which Eagleton-like ideologues and demagogues control literature departments, curricula and pedagogy is the extent to which literature is indeed dead at Catholic institutions. Students of such academic politicos are not taught to appreciate literature qua literature but are instructed only to articulate and evaluate its political platforms. Consequently, their literary studies and criticism are bereft of any anagogical level of meaning. There is no way that literature can inspire understanding of the "higher things" such as universal values, metaphysical truths and the Divine Logos. Such a loss of literature deforms literature curricula and departments in Catholic liberal arts institutions into illiberal training camps for the politicos' favorite ideologies. Illiberal education in literature is the demise of what was in the tradition of the perennial philosophy a profound medium for Catholic institutions to strive to fulfill their true missions.

Final Remarks

The after-effects of POMO have tilted Catholic higher education into a most precarious position. The current conditions are truly bleak, but need the forecast be as foreboding? Are there good reasons for hope?

The virtue of hope is not optimism, and it is certainly not pessimism. The pessimist whines, "Woe is me, my situation is not what I will it to be." The optimist, on the other hand, self-assuredly asserts, "My situation will be what I will." In both cases, it is what "I will" that is primarily operative, positively with optimism and negatively with pessimism. Hence, both pessimism and optimism are egocentric. Authentic hope, however, is not egocentric but ego-effacing. Hope is the humble deference to an order, a design, a Truth that transcends and is far greater than the ego. With hope comes the faith that Truth will prevail, and it does not depend entirely on what "will be done," but mainly on "Thy will be done."

The Truth is not power, but the Truth is powerful. Hoping with and having faith in the power of the Truth are why Catholic higher education and the perennial philosophy will survive to bury their undertakers.

References and Notes

1. Reprinted with permission from: "Postmodern Challenges to Catholic Higher Education" *("Postmodernistyczne wyzania dla katolickiego ksztalania na poziomie wxzszym")*, trans. by Agnieska Lekka-Kowahk in <u>Philosophy and Education *(Filozofi i Edukacja)*</u>, ed. Piotr Jarosynski, et al. (Lublin, Poland: Katedra Filozofi Kultury KUL, 2005) pp.45-53. This paper was also presented at the Third International Congress of Philosophy on the Future of Western Civilization, Theme: Philosophy and Education, Catholic University of Lublin, Lublin, Poland April 2004.

2. John Paul II. *Crossing the Threshold of Hope,* trans. by Jenny McPhee and Martha McPhee, (New York: Knopf, 1994) 54.

3.   For a fuller account of the impact of the "anthropocentric shift" see: Thomas A. Michaud, "Gabriel Marcel's Catholic Dramaturgy," *Renascence,* 55.3 (Spring 2003) 229-240.

4.   The term "perennial philosophy" has been and is used with a wide range of meanings. From Gottfried Leibniz (1646-1716) to Aldous Huxley (1894-1963) the term has been used to indicate a holistic integration of various philosophical and spiritual beliefs. In the context of Catholic tradition, the term is used to denote an Aristotelian-based philosophical realism which supports and complements the doctrines of the Faith. A recent discussion of the perennial philosophy as foundational to the Catholic tradition is offered by Curtis Hancock, "Faith, Reason and the Perennial Philosophy," in *Faith and the Life of the Intellect,* eds. Curtis Hancock and Brendan Sweetman (Washington, D.C.: Catholic University of America Press, 2003) 40-63. Hancock indicates (43-4) that Pope John Paul II aptly describes the universal, timeless and inclusive qualities of the perennial philosophy in *Fides et Ratio,* Sections 4-5: "Although times change and knowledge increases, it is possible to discern a core of philosophical insight within the history of thought as a whole. Consider, for example, the principles of non-contradiction, finality, and causality, as well as the concept of the person as a free and intelligent subject with the capacity to know God, truth and goodness. Consider as well certain fundamental moral norms which are shared by all. These are among the indications that beyond different schools of thought there exists a body of knowledge which may be judged a kind of spiritual heritage of humanity. It is as if we had come upon an implicit philosophy, as a result of which all feel that they possess these principles, albeit in general and unreflective way. Precisely because it

is shared in some measure by all, this knowledge should serve as a kind of reference point for the different philosophical schools ... On her part, the Church cannot but set great value upon reason's drive to attain goals which render people's lives ever more worthy. She sees in philosophy the way to come to know fundamental truth about human life. At the same time, the Church considers philosophy an indispensable help for a deeper understanding of faith and for communicating the truth of the Gospel to those who do not yet know it."

5.   This rendition of the Modem philosophical roots of postmodernism is more completely developed in: Thomas A. Michaud, "Introduction," in *Gabriel Marcel and the Postmodern World*, ed. Thomas A. Michaud, *Bulletin de la Societe de Philosophie de Langue Francaise*, Vol. VII, No. 1-2 (Spring 1995) 5-29.

6.   This description of postmodernism summarizes Michel Foucault's views on power, truth and politics as articulated in: Michel Foucault, "The Political Function of the Intellectual," trans. Colin Gordon, in *Philosophy: Contemporary Perspectives on Perennial Issues*, ed. E.D. Klemke, et al. (New York: St. Martin's Press, 4th ed., 1994) 601-606.

7.   Pope John Paul II, *Fides et Ratio*, 1998, #92.

8.   James Schall, S.J., *"Fides et Ratio:* Approaches to a Roman Catholic Political Philosophy." *The Review of Politics.* 62 (Winter 2000). Available http://www.moree.com/schall/revpol62.htm 1-12.

9.   Ibid. p.11.

10. Michael Novak, "Defining Social Justice." *First Things,* December 2000, p.11.

11. Ibid. p.11.

12. Ibid. p.12.

13. This point expresses Aristotle's views in a number of places in the *Poetics*, but especially sections 2.1 and 3.l. Richard Janko's masterful "Introduction" to his translation of the *Poetics* clearly explains how and why Aristotle believed that literature can teach virtue. The key concepts in this explanation are Aristotle's notions of *mimesis* and *catharsis*. The above-cited article, "Gabriel Marcel's Catholic Dramaturgy," offers a concise summary of these concepts and examples from the dramas of Marcel of how they can educate in virtue.
14. Terry Eagleton, *Literary Theory,* U. of Minnesota Press, 1996, pp. 171-2, 189.
15. Ibid. pp. 19-23.

Bibliography

Aristotle. *Poetics.* Translated and Introduction by Richard Janko. Indianapolis: Hackett Publishing Co., 1987.

Eagleton, Terry. *Literary Theory.* 2nd Edition. Minneapolis: U. of Minn. Press, 1996.

John Paul II. *Fides et Ratio.* 1998.

John Paul II. *Crossing the Threshold of Hope.* Translated by Jenny McPhee and Martha McPhee. New York: Knopf, 1994.

Novak, Michael. "Defining Social Justice." *First Things.* December 2000. 11-13.

Schall, S.J., Fr. James. *"Fides et Ratio:* Approaches to a Roman Catholic Political Philosophy."

The Review of Politics. 62 (Winter 2000). Available on-line at http://www.moree.com/schall/revpol62.htm 1-12

The Identity Crisis in Catholic Higher Education[1]
November 2008

The first sentence of a widely read 2006 book, Catholic Higher Education, reads, "A crisis is looming in Catholic education."[2] Though this work is a worthwhile study, its opening statement is misleading. A crisis is not merely "looming" in American Catholic higher education; the crisis is at its peak at many, perhaps most, of the 215 accredited U.S. Catholic colleges.[3] Simply stated, that crisis is the efforts to retain, redefine, reject or renew colleges' Catholic identity.

A study by the Higher Education Research Institute provides some details about the crisis. The study "compared results of a survey administered to college freshmen in 1997 with a survey given to the same students as graduating seniors in 2001."[4] Among other disturbing trends, the results showed that students attending Catholic colleges are more likely to increase in support for legalized abortion by 13.8% and for same-sex marriage by 16.2%. In regard to premarital sex, the increase in the agreement response to the following statement was 21.5%: "If two people really like each other, it's all right for them to have sex even if they've known each other only for a short time."

Data such as these are alarming, but they do not entirely depict the ominous complex of the Catholic identity crisis. How, for instance, did the crisis originally afflict Catholic higher education? Though dealing fully with this issue would extend beyond the scope of this presentation, a brief history of the crisis only since 1990, the year Ex Corde Ecclesiae was promulgated, will be helpful.

Some of Ex Corde's principal prescriptions for Catholic identity can be summarized as: Catholic colleges should 1) affirm Christian inspiration, 2) engage in research and reflection in light of the Catholic faith, 3) keep faithful to the Christian message, and 4) maintain an institutional commitment to service.[5]

Ex Corde was greeted by vigorous criticism on virtually every Catholic campus in the U.S. In 1996 the U.S. Bishops submitted an implementation plan to the Vatican, a plan that was perhaps swayed by the opposition, and the plan was rejected. In 1999 the Bishops re-submitted a stronger plan, though its actual results remain questionable.

That plan can again be summarized with four principal points: At Catholic colleges, 1) the Catholic faith should hold a privileged position, 2) all truth should be pursued so that Catholics are prepared for ethical leadership in a wide range of occupations and professions, 3) academic expertise should be applied to solving societal problems and advancing peace and justice, 4) Christian communities of prayer, sacraments and spiritual development should be fostered.[6]

Despite the opposition, Ex Corde was recognized as an apostolic constitution, which had to be taken seriously and, in some ways, followed. Consequently, in the early 1990s, many Catholic colleges initiated various types of academic majors and minors in "Catholic Studies," which they believed would be the preserves of Catholic identity and would be sufficient to fulfill Ex Corde's mandates. Though there was at first a mild burst of student and faculty interest in such programs, their popularity waned, and now after just a decade, many Catholic studies programs have folded or are limping along with few faculty and students.

What have actually emerged as the touted "saviors" of Catholic identity are various programs oriented toward service and service learning. These programs emphasize the service prescriptions from <u>Ex Corde</u> (see #4 above) and from the Bishops' 1997 implementation plan (see #3 above). Today almost every Catholic college in the U.S. has some sort of service and/or service-learning program. With this development, the issue now is whether such programs are delivering on their claims to be the resolutions of the identity crisis, or whether they actually signal the end of Catholic higher education within the profoundly rich Catholic intellectual tradition.

The noted Catholic historian, Robert Wilken, warns of a learning gap within Catholic higher education. He cautions, "when it comes to the intellectual life of the university, the lamp of Catholic thought is hidden under a basket."[7] The implication is that although with service and service learning a kind of piety and charity are evident, Catholic intellect and learning are not evident. Wilken further cautions that "if reasoning about the soul and God, and hence about what it means to be human, is excluded from the university, the intellectual enterprise makes itself a captive of the present…"[8]

That "present," as the Holy Father Benedict XVI teaches in his Regensberg lecture, assumes that reason has to do only with what can be established on empirical or mathematical grounds, and other forms of thinking are merely a matter of feeling, sentiments or faith. As Pope Benedict states, "In the Western world it is widely held that only positivistic reason and the forms of philosophy based on it are universally valid."[9]

The zealous promotion of service and service learning as the preserve of Catholic identity is marginalizing teaching and learning within the Catholic intellectual tradition by advancing a piously heartfelt but intellectually "headless" social activism.

The traditional model of the Catholic "contemplative in action," which encourages the complementarity, the union, of faith and reason as the source of social action, has become lost with the current distortion of the very Catholic mission of the colleges.

The ultimate mission of Catholic education is to guide the formation of persons and the salvation of their souls. St. Ignatius Loyola believed, in fact, that teaching in Catholic schools was a spiritual work of mercy: instructing the ignorant, so that students could knowledgably integrate their faith into their lives and contribute to the common good of society.[10] Current service and service-learning programs, however, appear to ignore that spiritual work to focus exclusively on their politicized versions of the corporal works of mercy, regardless if those works actually accord with Catholic teaching.

A stark example of how service and service learning are becoming increasingly politicized to conform to a social reformist agenda, which is not necessarily Catholic, occurred at a 2008 meeting of the U.S. Association of Catholic Colleges and Universities dedicated to a national Catholic Social Ministry gathering. The published Notes from that gathering are telling.[11] The topics included, "Resources for a Cooperative Alternative to Competitive Society", which called for the rejection of the competitive paradigm for business enterprises in favor of an alternate paradigm which stresses community and will help us move past winners and losers. Another topic was "Catholics and the Changing Climate," which challenged Catholic activists to "green up" and find religious language and symbols that will motivate colleges, faculty and students to act for this cause since it is "one of the most important social justice issues of the 21st century."

Yet another topic dealt with "My Church Right or Left –
The Prospect of Purple Politics," which concentrated on,
among other things, how to seek constructive dialogue over
Faithful Citizenship with those who simply want to focus on
the life issues within Catholic social teaching. Faithful Citizenship is the November 2007 document from the U.S. Conference of Catholic Bishops.[12] This document is being criticized
vehemently by the Catholic Left because it emphasizes that the
life issues, such as abortion, euthanasia and stem cell research,
are intrinsic evils, and they should be given the moral gravity
they are due when a Catholic votes for political candidates.

As an example of the "headless" approach discussed earlier,
the Notes, moreover, urge: "In order to mobilize students…we [should] build a discourse that centers on the student's passions and emotions." This statement not only expresses how service, as the basis of Catholic identity, is a captive of the present attitudes toward reasoning, but it also is disturbingly reminiscent of Adolf Hitler's words to the effect that,
"Reason confuses people, but emotion is sure."[13]

The Notes continue with the topic, "Service Learning and
Educating for Social Justice," which describes service learning
as "one of the most exciting and dynamic pedagogical tools in
educating for justice." This enthusiasm for service learning car-
ries over to the final section of the Notes wherein "experiential
learning," typically a synonym for service learning, is hailed as
the starting point for the social ministry agenda.

"Experiential learning" is the label the secular humanist
American philosopher John Dewey used to define his progres-
sive pedagogy.[14] As Fr. John Hardon explained, however,
Dewey was committed to an ideology of socialistic naturalism,
the first postulate of which is the denial of a personal God.
"Accordingly, the only religion which progressive education

recognizes is the 'religion' of social improvement and the progress of civil society."[15] Deweyan experiential learning, then, serves a socialistic ideology, which is believed in as a civil religion, the only sort of religious passion that can engender social unification and a state-consciousness.

Experiential learning was also the foundation of the so-called "critical pedagogy" of the Brazilian liberation theorist Paulo Freire. Freire prescribed the active involvement of students in real experience to serve his socialistic ideology of "radical democracy" by creating an effective praxis for social reform and liberation among learners.[16]

Almost every Catholic college today has adopted experiential learning as the basis for service and service-learning programs, many operating under such titles as "Applied Catholic Social Thought," "Institute for Catholic Social Justice Education," and "Center for Service and Social Action". As indicated above, moreover, such programs are typically promoted as the bases for Catholic identity, and though it is risky to over-generalize, they are commonly faithful to a politicized ideology of progressivism and liberationism. They stir the emotions of students, committing them to a passionate praxis, which, however, is not complemented by reasoned instruction in the Catholic Faith within the programs themselves, or even within the overall curriculum. As the colleges become more and more dedicated to these programs as the locus of their Catholic identity, their Catholic mission and the Catholic Faith itself become more and more distorted as a type of civil religion.

A civil religion of any sort substitutes ideological zealotry and social activism for what is truly the final end of human existence, the beatitude of salvation. Without rational instruction in the metaphysics of the Catholic intellectual tradition and appreciating faithfully the teachings of revelation, Catholic higher education will no longer be, as Pope Pius XI taught, "preparing man for what he must be and for what he must do here below, in order to attain the sublime end for which he was created."[17]

References and Notes

1. Presented at the International Congress on Catholic Education: Problems, Risks and Rewards, University of Media and Social Culture Torun, Poland, November 21 & 22, 2008.
2. Melanie Morey and Fr. John Piderit, *Catholic Higher Education: A Culture in Crisis* (New York: Oxford U. Press, 2006)1.
3. This number is cited by the Association of Catholic Colleges and Universities. www.thehighschoolgraduate.com/editorial/catholic_college.html).
4. Deal Hudson, "Are Your Kids Safe in a Catholic College?" www.catholicity.com/commentary/hudson/collegesurvey.html).
5. This summary of *Ex Corde's* principal points closely follows the summary in Richard Yanikoski, "Do Catholic Universities Make the Grade?," Monday, June 23, 2008 (URL = www.uscatholic.org/life/2008/06/do-catholic-universities-make-grade?page = 0%2CO.
6. Ibid.
7. Robert Louis Wilken, "Catholic Scholars, Secular Schools" *First Things* (January 2008). www.firstthings.com/article.php3?id_article = 6104.
8. Ibid.
9. This statement from Pope Benedict XVI is quoted in Wilken's article, "Catholic Scholars, Secular Schools."

10. The historian of the Jesuit order, John W. O'Malley, makes this point about St. Ignatius and the early Jesuit schools in "How the First Jesuits Became Involved in Education," in *The Jesuit Ratio Studiorum*, ed. Vincent Duminuco, S.J. (New York: Fordham U. Pr., 2000) 56-74 at 64.

11. Notes on The Association of Catholic Colleges and Universities March 2008 Catholic Social Ministry Gathering http://accunet.:4acom/:4qa/bb/ index.cfm?page-topic & topic ID = 24.

12. *Forming Consciences for Faithful Citizenship: A Call to Political Responsibility from the Catholic Bishops of the United States*, U.S. Conference of Catholic Bishops, November 2007. www.usccb.org/faithfulcitizenship/FC Statement

13. See, 50,000 Famous Quotes at http://www.great-quotes.com/cgi-bin/db.cgi?db=db&uid=default&Category=CHANGE&mh=10&sb=---&so=ASC&view_records=View+Records&ww=on.

14. See Fr. John Hardon, S.J., "The Dewey Legend in American Education," (URL = http://catholic education.org/articles/education/ed0045.html)

15. Ibid.

16. Peter Deunov, "Experiential Education" (URL = http://sthweb.bu.edu/index.php?option=com_awiki&view=mediawiki&article=ExperientialEducation

17. Pope Pius XI, "Christian Education of Youth," in *Five Great Encyclicals*, ed. Gerald Treacy, S.J., (New York: Paulist Press, 1939) 39. Quoted in Fr. John Hardon, S.J., "The Dewey Legend in American Education."

Reflections on
the "New Progressivism" in Education[1]
April 2013

ABSTRACT

This philosophical essay identifies and critiques some basic principles and practices of the "New Progressivism" in US education today. An overall aim of these critiques is to offer some reasons why citizens' dissatisfaction with "government education" is contributing to the increase in homeschooling and alternative education. Various basic principles of the New Progressivism, some express large philosophical ideas and others very specific agendas, are explained and then exemplified with anecdotal situations which expose the principles' flaws in conception and practice.

The title of this essay implies at least three themes which will be addressed, though each with varying degrees of emphasis. First of all, this essay is just that, an "essay," or more precisely, a "philosophical essay." It does not offer detailed accounts, penetrating textual studies or in-depth social scientific analyses of the New Progressivism and U.S. Education. It does, however, communicate philosophical observations emerging from over four decades of experience in higher education, and higher education is, in fact, the ultimate source from which U.S. education flows. University departments and colleges of education, which teach teachers at all levels how and what to teach, have enormous influence, indeed, power over the educational system. To reflect, then, on the philosophical bases of the university-governmental complex of U.S.

education from the perspective of extensive higher education experience enables one to assume a vantage point for a comprehensive, critical purview.

U. S. education has been defined and governed by higher education's departments and colleges of education for almost a century. For the primary and secondary schools, public and even the majority of private schools, require certifications of teachers which can only be obtained from the university education programs. In addition, national accrediting organizations, teachers' unions, and federal and state educational governing boards and agencies, heavily regulate, if not micro-manage the educational system. U.S. education is predominately "government education" which is controlled by teachers, administrators and educrats, whose pedagogies, policies and authority are ultimately derived from the departments and colleges of education. Their political and educational philosophies rule, and conformity, obedience is mandatory.

The rapid growth of homeschooling and other alternatives, such as on-line schools from the primary through college levels, is in large part a reaction against government education. Citizens, whose philosophical positions and religious credos oppose the government system, have taken it upon themselves to establish their own options. These efforts, unfortunately, have been beleaguered by the government system and strongly challenged by the university education establishment. The movement, nevertheless, continues to grow, resisting conformity at every step, and "gaming the system" when it can to secure their freedom to educate as they choose.

The second theme implied by this essay's title is that if a "New Progressivism" is being stipulated, there must have been an "Old Progressivism." Obviously, then, the question arises: What is the difference between Old and New Progressivism in education? Addressing this question leads into the third theme implied by the title, namely what some of the philosophical disabilities with the New Progressivism are, which, as already mentioned, have caused citizen opposition and contributed to the growth of homeschooling and other alternative ways of education.

The Old Progressivism has historical roots which extend as deeply as the European Enlightenment with Modern Rationalism and Positivism. To express it in sketchy "broad strokes," its origins are with thinkers and works such as Marquis de Condorcet's Outlines of an Historical View of the Progress of the Human Mind (1795), August Comte's Course on Positive Philosophy (six volumes, (1830-1842) and System of a Positive Polity or Treatise on Sociology and Instituting the Religion of Humanity (1851-1854). Comte's friend, John Stewart Mill, was also a main figure in this lineage with the later editions of his Principles of Political Economy and Some of the Applications on Social Philosophy (original edition 1840, "Chapters on Socialism," 1874).

U. S. Progressivism arose in the late 19^c and early 20^c, and it adapted European views, such as those of the aforementioned works, to its indigenous pragmatism, especially in regard to educational philosophy. Principal thinkers such as John Dewey and William James advocated a reformist social agenda, which could be operationalized. One of the main means of such reform was through reform of the schools and teaching. Dewey's educational Progressivism spawned a transformation of schooling, which, in fact, was in many ways sorely needed. Dewey's views called for "child-centered" and "social reconstructionist" approaches so that schools could become more effective agencies of a democratic society.[2]

Though Progressive educational reforms were significant in the first half of the 20^c, they were moderate in comparison to the more extreme post-WWII changes in the 1950s, 1960s and continuing to today. The Old Progressivism was superseded by the New Progressivism, with a specific difference being the extent of the politicization of educational approaches. To be sure Progressive education was always bound to politics and government reform, but the ways in which progressivism instantiated its politics in education became thoroughly ubiquitous leading to the university-governmental complex the U.S. has today.

The social reconstruction agenda of the Old became sociocultural engineering through schooling. Schools are not just more effective agencies for a democratic society, but are institutions for the political formation of students, and university educational programs are the centers which train the teachers, administrators and educrats to carry out the New Progressivism's political designs.

The philosophical platforms that subtend the university-governmental complex of the New Progressivism are, to put it mildly, disturbing. They are fraught with shallow, ill-formed views which can confuse and debilitate the minds of impressionable students. But what are those views and what principles do they embody? Experience has taught me there are at least four BIG principles that drive and advance New Progressivism in education. Those four BIG principles are:

1.   Collectivism Triumphs over Individuals.

Progressivism's fundamental objective is to achieve the greatest political and economic good for the greatest number of people. This aim is coupled with the supposition: the good of the many outweighs the good of the few.[3] For Progressives, these axioms establish their concept of the common good, which is clearly a majoritarian precept.

Connected with their devotion to such a common good are their efforts to seek social and economic justice above all else, and to secure government by, of, and for the people. Progressives, accordingly, favor large central government authority, interventionist economics, a mixed political economy of capitalism and socialism, though weighted in favor of socialism, and government redistribution of wealth.[4] They oppose what they perceive as government by corporations and the excesses of individual wealth and property. The common or collective good for the people is a primary value and any individual good is truly good only if it serves the collective.

It seems at points, however, that Progressivism's preeminent collective is undermined by their individualized pro-choice stances. This is actually not so, and it is most clear in the government schools. Some illustrations from experience will show what this means.

For many years, I designed and conducted leadership and ethics seminars for primary and secondary school teachers. In these seminars I typically raised controversial topics which I knew would challenge the teachers, since they were topics that were directly related to policies at their schools. In one case, I focused on the issue of having students sing traditional Christmas carols during the Christmas season. After much spirited discussion among the groups one teacher stood up and stridently stated that her school's policy is to ban any carols, like Silent Night, that have religious meanings. I asked why and whether she agreed. She responded that she agreed entirely and explained that if one student is offended by singing such carols and chooses not to sing, then the whole school should not be allowed to sing them. I then asked what if all of the school's students except that one really want to sing the traditional carols. She insisted that she was strongly pro-choice for individuals, and no school group should impose their choices on any individual. Her colleagues voiced their support for her "courageous" stance.

I accepted their views for the moment, but later in the seminar, I raised another issue. Suppose in a sex education class, a 14-year-old student brings a letter from his parents that he does not want to attend classes which teach him such things as putting on condoms correctly, teach him that only homophobes oppose same-sex marriage, and teach him that sexual abstinence is impossible to live up to. The teachers buzzed for a while, and then one stood and stated that his school's policy is that the student would be allowed to leave the class and do homework in the library, but the class will continue. I then asked the obvious question: Why with a pro-choice policy, would the Christmas carols be banned because of the choice of one individual student, and the sex education classes continue, though without the offended student?

The teachers poured various answers upon me, and the gist of all of them was that the Christmas carols do not serve the common good of education while the sex education classes do. It was confirmed for me that Progressive education's politicized common good was not in any literal sense the good of the many. Their common good was what they believed served their agenda for what the collective ought to be taught, regardless if their desired collective was really not of, by and for the people.

Progressive education is fraught with such flawed philosophy. Collectivism triumphs over the individual or even the majority of the individuals only to make the collective conform to the morality and politics the Progressives aim to instantiate.

2.   Utopianism and the Limitless Perfectibility of Humanity.

Progressives' zealous belief in collectivism, even when it makes little logical sense, is related to their undaunted commitment that a society, a nation and even the world can be engineered into a utopia wherein egalitarianism, peace and justice reign, and evil is eliminated. Like the "New Prometheus," Progressives further believe that their government education systems, as well as a "nanny state" which regulates out of existence all risks, such as health, motor vehicle, and employment, can transform and perfect humanity. Their vision of utopia through government engineering is their supreme value for the collective. If individuals do not accept their utopian vision, no matter even if it is the majority, they are, for the Progressives, just not enlightened, not fully evolved and have to be engineered by government education and legislation to be made to conform. They must learn to hope and change properly, in order to abide by the superior vision of the Progressives, because that vision is the only way in which utopian ideals can be achieved and evil eliminated. Progressive utopianism is the moral standard: whatever serves that vision is good, whatever contradicts it is evil.

Today, after the horrific shooting tragedies in Newtown, Connecticut and Aurora, Colorado, Progressive educators are convinced that madmen with guns must be eliminated to secure the path to utopia. It is not the madmen on which they focus, however, but it is the guns which must be eliminated. Progressive educators throughout the U.S. now believe that all students of any age must be engineered to reject, if not despise guns or any weapons, for that matter, which includes even imaginary guns and weapons. Their zeal has resulted in some bizarre cases.

A seven-year-old child was punished by suspension from school for chewing on his pastry in such a way that according to his teacher it sort of looked like a hand gun. The child's protests that he never intended to chew his pastry into a gun shape were dismissed as irrelevant. Another young child playing an imaginary game with an empty box on the school playground was also suspended. He was pretending that he was a virtuous warrior and had trapped all evil in the world in the box, and then exploded the box destroying all the evil. The child, of course, could not understand that the imaginary evil he pretended was the wrong sort of evil the Progressive teachers and administrators imagined as threatening their utopian vision. The Progressive imagination of evil punished and suppressed the child's imagination: even the imaginations of children should be engineered when they do not align with Progressives' imagined utopia.

3.   Nature Is a Construct.

This principle in regard to practice is interpreted quite literally. Physical and biological nature is defined by the Progressives in whatever manner fulfills their utopian designs. Nature becomes, then, a malleable, fluid phenomenon configured by political conceptions. Laws of nature are not firm but are constructed and reconstructed to support the Progressives' agenda, including within educational curricula. Certainly, the

New Progressivism is an extreme politicization of Dewey's re-construction in philosophy, society and education.

Two of the most troubling examples of the politicized re-construction of nature are in regard to sexual biology and en-vironmental science. In sex education classes, Progressives teach that homosexuality is genetically determined. A homo-sexual has no choice in regard to his or her sexual identity and practice. In this way, homosexuality is constructed as a natural phenomenon, and homosexual practice should not be de-nounced as immoral because a homosexual is only doing what comes naturally. At the same time, however, Progressives teach that sexual gender is a social construct. They even posit five diverse genders which ought to be socially and politically rec-ognized, namely, heterosexual, lesbian, gay, bisexual and transgender.

It is indeed the case that social influences do contribute to forming gender roles, but to maintain that gender is entirely a social construct is simply to ignore the laws of nature regarding genetic and chromosomal make-up: xx is female and xy is male. Progressives, therefore, on the one hand appeal to "genetic de-terminism" to claim that homosexuality is "natural", and, on the other hand, dismiss natural genetics and chromosomes to support their politics of gender diversity. This contradiction does not matter because for them nature is such a malleable construct. Natural science is politicized science in service of educating students in the social justice of sexuality and gender that the Progressives advocate.

Another area in which nature is constructed to advance the Progressive agenda is the phenomenon of "global warming." Students are taught as unassailable fact that human-caused global warming, or climate change, is a dire threat to global justice. Rich nations are destroying the planet with their carbon pollution and causing poorer nations and people to suffer the threats of massive natural catastrophes, like hurricanes, tsunamis, and droughts. Rich nations should therefore be punished and be made to pay poor nations for "carbon credits" to compensate for the injustice they are perpetrating. This process would redistribute the wealth of rich nations to poor nations in order to rectify the evil injustice.

In schools the students are taught that the planet must be saved from global warming and the global redistribution of wealth is the way to do it. Students are not taught, however, the "inconvenient truth" that there has not been any global warming for about a decade and a half. As the Economist magazine reports, "Over the past 15 years air temperatures at the earth's surface have been flat while greenhouse emissions have continued to soar." The Economist continues that, "The world added roughly about 100 billion tons of carbon to the atmosphere between 2000 and 2010. That is about a quarter of all the CO_2 put there by humanity since 1750."[5]

The warming trend has stopped, at least for 15 years, which contradicts the models and forecasts of the climate change experts. But this is not taught to students and is not communicated by Progressive political leaders. The data do not conform to the agenda, so they are simply dismissed. Schools continue to make students fearful about the looming global warming cataclysms, organize special "Earth Day" events to inspire students' pursuit of economic justice, and praise students who are striving to make themselves and their families "Go Green." To paraphrase the Protagorean dictum, Progressive politics is the measure of all natural things.

4.   Moral and Epistemological Relativism

In his January 2013 State of the Union Address, President Obama, the Progressive in Chief, exhorted the nation that Americans should not "mistake absolutism for politics . . . ". His words were directed at other politicians and citizens who hold to certain objective truths and firmly, absolutely establish their political principles upon such truths. Though Obama did not say explicitly that a "right to life" political position based on the absolute evil of abortion was such "mistaken absolutism," the implication was apparent. Obama's denunciation of absolutism thrilled the Progressives, for whom moral and epistemological relativism are trademarks of their beliefs and their university-governmental educational complex.

Progressive relativism permeates education in a variety of pernicious ways. One clear example is the cult of "critical thinking" that has ascended. John Dewey championed teaching critical thinking as a necessity for accomplishing his educational reform.[6] What it has become, unfortunately, bears little resemblance to the logic and rhetoric he advocated. So, then, what does "critical thinking" mean today in Progressive education?

An anecdote from experience will serve to show how critical thinking is understood in the university. At a university faculty meeting a few years ago, the faculty decided to make critical thinking a key learning outcome for all students. A colleague then asked, but what is critical thinking? Another colleague from the Psychology Department spoke and said bluntly that to teach critical thinking, we must teach skepticism. The psychologist continued with words to the effect that to think critically, the students must learn to be skeptical of all truths; they must learn to be skeptical of so-called objective, universal and absolute truths; they must learn to question what is fact and question all authority. Most of the rest of the faculty murmured agreement with the psychologist, but I was actually frightened. I asked why critical thinking was not logical reasoning, which is a cognitive tool for inquiring into truth. The "truth" part of my claim was strongly denounced since, of course, truth is unattainable. Then, various faculty also began to reject the "logical reasoning" part of my statement, since for them critical thinking can be done by the imagination without involving logic or reasoning whatsoever. At this point I realized that serious philosophical discourse was just impossible.

For Progressives, critical thinking today is a Sophistic exercise, imaginative opinions replace reasoned argumentation. There are no criteria, no logical principles, no rules for correct reasoning to assess these opinions, except whether they advance or obstruct the political agenda of Progressivism. A student is assessed as having advanced critical thinking skills if he or she can accurately express, in writing or orally, the politically correct views of the Progressives. Critical thinking has become another construct fabricated to serve the Progressive vision.

In line with the relativistic construction of critical thinking is the way in which social research design and methods are defined and taught by Progressives. In Colin Robson's widely used university textbook entitled ironically, Real World Research, he offers an enumerated list of the traits of "A Realist View of Science." Trait #1, the prime directive, reads, "There is no unquestionable foundation for science, no 'facts' that are beyond dispute. Knowledge is a social and historical product. 'Facts' are theory-laden."[7]

Epistemological relativism and constructivism permeate this directive. With Robson's popular view, any sort of scientific research begins in skepticism, there are no basic facts, no foundational truths and all knowledge is relative to the time and social conditions in which it is asserted. This is today's Progressive version of scientific research and realism. With such beginnings in skepticism, how can the ends of scientific research be anything but more skepticism?

In regard to Progressivism's moral relativism, another example from the Leadership and Ethics seminars I conducted for teachers will be illuminating. In introducing the Ethics portion of the seminar, I asked the teachers if they accepted objective, universal standards for right and wrong, good and evil. A secondary school Social Studies teacher at a back table with his colleagues raised his hand and proclaimed that there was no real right and wrong in ethics; it was all relative to different cultures. If something is wrong for one culture, then it is wrong for that culture. The exact same thing could be right in another culture, and thereby it is right for that culture. We should not, moreover, ever impose our cultural standards on a different culture because to do so would be to disrespect that other culture. There are no higher ethical standards that can and should be applied to all cultures. His tablemate colleagues and many other teachers in the room voiced their agreement, and I was dismayed to realize that their young students are victims of their Progressive confusion.

After collecting my wits, I asked the Social Studies teacher whether he would agree that human slavery, the buying and selling of human beings, is always wrong. At first he seemed stunned by the question, but then, perhaps pursuing a foolish consistency, he exclaimed, "No! It depends on the culture. If a culture accepts slavery, then it is right for them, and no one from another culture that thinks slavery is evil should judge the slavery or try to eliminate it." At this point, a table in front with mostly African-American teachers erupted. They vociferously and aggressively challenged the Social Studies teacher, and he and his like-minded colleagues in the room tried to defend themselves. I stood back and let the debate melee run its course. The African-Americans and their supporters won: human slavery is always wrong. After things had sufficiently calmed down, I resumed discussing ethics, though with the principled basis that there really are some universal right and wrongs.

This scene was a clear illustration of the moral and epistemological confusion which Progressivism imposes upon students. Without education in genuine critical reasoning, without an appreciation of truths in science, and without an understanding of the perils of relativism, Progressives and their educational systems should ultimately implode, collapse in upon themselves. This implosion, however, will likely not happen as long as the Progressives continue to control the universities, advance their seductive collectivist utopian vision, and maintain their politics within the university-governmental educational complex.

This essay has hopefully exposed and illustrated the deteriorating condition of US education in the grips the New Progressivism. The homeschooling and alternative education options are legitimate and growing, but truly at this time they are nothing but an irritant for the Progressives. As the theme of this World Congress specifies, education is at a crossroads, though Progressives are presently turning it in the direction of their imagined utopia. Only solid commitment from educators and graced wisdom can nudge Progressivism away from veering toward and finally crashing within the dystopian future they want for all of us

References and Notes

1. This paper was presented at: "Philosophical Reflections on the 'New Progressivism' in Education," The <u>Twelfth International Congress of Philosophy on the Future of Western Civilization</u>, Theme: Education at the Crossroads, John Paul II Catholic University of Lublin, Poland, April 2013.
2. "A Brief Overview of Progressive Education," http://www.uvm.edu/~dewey/articles/proged.html.
3. "Educational Progressivism," http://www.progressiveliving.org/ progressivism
4. "Progressivism's Journal," http://progressivism.livejournal.com/profile
5. Reported in "Global Temperature Not Up" by Rich Lowry," *Wheeling Intelligencer*," 4/3/13. References are from "Global Warming Apocalypse: Perhaps a Little Later," *The Economist*, March 30, 2013.
6. See *ibid*. Footnote #2 above.
7. Colin Robson, *Real World Research*, Third Edition (The Atrium, UK: John Wiley and Sons, Ltd., 2011) p. 61.

Progressive Higher Education:
Through Homogeneity to Ideal Diversity[1]
June 2017

ABSTRACT

This essay exposes the ways in which the Progressive pursuit of 'diversity' in U.S. higher education is not actually diversity at all but ideological homogeneity. After citing numerous instances of diversity mongering on campuses, an axiological analysis of Progressive diversity is offered to show clearly why and how their diversity is really uniformity. Throughout the essay, much attention is given to Progressive diversity and Catholic education, since such diversity and Progressivism in general are dealing perhaps a mortal blow to the future of Catholic higher education.

Progressivism reigns in U.S. higher education. This is true of both public and private education, including religiously affiliated institutions. With Catholic institutions, there are 210 schools which award baccalaureate and graduate degrees,[2] but only about 9% of them could be called "traditionally Catholic," and, thereby, not entirely under the rule of Progressivism.[3]

Progressivism is a multifaceted ideology encompassing economic collectivism, multicultural utopianism, constructivism, and moral and epistemological relativism. This essay, however, will not offer a critique of those facets as that already has been done at this Future of Western Civilization International Congress series. The papers are, "Diversity within United States' Culture and Politics" (2011),[4] and "Philosophical Reflections on the 'New Progressivism' in Education" (2013).[5] This focus, then, will be an extended axiological analysis of the Progressive dedication to, or perhaps obsession with, diversity.

Progressive "diversity" in higher education is actually a mere shibboleth, a value-laden ideological catchword that inspires the loyalists but actually lacks substantial meaning. The diversity to which Progressives are devoted denotes their ideal of a university, and society in general, committed to multiculturalism with total equality as the supreme value. Such equality requires a reformation to eliminate the oppression of the victimized, those groups that have been oppressed because of their ethnicity, religion, race, gender and sexual identity. And, of course, this reformation for equal justice is only possible by conforming fully to all facets of the ideology of Progressivism. Progressive "ideal diversity" cannot and does not tolerate any opposition from those who are deemed 'oppressors.' The ideas, the philosophies, the teachings, the political votes, and even the very presence of oppressors within Progressive educational institutions and society at large, must be suppressed, eliminated, if the reformation is to win its cause for equal justice. Only unadulterated purity, undifferentiated homogeneity, can achieve the realization of the Progressives' ideological utopia.

This critical analysis of Progressive axiology proceeds by: 1) Citing and commenting on a number of recent incidents at higher education institutions, both at public and Catholic schools; 2) Examining in detail the Progressive axiology and its consequences; and finally, 3) Offering some remarks on what the future could hold for Catholic higher education within the reign of Progressivism.

Diversity Disturbances

The Progressives' zeal to achieve their ideal diversity through ideological conformity and suppressing the oppressors is causing grave consternation about the interchange of ideas and free speech in higher education. It has also led to questions regarding the maturity of university students, faculty and administrators who are fully supportive of some bizarre demonstrations and raucous, even riotous, uprisings on campuses.

Progressives, however, appear to be indifferent to any criticism. They, especially the students, self-identify as mature, serious persons who are morally enlightened. To borrow some terms from Aristotle but use them in rather satirical ways, the Progressives believe firmly that they are the spoudaioi, the moral exemplars. Their values and beliefs are beyond the good and evil of the bourgeois masses. Those who disagree with, criticize or oppose them are the deplorables, the phauloi who are afflicted with a low or base morality. The phauloi must not challenge but always defer to the spoudaioi, and if they don't, they must be silenced. On too many campuses, the Progressive spoudaioi have stifled, even anathematized, free intellectual discourse and authentic inquiry for truth.

The campus disturbances urged by the Progressives are widespread. They include:

- Southern Illinois University hosted a month-long series of student "nap-ins" to help guide them on their "internal journey to diversity." There are four two-hour nap sessions in which students can dream about diversity, and then upon waking, write about their dreams on a shared scroll.[6] Progressives, apparently, are not deterred that their ideal, utopian diversity belongs in a dream-world, even if might be nothing more than a pipe-dream.

- Cornell University held a "cry-in" for students who were terrified by the election of President Donald Trump. Cornell staff provided the weeping and wailing students with tissues and hot chocolate to comfort them in their sorrow.[7] The University of Kansas announced to students that they can visit therapy dogs every other Wednesday for consolation over the horrible Trump victory. The Progressive *spou-daioi* evidently believe that their public grief disturbances should be a moral exemplar for all.[8]

- At Pierce College in Los Angeles a student was told to stop handing out free copies of a Spanish-language edition of the U.S. Constitution. He was instructed to apply for a permit to distribute the pocket Constitution in the "free speech zone" only. And, if he did not comply, he would be asked to leave campus. Progressive control of campus speech must be absolute, even if it regards distributing the very document that establishes the law protecting free speech.[9]

- The disturbance at elite Middlebury College is perhaps the most extreme example of a Progressive war on free speech through a suppression of a diversity of ideas. The enemy was the noted conservative social scientist Charles Murray, author of The Bell Curve about groups' IQs and Coming Apart about the struggles of the white working class from 1960-2010. Irate student protestors prevented the start of Murray's talk by yelling and slamming furniture. Murray was moved to another venue. His talk was delivered, although the ending discussion with Professor Allison Stanger, who was to debate Murray, had to be moved to yet another room for a live-streamed presentation. When protestors found that room, they pounded on the windows and pulled fire alarms. Murray and Stanger exited at the end of the live-stream but were assailed by the protestors who shoved and grabbed Stanger, pounded on their car and obstructed its departure. Stanger went to the hospital and wrote later that she feared for her life.[10] The speech thuggery of the Middlebury protestors is consistent with their "beyond good and evil" values and their objective to silence and eliminate the opposition.

In spite of Pope Francis's warnings and admonitions about Progressivism, most Catholic universities have let themselves become as subordinate to the Progressive reign as any other school. In 2013, Pope Francis sharply denounced the "hegemonic uniformity" of "the single line of thought" spawned by a "spirit of adolescent progressivism": it is a worldliness that will negotiate everything, even the faith. With such immaturity, the mentality is that "any move forward and any choice is better than remaining within the routine of fidelity."[11] Catholic universities, nonetheless, are negotiating their faith and values to show that they too are worthy of being morally enlightened Progressive spoudaioi.

- A student government representative at Catholic Duquesne University urged the University to withdraw its plans to invite the popular fast-food restaurant, Chik-fil-A, to open a franchise on campus. Students were upset that the restaurant chain's CEO has publicly supported traditional marriage, although the chain's policy and practice on serving customers and hiring employees upholds non-discrimination. The Progressive students can't allow a genuine diversity of moral values, even when the value conforms to the Catholicism of the university they have chosen to attend.[12]

- A College Republican student group at the Vincentian DePaul University was prohibited to advertise a meeting with a flier that read, "Unborn Lives Matter." DePaul's President Rev. Dennis Holtschneider stated that the poster was an example of "bigotry that occurs under the cover of free speech." Rev. Holtschneider clearly believed that the conservative students' flier intended to wound the "Black Lives Matter" group on campus. Rev. Holtschneider explained that De Paul does allow diverse thought on campus, as long as it isn't "meant to cause distress." Within the blinkered ideological absolutism of regnant Progressivism, there is not the slightest cognizance of the wicked irony that a Catholic university censors students who seek to promote the moral values of Catholicism itself.[13]

- Student protestors at Notre Dame University oppose the University's invitation to U. S. Vice President Mike Pence, a native and former governor of Notre Dame's state of Indiana, to be the 2017 graduation commencement speaker. As a student leader said, she and her peers felt "unsafe" and threatened "by someone who openly is offensive but also demeaning of their humanity and of their life and of their identity." In 2016 Notre Dame awarded then VP Joe Biden, a Progressive Catholic, the Laetare Medal for outstanding service to the Catholic Church and society. Progressive students now, however, can't even abide the presence of a public official like Pence whose values do not conform. It disturbingly recalls Robespierre's Reign of Terror and his Committee for Public Safety: Notre Dame Progressives basically want Mike Pence banned because he presents a public safety hazard.[14]

- In October 2014 a philosophy class, Theory of Ethics, at Marquette University became the scene of a Progressive LBGT diversity disturbance. An undergraduate student talked to the instructor after class expressing his view that same-sex married couples should not be allowed to adopt children. He did so because he wanted to explore the issue of children's rights to a mother and father, and because the instructor had not allowed a discussion of the issue in class. During the one-on-one discussion with the student, the instructor apparently became frustrated proclaiming, "In this class, homophobic comments, racist comments, will not be tolerated," and then invited the student to drop the class.[15] This disturbance has since escalated into a major case, with the suspension of a traditionally Catholic Marquette professor who advocated on behalf of the student. National Catholic and conservative foundations became involved and a court case is still pending. When it comes to their diversity agenda, the Progressive academy will not let Catholicism, philosophical integrity, or the best interests of students hinder their cause.

- As a final instance of a diversity disturbance, it is important to show that U.S. Catholic universities are far from alone in their Progressive obeisance. In March 2017, at the Catholic University of Louvain (UCL) in Belgium, a philosophy lecturer was suspended by the administration for distributing a pro-life paper to his students. The lecturer indicated that he says to his class "repeatedly that no one should feel forced to agree with me." He lamented that, "I did my job, and I'm now under a disciplinary procedure which doesn't make any sense to me." In a press release, the University justified its action by claiming, ". . . in the spirt of the Act decriminalizing abortion voted in 1990 [in Belgium], it (UCL) respects the autonomy of women to make this choice, in the circumstances specified by the legislature."[16] The Progressive Caesars obviously believe that the morality of their ideology is due <u>everything</u> academic, and all teaching, values, and student learning must be rendered unto the Caesars.

The Transvaluation of All Values

Friedrich Nietzsche's transvaluation of all values called for a reassessment of bourgeois Christianity since, among other ills, it repressed sexuality and promoted the weaknesses of humility and piety. Within higher education, Progressives are prosecuting a transvaluation with their ideal diversity as a principal value. In Progressive axiology, equality is the supreme value. Social justice is their end and selective tolerance is a means for achieving egalitarian diversity. Their tolerance is selective because what opposes their agenda is unjust and not to be tolerated. Their ideal diversity, for example, prizes free speech only insofar as it does not cause any distress within the ideological homogeneity of their diversity safe zones.

This Progressive axiology is clearly articulated by Lynn Pasquerella, President of the Association of American Colleges and Universities (AACU). The AACU is a highly influential organization which in many ways contributes to establishing the guiding principles for government funding, student grants and loans, and accreditation of colleges and universities by national organizations. This accreditation aspect is very important as without accreditation, no institution can receive government funding for student grants and loans.

In her statement of April 4, 2017, "Free Expression, Liberal Education and Inclusive Excellence,"[17] Pasquerella identifies the Progressive academic mission of the transvaluation of the historically oppressive U.S. society. As she states,

> . . . if we fail to help our students connect their education to broader societal issues, in ways that inspire them to lead change in a society still challenged by profound inequities, we abnegate our responsibility to promote engaged citizenship, cultural empathy, pluralism, and diversity as the foundation for our nation's historic mission of educating for democracy.

The AACU affirms that quality in liberal education is bound to equity, and with cultural empathy, tolerant inclusivity, and sensitivity to universal victimization, higher education must realize that:

> None of today's students arrives on college and university campuses devoid of past experiences, pain, and suffering that influence their worldviews. Redressing past and present injustices mandates aligning our expertise as teachers, scholars, researchers, and artists to rewrite the dominant narrative that consigns to the lower shelves of history the contributions of marginalized groups that have shaped American society in profound, albeit often unacknowledged, ways.

Tolerant inclusivity, a means to achieving diversity justice, is a criterion for determining the parameters of free speech and a free exchange of ideas. As Pasquerella says:

> . . . a complex identity politics has fueled controversies over the legitimacy of "safe spaces," the disinvitation

and shouting down of speakers, and a pervasive en-
forced illiberalism on campuses. Student support
around a wide range of diversity and inclusion issues
highlight the extent to which the conclusions we draw
regarding whether arguments and assertions in support
of limiting speech are rational and warranted depend,
in part, on whose stories are being told and who is doing the speaking. They offer a counternarrative to the
dominate discourse that has traditionally marginalized
the voices of women, students and faculty of color, religious and ethnic minorities, and members of the
LBGTQIA[18] community. . . . These protestors regard
their actions as justified on the grounds of necessity
and attempts to stop them as further silencing those
representing the most vulnerable members of society.

To paraphrase George Orwell from *Animal Farm*, it appears
that for the AACU, everyone on campus has free speech, but
some have more free speech than others.[19] Those with heightened free speech are the representatives of the vulnerable. Silencing oppressors is justified since they are merely phauloi,
and the heroic protesting spoudaioi have the morally superior
just cause of Progressive ideal diversity. The Progressive Reich
has been formalized, legitimized and institutionalized by the
AACU.

Hoping Against Hope

The origin of this section title is Biblical from Romans 4:18.
The aged, physically decrepit Abraham had been promised by
God that he would become the father of many nations. For
Abraham, this seemed hopeless, but he maintained his faith.

Abraham "hoped against hope"[20] that God's promise would be fulfilled.

It is scandalous and grossly dispiriting that a mere 9% of U.S. Catholic universities are, in varying ways, solid in maintaining the Catholic tradition. The Catholic educational charism of moral and intellectual formation is certainly an endangered species on the brink of extinction. Is there any hope for recovery?

There is perhaps a slight ray of hope and this is emitted by U.S. governmental tradition itself. Even the AACU affirms that according to U.S. Constitutional law, private universities, such as Catholic institutions, are not bound by First Amendment free speech considerations, "except under certain specified state laws." Private institutions can "constrain speech in classrooms, open forums and through the refusal to grant the use of their facilities. They are permitted to do so if the restrictions constitute reasonable regulations, consistent with their missions, and are deemed necessary to achieve their objectives."[21]

If Catholic institutions take their charism seriously, they do not, by law, have to make an idol of a Progressive-styled social justice mission and can faithfully self-identify as Catholic. They can hire the faculty and administration they choose, include or exclude guest speakers according to their sympathies with Catholicism, require faculty to teach content consistent with Church teaching, and, unless and until there are radical revolutionary changes undermining Constitutional laws, continue to receive government funding. Again, by law, no Catholic institution has to permit administrators, faculty or speakers to spew anti-Catholic propaganda simply in order to ensure the Progressive supreme value of a so-called 'equal balance' of views.

In order to recover, Catholic schools will have to be open to the grace of the kind of courageous faith that empowered Abraham to hope against hope. This will not happen en masse with Catholic schools, but its rate of occurrence will be slow, gradualistic, one controversial issue, one Catholic institution at a time. And, believing in a teaching from *Ex Corde Ecclesiae* can help with spiritual resolve:[22] *Ex Corde* extols dialogue, including between faith and reason and "the gospel and culture." But it's the responsibility of a Catholic university to aim this dialogue toward the pursuit of truth. As Saint John Paul the Great taught, the "privileged task" of a Catholic university is "to unite . . . the search for truth, and the certainty of already knowing the fount of truth." Having faith that God is the fount of truth must necessarily illumine any Catholic institution's chances of recovery.

References and Notes

1. This paper was presented at: "Progressive Higher Education: Through Homogeneity to Ideal Diversity," Sixteenth International Congress of Philosophy on the Future of Western Civilization, Theme: The Catholic University: Risks and Opportunities, June 8-9, 2017, John Paul II Catholic University of Lublin, Lublin, Poland
2. This 2016 statistic is based on the Association of Catholic Colleges and Universities, https://www.accunet.org/14a/pages/index.cfm?pageid=3797.
3. This figure is based on Cardinal Newman Society's, "Recommended Colleges," https://cardinalnewmansociety.org/recommended-colleges/

4. Thomas Michaud, "Roznorodnosc w kulturze: polityce Stanow Zjednoczonych," in *Emigracja I cywilizacje*, Czlowiek w Kulturze, 23 (2013), pp. 63-73

5. Thomas Michaud, "Filozoficzne refleksje nt. 'Nowego Progressywizmu' w edukacji," Philosophical Reflections on the 'New Progressivism' in Education," The Twelfth International Congress of Philosophy on the Future of Western Civilization, Theme: Education at the Crossroads, John Paul II Catholic University of Lublin, Poland, April 2013.

6. Reported by Anthony Gockowski at: https://campus-esform.org/?ID=8896

7. Reported by John Hayward at: http://www.breitbart.com/big-government/2016/11/16/5-most-absurd-way-the-left-has-responded-to-the-2016-election/.

8. Reported November 11, 2016. http://breaking 911.com/colleges-offer-hot-chocolate-therapy-dogs-play-doh-students-trump-victory/

9. Reported by Sheriff David Clarke, Jr. at: http://www.patheos.com/blogs/davidclarke/2017/03/college-students-banned-handing-constitution-unless-free-speech-zone/

10. This brief account of the Middlebury College disturbance is based on the editorials: Rich Lowry, "It Will Go Down As 'Battle of Middlebury College'," Wheeling Intelligencer, 3-11-17; Laura Hollis, "The Left's Revolutions Always Turn Out Like This," Wheeling Intelligencer, 3-14-17; Thomas Sowell, "Real Lessons of Middlebury, Wheeling Intelligencer, 3/15/17.

11. Pope Francis made the remarks in his daily homily, 18 November, 2013. See: http://www.asianews.it/news-

en/Pope-God-save-us-from-the-hegemonic-uni-
formity/%E2%80%9D-of-the-one-live-of-thought-fruit-
of-the-world-that-regoliates-everything-even-faith/.

12. Reported at: http://www.wtae.com/article/donald-
trump-jr-mocks-duquesne-university-students-concern-
over-chick-fil-a/927547.

13. Nicholas Hahn, "What Passes for 'free' speech on a Catholic campus," The Detroit News. October 24, 2016.

14. Michelle Malkin. "Inciting Violence on Campus," Wheeling Sunday News-Register, April 16, 2017.

15. This account of the Marquette disturbance draws from:
Robert Oscar Lopez, "Catholic Higher Education in Ru-
ins," 15 December, 2014, *Religion in the Public Square* at
www.thepublicdiscourse.com/2014/12/14192/.

16. Reported by Miciah Bilger, "This Catholic University has
Suspended Pro-Life Lecturer for Opposing Abortion,"
March 31, 2017, at: http://www.lifenews.com/category/
international/.

17. Lynn Pasquerella, "Free Expression, Liberal Education
and Inclusive Excellence," April 4, 2017, at:
http://www.aacu.org/about/statements/2017/free-ex-
pression. All of the following quoted material is from this
document.

18. The acronym LBGTQIA stands for: Lesbian Bisexual Gay
Transgender Queer Intersex Asexual.

19. George Orwell, Animal Farm (New York: Signet Classics,
1996). The famous quote is on p. 134: "All Animals are
equal, but some are more equal than others."

20. The New American Bible (Nashville: Thomas Nelson Pub-
lishers, 1983) Romans, 4:18, p. 1216.

21. Ibid., Note #16 above.

22. The following remarks include quotes from <u>Ex Corde</u> cited in and other paraphrased material from Adam Cassandra, "Free Speech Doesn't Require Colleges to Sponsor their Opponents," at: http://thefederalist.com/2016/06/01/free-speech-doesn't-require-colleges-to-sponsor-their-opponents/.

Happiness Lost: The Ravages of Nihilism[1]
June 2018

In this past Spring 2018 semester the most popular class ever at Yale University was held, PSYC 157: Psychology and the Good Life. About 1200 students, nearly one-fourth of all Yale undergraduates, were enrolled.[2] The subject matter was happiness. Dr. Laurie Santos, the course's professor, focused on both positive psychology, the characteristics that allow humans to flourish, and behavioral change, in order to motivate students to live by the courses' lessons. Santos calls the lesson-based changes "rewirement assignments.[3] She explains that, "Students want to change, to be happier themselves, and to change the culture here on campus."[4] She continues by speculating that the interest in the class is so great because in high school the Yale students "had to deprioritize their happiness to gain admission to the school, adopting harmful life habits that have led to "the mental health crises we're seeing at places like Yale!"[5]

Why is this class with its huge enrollment so remarkable? Why should this "happiness course" phenomenon receive serious philosophical attention? The principal reason is that what happens at Yale is often a bellwether sign for cultural conditions, and in this situation, it is the culture of millennial generation students.[6] Generational cultures contribute to defining civilizations, and if millennials are grossly unhappy and clueless as to what authentic happiness is, then their generation portends, to some degree, a civilizational crisis: 'happiness lost' must be recognized as a symptom of civilizational decline.

The course, moreover, is hailed as a panacea for millennial mental health problems. Millennials are probably the most medicated, most in-therapy, most depression-suffering, most tech-dependent, and most in-debt generation in history. Rachelle Hampton in her article titled, "'Happiness 101' Courses Are a Necessary Stop-Gap for the Campus Mental Health Crises" states that,

> Almost 50 percent of students surveyed by the American College Health Association in 2016 reported feeling that things were hopeless – and almost 37 percent reported feeling 'so depressed that it was difficult to function' during the previous 12 months. Clearly, colleges must make their mental health services more robust; but in the meantime, classes like Santos' are filling a huge need – just ask the 24 teaching fellows hired to help manage her massively attended course."[7]

So, why are millennials so unhappy, so depressed? Why don't they have some understanding of what happiness really is? And, will 'Happiness 101' courses and more extensive mental health services really make a difference?

William Donohue observes that it is not only Yale, since courses in positive psychology are immensely popular all over the nation, and all have a common goal, namely to make students happier.[8] Positive psychology is predicated on affirming that happiness can be taught and learned in a course. Donohue, however, questions that claim. He argues that,

> Happiness can be acquired but to say that it can be learned, and taught in a classroom, is not only a stretch, it is deceiving. No one doubts there are aids, exercises, and tips that can be tapped when we are down, but there are no shortcuts, or cheat sheets, that can be accessed to make us happy.[9]

Positive psychology's clever behavior modification rewirement techniques, such as getting more sleep, dismissing class so students could intentionally relax without worrying about their studies, and the personal self-improvement "Hack Yo'Self Project," might indeed be worthwhile stress-reduction and overcoming-the-blues measures. But is happiness, the good life, nothing more than the stress-free, I'm-in-a-good-mood life? Positive psychology, as Donohue implies, is rather shallow in regard to understanding what happiness really is. In addition, it is questionable whether positive psychology and its "pitch-professors" understand fully the depths of the millennials' happiness dysfunctions.

For instance, Clapit, a social media entertainment network, reports on a December 2016 survey it commissioned from YouGov PLC, a third-party professional research and consulting organization.[10] The survey's 2,450 respondents revealed that: one in twelve millennials would completely detach themselves from their family to become famous; one in 10 would rather be famous than go to college or even graduate; one in nine would rather be famous than get married; and one in six would forego having children for the possibility of fame.[11] Clearly, there is a more profound happiness problem with millennials than what positive psychology addresses. With the growing belief that fame, which is fake happiness, ephemeral, not under one's control, and entirely dependent on others' view of oneself, is really happiness, then millennials are truly suffering from a more disturbing existential malignancy. What is their cultural malady?

Not to dismiss serious cases of clinical depression and other mental illnesses, the millennial cultural affliction can be philosophically diagnosed as existential dread which causes a low-grade nihilism. This dread is a creeping feeling of unheimlich-keit, to borrow a Heideggerian term: it is a sense of "not-at-homeness" within reality; it is an unsettling anxiety; an inarticulate fear and trembling about what is truly real.

The millennial mind and their cultural disposition have been shaped by a barrage of uncanny constructs that have alienated them from the real. They are required to self-identify. They must choose their own sexual-construct identity since the reality of biological nature is not a valid determinant. They must self-identify within an appropriate racial/ethnic group or tribe, and accept the de-individualizing construct-traits of the group, including the racial/ethnic, moral or immoral traits of being privileged or oppressed. They must live with the climate-change construct of planetary ecological apocalypse unless they affirm the "inconvenient truth" and identify with save-the-planet politics. They must create themselves on social media. Their virtual "identities" must conform to the construct-mores of their millennial culture, or else they won't get enough "likes," "retweets" and "reposts" to confirm their worth as a person.

Millennial existential dread is felt because they have little sense of the real. Their construct-mediated selves are alien to who and what they are as real human persons. Because they are not engaged with the real, the separation anxiety they feel can bring on the low-grade nihilism. It is "low-grade" because it is not typically an all-consuming nihilism which paralyzes them, rendering them morbidly inactive. They continue with their lives, their survival, but fail to experience a durable happiness. It is the nihilism of a metaphysical, epistemological and moral relativism that occludes any appreciation of the nature of Being, the joy of discovering Truth, and the confidence in the rectitude of virtues over the turpitude of vices.

The classical notion that human persons flourish, experience happiness, when as individuals they fulfill their human potentials in virtuous ways is unknown to millennials. In fact, they would greet such a proposition with skepticism, disbelief, and even scorn.

Millennials' constructs cannot reckon with a moral order of virtues, much less admit that there is some sort of objective, universal truth of their human being and of Being in general. Still, their nagging dread intimates that something is missing, and although their constructs are felt to be inadequate, they cannot find the real happiness they desire. They may endeavor to "hope against hope" for happiness, but, finally, hopelessness prevails. For the millennials, happiness has been lost, and a generational culture without authentic happiness bodes very ill for the civilization of which it is a part.

References and Notes

1. This paper was presented at: "Happiness Lost: The Ravages of Nihilism," <u>The Seventeenth International Philosophy Congress on the Future of Western Civilization,</u> Theme: Civilization of Freedom or Civilization of Totalitarianism, June 4-8, 2018, John Paul II Catholic University of Lublin, Lublin, Poland.
2. David Shimer, *Yale's Most Popular Class Ever: Happiness,* The New York Times, https://www.nytimes.com/2018/

01/26/nyregion/at-yale-class-on-happiness-draws-huge-crowd-laurie-santos.html.

3. Ibid.

4. Ibid.

5. Ibid.

6. The exact dates which bracket the millennial generation are somewhat fluid and debatable, however, the years 1982-2004 stipulated by William Strauss and Neil Howe are a common benchmark (See, https://en.wikipedia.org/wiki/Strauss-Howe_generational_theory).

7. Rachelle Hampton, *'Happiness 101' Courses Are a Necessary Stop-Gap for the Campus Mental Health Crisis,* January 30, 2018 at: https://slate.com/human_interest/2018/01/happiness-101-college-courses_are-a-mental-health-stop-gap-html

8. William Donohue, "Happiness Eludes College Students," in *Catalyst* (Vol.45, No. 2, March 2018) p.3.

9. Ibid.

10. Kayla Inserra, "The New Dream Job: More than a Quarter of Millennials Would Quit their Job to Become Famous," January 2017 at: http://clapit.com/press/the-new-dream-job/

11. Ibid.

Section VII

Short Story

Section Introduction

I decided to include this short story in this volume because it created such a memorable time for my colleagues and friends, American and Polish. Still, it wasn't just the story, it was Piotr Jaroszynski's version of it and its subsequent publication in a high-end glossy magazine that affirmed the story as a tale of our international and philosophical comradery. It was an entertaining story, but Piotr's rendition of it gave it a depth that I had not previously realized.

One evening after dinner in Lublin, Poland, Spring 2004 our host, Piotr Jaroszynski, asked me to tell a story. It was my first time in Poland and I gathered that it was a sort of custom to invite guests to tell stories, especially when they are American-English speakers and the professors and graduate students desire to hear and practice their "American." I responded that I did have a story to tell. It was one that I had told before and it was a true story from my college days.

In May 1973 a buddy and I hitchhiked across the USA from Fairfield, Connecticut to San Francisco, California and back to Connecticut. The trip took about a month. I wanted to experience the country, we had friends in San Francisco we were going to visit, and I was also curious to see where in the San Francisco area my parents lived when I was born in 1952. I had done much hitchhiking throughout New England, so I learned some of the ways of the road. In the early 1970s, hitchhiking

was not uncommon; it was a different country then, more innocent and welcoming perhaps. Nevertheless, no experience
could have prepared me for the extraordinary events as related
in the story "Chicano."

Chicano
By Prof. Piotr Jaroszynski

Appeared in Polish in the magazine, *Polonia*, February 2006,
pp. 70-71.

Original Translation by Raphael Lizut
Edited Translation by Thomas A. Michaud

There are insignificant stories, which are easy to forget, but
there are also stories whose images have such great power that
it is hard to be free from them; they constantly come back to
mind. While a movie offers us ready-made pictures, and there
is not much left for the personal creativity of the audience, a
story allows each listener to imagine it in his way, yet not entirely freely. I rank a good story above a movie, because a
movie makes all the details unambiguous, and I am just a pas-
sive observer. In reading a book or listening to someone's
story, however, I instantly create a kind of world, which becomes my world. This sort of magical effect was cast on me by
the story of . . . Chicano.

It was in the early 70's - started Tom from West Virginia, a
heavy-set guy with a cheerful face, now a professor of philosophy, at that time a student - and I was slim and I liked to
hitchhike. Drivers eagerly gave us rides. It happened when my
friend and I were on our way to California. We picked a route
(Highway 40) which went through the Mojave Desert. We were

told that it takes a whole day to go through, that it is easy for a vehicle's engine to break down, and that the desert likes to play tricks, especially in a place called "Devil's Playground." But this was nothing to us. We were young, and when you are young, any danger is just another adventure.

In the early morning we were trying to hitch a ride in the town of Needles: a gas station, McDonald's, a hotel and a few houses. Ahead, stretching to the line of the horizon was the desert. It wasn't hot yet; we even felt a nice chill. There was no one on the road. We were joking. When you are young it is easy to turn everything into a joke. Finally a van came. The driver stopped and invited us to climb inside. And inside – a bunch of laughing cadets from the Air Force Academy. With military people – generally coarse types -- it doesn't take too much to find a reason to laugh.

We only just pulled out, when we stopped again . . . the next hitchhiker. He came out of nowhere; we did not see anybody on the road before when we were hitching. It was a Chicano. All of us became silent for a moment. Chicano was solemn and concentrated. He did not say a word. He looked about 30 years old. The van moved on and the atmosphere loosened up again. As we were talking and laughing, I decided to sound out Chicano. It was not easy, he was answering quite tersely. He did not look at me, he did not look through the window; he did not look anywhere, maybe only inside himself. I like those kinds of people because I believe they hide some sort of mystery. And I was intrigued by that -- I was young. Finally, I succeeded.

Chicano was just released from jail after four years -- from the State Penitentiary in New Mexico. He was busted for smuggling marijuana from Mexico to the US. Living near the border you can get rich fast, and a lot like him were involved in the business. But he didn't admit that he was guilty. He claimed that he was paid by a guy in Mexico he hardly knew to deliver a suitcase to a house in New Mexico. When he got to the house, cops surrounded him. He had been set-up; he didn't know what was in the suitcase. He said he was a decoy; the drug-dealers themselves told the cops where he was going with the suitcase so the dealers could bring in their large shipment somewhere else. I believed him and I didn't believe him. Nevertheless, I looked at him suspiciously and even with fear. One can't read from the appearance of some people what they really think, what they intend or what they will do.

Through the windows of our van, we could see the vast desert; it was getting hotter and hotter. There was not even a cloud in the sky. After around three hours of driving, we approached the storied "Devil's Playground." And then it happened: the engine overheated. The driver had to stop the van. It was incredibly hot; the temperature was over 100oF in the shade; just imagine how hot it was in the sun. You don't even want to think about it. It turned out that the water pump was broken. Now, we needed a couple of things: first, a new pump, and second, water. To get a new pump, somebody had to return to the town. The driver and another cadet quickly volunteered. They soon got a ride in a truck heading back towards Needles.

But what about water? Along the desert highway every 5 miles or so there are water stops with large metal barrels of water. This is just in case a vehicle's cooling system failed - something which often happened in this temperature. The closest, maybe two miles away, was ahead of us, but no traffic was moving in that direction. We all knew that someone would have to walk through the desert in the heat. There was nothing

around, only a few cacti here and there and lots of lurking liz-
ards, snakes and scorpions. My friend and the cadets became
silent. They were obviously scared, so I on impulse volunteered. And then Chicano raised his hand. I was glad, but at
the same time I felt shivers down my spine. Being alone with
this guy who just got out of prison was not something I desired; but still it was better than walking alone.

We grabbed some empty jugs, a finished gallon bottle of
cheap wine and some plastic juice quarts, and started to walk,
Chicano in his flannel shirt, gazing at the vastness, silent, and
me, ready to talk, but a little bit worried. Anyway, how can you
talk in heat like this? It was now probably more than 1100F in
the shade and we were walking in the sun. Even now, I can feel
this oppressive beastly heat.

After about two hours we reached the place where the water
barrels should be, but we beheld an uncanny sight. We rubbed
our sun-dried eyes with stunned disbelief. We didn't know
whether it was real or some kind of mirage. We didn't see a
water barrel but some type of living creature – black and yellow, pulsing, not like anything I'd ever seen, ancient. We came
closer and closer. And finally, we knew. It was not a mirage.
The whole barrel was covered with a thick layer of black- and
yellow-colored wasps, which were attracted probably by the
scent of the water and were trying to get inside the barrel. They
were mad because the barrel was closed tightly. In order to get
to the water, the barrel needed to be open. And only a man
could do it . . . But the man would have to face hundreds,
maybe thousands, of angry, venomous, vicious insects. What
could we do? I felt completely helpless. Suddenly Chicano said:
I will open.

He completely surprised me. I looked at him incredulously
while he took off his shirt, did some focused stretching-type

exercises, and then picked up our jugs, some in each hand. Now, extremely slowly, he started to move towards the barrel. Each move he made, with his hand or with his leg, was unimaginably slow. Sometimes I thought that he wasn't moving at all. But that was not true, he was moving, inch by inch. I closed my eyes because I didn't want to see what would happen if the wasps attacked him. Definitely, he would be stung to death. I then forced myself to open my eyes; he was getting closer and closer to the barrel. And finally, after several minutes, which seemed like long hours, he reached his destination. He was standing over the barrel.

Suddenly the wasps, one after the other took off, not to fly away, but to land on him. I was absolutely petrified. I couldn't take it. I wanted to run. After a few moments Chicano was completely covered with the "yellow jacket" wasps. He looked like some kind of strange Jurassic reptile. I could hear their ear-numbing buzzing, each one equipped with a poisonous sting; they were huge, dangerous, terrifying. Chicano still did not move.

But then he delicately set down our jugs and very cautiously started to open the barrel's lid. He picked up our jugs and sank them in the murky water. When they were full, Chicano raised them out of the water, took a deliberate step back and carefully turned around to face me.

I can see even now in my mind's eye the image of his face hidden by a living mask of wasps. The mask crawled over his nose, his tightly shut eyes, his pursed lips and firmly set jaw. He started to walk ever so slowly towards me. With each step, the wasps, one after the other, took off and buzzed back to the barrel. Eventually all of them returned to swarm the barrel, and once again, in front of us there was a black and yellow, prehistoric monster, whose body was vibrating in some sort of eternal rhythm. Chicano was not stung even once. We were saved.

It was late evening when our van reached the first town on the other side of the desert, and it was Barstow. Chicano asked the driver to stop. Then he got out, disappeared into the dark vast, and we took off.

That was the end of Tom's story, but the picture of the wasps stayed in my imagination for a long time, even becoming more and more vivid. Certain scenes faded but gradually came back more strongly. They gave me the feeling that I was actually traveling through a desert with wasps all around, searching for their victims. And the hellish heat!

Did Chicano really save you? I asked Tom. Yes, replied Tom, he appeared and disappeared in that Devil's Playground. When you are young - added Tom - you never know who is going to save you.

Author's Bio

Thomas A. Michaud, Retired, Dean, School of Professional Studies and Professor of Philosophy, West Liberty University (WLU) earned his M.A. and Ph.D. from Marquette University and his B.A. (Honors) from Fairfield University (CT). He has taught at Wheeling Jesuit University, Marquette University, Mount St. Mary's University (MD), Siena University (NY), and Rockhurst University (Kansas City, MO). His international experience includes a Smith Fellowship for the Husserl Archives at the University of Louvain (Leuven), Belgium, a Senior Fulbright Lectureship for the Federal University of Rio de Janeiro, Brazil, and the inaugural lecturer for the Rev. Jacek Woroniecki Memorial English Language Lectures in Philosophy, John Paul II Catholic University of Lublin, Poland.

Emphasizing his "common sense" approach, he has held seminars in leadership and ethics for many government and civic groups, professional associations, non-profit organizations, and educational institutions (including Duke Univ.'s Fuqua School of Business MBA program). In addition, Tom has designed and delivered extensive leadership ethics education programs for Wheeling Pittsburgh Steel Corp., Columbia Gas Transmission Corp., Columbia Gulf Transmission Company, Columbia Natural Resources Corp., Cabela's Distribution Center and Dermox Corp.

He is the recipient of a WV Humanities Council Research Fellowship, former Director of the WV Business and Professional Ethics Project, a Kettering Foundation Contract Scholar, and a past-President of the Gabriel Marcel Society. He is also past-Vice President of the WV Humanities Council, and a former member of the Executive Council of the American Catholic Philosophical Association.

Besides writing a business ethics and leadership column (1996 to 2007) for The State Journal (WV's leading business newspaper), he also has regularly written editorials for Nasz Djiennik (a Polish Catholic newspaper). His course text, *The Virtues of Business Ethics*, is published by Copley Custom Publishing Group, Third Edition, 2010. His numerous papers, articles and reviews include publications in *Philosophy Today*, *Renascence*, *The Review of Metaphysics*, *The Philosophy Research Archives*, *The Inter-American Review of Bibliography*, *Studia Gilsoniana*, *Man in Culture*, *The Kettering Review*, *Higher Education Exchange*, *Studia Philosophiae Christianae*, *Business Ethics Magazine* and *Ethics West Virginia*. The anthology he edited and introduced, Gabriel Marcel and the Postmodern World, appeared as a special double volume of the Journal of the American Society of Philosophy in the French Language. He was also the Guest Editor for and a contributor to the Gabriel Marcel special issue of The American Catholic Philosophical Quarterly.

Dr. Michaud regularly designed courses for, taught in, developed and implemented various types of non-traditional, accelerated adult degree completion programs. These include both undergraduate and graduate (Master of Science in Organizational Leadership, MBA, Executive MBA, Master of Professional Studies- MPS) programs. As Dean, Michaud essentially started the WLU School of Professional Studies (SPS), initiating its programs (Bachelor of Leadership and Administration, Professional Studies course concentrations, Master of Professional Studies in Organizational Leadership and Justice Leadership) and contributing to the management of the WLU Highlands Center.

www.ingramcontent.com/pod-product-compliance
Lightning Source LLC
Chambersburg PA
CBHW052123270326
41930CB00012B/2730